RETHINKING ISLAMIST POLITICS

D1646037

Rethinking Islamist Politics

Culture, the State and Islamism

SALWA ISMAIL

I.B. TAURIS
LONDON · NEW YORK

Published in paperback in 2006 by I.B. Tauris & Co Ltd
6 Salem Road, London w2 4BU
175 Fifth Avenue, New York NY 10010
www.ibtauris.com

In the United States of America and Canada distributed by
Palgrave Macmillan a division of St. Martin's Press
175 Fifth Avenue, New York NY 10010

Published in hardback in 2003 by I.B. Tauris & Co Ltd
Copyright © 2006 Salwa Ismail

Library of Modern Middle East Studies 19

ISBN 1 84511 180 X
EAN 978 1 84511 180 9

A full CIP record for this book is available from the British Library
A full CIP record is available from the Library of Congress

Library of Congress Catalog Card Number: available

Typeset in Aldus by Hepton Books, Oxford
Printed and bound in India by Replika Press Pvt. Ltd.

Contents

Preface to the Paperback Edition

In the wake of the events of September 11, 2001, the Madrid bombings in 2004, and the more recent violent attacks in Cairo, Sharm al-Shaykh and London in 2005, the phenomenon of Islamist militancy and violence continued to occupy a central place in scholarly writings on the Middle East and Muslim societies. In some of these writings, Islamist activism, aimed at targets in Western countries, has been construed as an affirmation of the 'clash of civilisations' thesis. Furthermore, in the discourse of western political leaders such as Tony Blair and George W. Bush, the attacks are presented as directed against Western ways of life, Western democracies and the values of freedom and liberty that are said to inhere in these democracies. This framing of the confrontational stance of some radical Islamist groups vis-à-vis Western governments excludes any attempt to situate militant Islamist activism in its historical and political context. Indeed, the claim that the most radical groups – even al-Qaʿida – aim to change western ways of life appears unfounded. The points of contention with Western governments invoked by al-Qaʿida's leader, Usama bin Laden, revolve around the long-standing issue of the Palestinian right to self-determination and the presence of American troops in Saudi Arabia. While bin Ladin's sincerity with regard to these issues is often disputed, it is difficult to deny the resonance that the reference to these causes has among Muslims in diverse settings. The USA's continued support for Israel, even when the international community condemns its violation of Palestinian human rights and its settlements policies, along with the US-led attack on Afghanistan, the American and British war against Iraq and subsequent occupation of that country, constitute the key issues of contention in relations with Western governments, in particular, the US government. While these issues organise opposition to Western governments, they do not explain the resort to violence. In this respect, we should note that the majority of Muslims and non-Muslims who oppose Western interventionist policies in the Middle East, as well as US support for authoritarian governments in countries like Egypt and Saudi Arabia, do not advocate the use of violence.

The essays that make up this volume aim at providing an account of Islamist activism focused on the infrastructures of action, that is, the bases upon which Islamist activism develops. One of the main arguments is that Islamist activism cannot be explained by invoking Islam as a unitary entity referring back to the sacred Text and the founding period of Islam. Instead, I propose that we examine the socio-political and historical contexts of activism, paying attention not only to macro-level factors such as state structures and policies, but also to micro-level processes in the everyday life of social actors. Hence, in a number of the essays, I focus on the neighbourhood level at which Islamist activists mobilise, showing how they appropriate existing urban spaces, investing themselves in positions of arbitration, claiming roles of welfare providers and engaging in the overseeing of public morality. All such strategies and modes of activism exist in the everyday life of communities and become invested with Islamic symbolism.

How should we view or approach the deployment of signs and symbols from Islamic traditions to justify activism and render it in Islamic idioms? The various discourses articulated by Islamists generate meanings in relation to particular historical settings and not outside them. The subject positions they make available are historically bounded. We should also note that the discursive field of Islamism comprises a wide range of articulations that are neither coherent nor homogeneous. They do not all buttress the idea of the Islamic state. The heterogeneity of Islamist movements has been reinforced by competing and conflicting discursive productions of Islamist and Muslim identities. Adopting a historical and historicising approach to Islamist movements entails acquiring knowledge of micro-practices of mobilisation anchored in the everyday life. In other words, we should pay attention to specific histories and abandon generalisations about the inherent nature of Islamic beliefs.

Since completing the research and writing of *Rethinking Islamist Politics*, a number of studies of Islamism have appeared in print, making significant contributions to the understanding of Islamist politics and the processes of re-Islamisation. Some of these studies have turned their attention to Islamism as a lifestyle tied up with the actors' socio-economic positions. Examining consumerist re-Islamisation in areas of education, leisure and fashion, these studies bring to focus the dynamic nature of Islamism and how it is mediated by global and local forces (for example, see Chapter 3 in Navaro-Yashin 2002). Further, studies of Islamist and Muslim self-representation in the public sphere underscore the ongoing debates among Muslims on how religion should inform their public selves (Çinar 2005, Moallem 2005).

The space/time compression that marks globalisation, according to some scholars, is at work in the links that bring together Muslims of different national backgrounds – in, for instance, the Middle East, South Asia, Europe and the US – to a shared space and time. This development may support the *umma* in the imaginary, but may also crystallise dissent and disagreements. Indeed, contemporary Muslims are engaged among themselves and with non-Muslims in dialogues on the role of religion in the public sphere and in politics. Rather than holding onto static views of their religion, in these dialogues contemporary Muslims challenge received ideas and established authorities. We should pay attention to the ongoing debates and mind the unfolding conversations.

S.I., September 2005

References

Çinar, Alev. *Modernity, Islam and Secularism in Turkey: Bodies, Places and Time*. Minneapolis: University of Minnesota Press, 2005.

Moallem, Minoo. *Between Warrior Brother and Veiled Sister: Islamic Fundamentalism and the Politics of Patriarchy in Iran*. Berkeley and Los Angeles: University of California Press, 2005.

Navaro-Yashin, Yael. *Faces of the State: Secularism and Public Life in Turkey*. Princeton: Princeton University Press, 2002.

Preface

The Middle East of the late 1970s saw the beginnings of developments, which, on the surface, indicated the growing appeal of religion
among people in the region. In Egypt, to take one example, this was
reflected in such things as the increased circulation and visibility of
Muslim Brotherhood publications (*al-I'tisam* and *al-Da'wa* could
more often be found in peoples' homes), the burgeoning popularity
of study circles in Cairo mosques (especially that associated with the
Mustafa Mahmud mosque) and the increased adoption of the veil. In
observing these and other developments, specialists of Middle Eastern politics and societies who, consistent with their modernisation
frameworks, had predicted the decline of religion, were faced with an
unaccounted for phenomenon. In their search for explanation, they
by and large cast Islam as agent. That is, Islam was made to assume
the role of a puppeteer, working behind the scenes, moving Muslims
to act in one way or another. This way of accounting for Islamism
has shaped much scholarly and journalistic writing about the phenomenon over the past thirty years. The results of this scholarship,
in the way of explanation and understanding, have been deeply un-
satisfying. Of course, this usage of Islam betrays theoretical prejudices
inherited from the Orientalist tradition and, although many scholars have written excellent critiques of this tradition, it continues to
have considerable influence on the ways social scientists and others
account for anything 'Islamic'.

The writing of this book was inspired by the 'injunction' to not use Islam as agent. In particular, it owes much to Talal Asad's idea of Islam as a discursive tradition. Chapter one reviews the construct of Islam as it appears in some of the more influential accounts of Islamism. Other, competing, accounts are also scrutinised. In the light of this examination, I suggest the elements of a critical perspective for studying Islamist politics and Islamism. Integral to this perspective is the idea of the sociality and historicity of religion – an idea that has crystallised with some recent anthropological studies of Islam in specific settings.

These essays began as an attempt to deal with particular pieces of the puzzle. One such piece was the articulation of Islamist discourses that differed in their constructions and preoccupations and supported different modes of action in relation to government. These differences could not be accounted for or comprehended within the perspective that identified Islamists in terms of common slogans and a common declared objective of establishing the Islamic state. Using classifications and qualifications to distinguish militant from quietist Islam has also proven to be of limited analytical benefit. In treating Islamist groups as social and political forces, my analytical focus goes beyond classification to include different levels of action, modes of interaction and identity formation within Islamist movements. This differentiated reading of Islamism is presented in chapters two and three. Both chapters are concerned with different articulations of Islamism, particularly the conservative discourses and associated actors and activism. Chapter two highlights the organising principles of the conservative discourse in Egypt and shows how conservative Islamism plays a vital role in structuring the political field, neutralising the militants and converging with state-sponsored Islamisation. Chapter three looks at the convergence and divergence that results from the actors' strategies and patterns of interaction. It examines the emergence of public morality as an area of convergence among various Islamist actors, identifying two nodal points for the analysis of this development: power processes involved in redefining orthodoxy and the practices of power and control in popular culture.

Chapters four and five look at Islamist movements as social movements that are inscribed in their social and political settings.

Cairo is one of these settings marked by particular socio-spatial determinants that shaped the development of the movement there. The resources provided by the setting and the structure of opportunities and limitations that characterise it are probed to understand the bases of Islamist activism in the popular neighbourhoods of Cairo. The urban settings in Algeria and Tunisia, covered in chapter five, provide a focal point of comparative understanding. The approach adopted in this chapter aims at bridging macro and micro levels of explanation. Towards this end, Islamist activism and militancy in Tunisia and Algeria are analysed in terms of the interplay of determinants at the macro level (social formation, national economic and political structures) and the micro level (network processes within the Islamist movements, modes of implantation in urban spaces, and cultural and ideological practices). In both chapters four and five, the analysis underlines how, in Egypt, Algeria and Tunisia, macro changes in labour markets, housing policies, etc., have interacted with micro processes such as informal employment and informal housing to produce the setting for Islamist activism and militancy.

The analysis of the potential and limitations of Islamist movements in chapter six is undertaken in relation to the thesis of the failure of political Islam. The purpose here is not to support or refute the idea that political Islam has failed but instead to reveal the projections built into this type of assessment. The view of a homogenising and homogenous Islamism rests on the idea of a 'true' Islam and hearkens back to the construct of Islam as essence, a construct we would be better off abandoning. The argument here is that Islamism, as a process, has a dynamic unfolding that entails hybridity and ambiguity. While these are seen elsewhere as signs of the coming of a post-Islamist society, they are treated here as part of the unfolding dynamic common to social movements and contestation politics.

In the course of my work, I have received support from many friends and colleagues, some of whom read and commented on parts or all of the essays. For reading earlier drafts of some chapters, and his insightful and thought-provoking contribution to our many discussions, I thank Ali Haouchine. Mervat Hatem encouraged me to develop my writing on Islamism into a book and commented generously on chapters three and four. I am grateful for her moral and intellectual support. I also benefited from Mohamed Saleh Omri's comments on chapters four and five. The support of my colleagues Zuleikha Abu Risha, Nelida Fuccaro and Kamil Mahdi has been greatly appreciated. I also owe thanks to Beaudoin Dupret, Jean-Noël Ferrié and Faird Ben Ali for their contributions at different stages of the work. Abdel Kader Zghal, Mohammed Kerrou, Morched Chabi, and Isabelle-Berry Chikhawi shared their knowledge of Tunis with me.

Some of the writing was made possible by the time off from my teaching duties granted during the 1997–98 academic year. My former head of department at Exeter, the late Peter Butler, was instrumental in arranging this relief for me and I am deeply indebted to him. I would also like to acknowledge my department's financial support for research travel. I am grateful for the research facilities and the institutional help of URBAMA in Tours, IREMAM in Aix-en-Province, CEDEJ in Cairo, IRMC in Tunis and CEMAT in Tunis. In my quest for material, I was greatly aided by Paul Auctherlonie, the Middle East Librarian at the University of Exeter.

Chapters two, three and four were originally published under the following titles: 'Confronting the Other: Identity, Culture, Politics and Conservative Islamism in Egypt,' in *International Journal of Middle East Studies*, vol.30 no.2 (1998): 199–225; 'Religious "Orthodoxy" as Public Morality: The State, Islamism and Cultural Politics in Egypt,' in *Critique: Journal for Critical Studies of the Middle East* 14 (Spring 1999): 25–47; 'The Popular Movement Dimensions of Contemporary Militant Islamism: Socio-spatial Determinants in the Cairo Urban Setting,' in *Comparative Studies in Society and History* 42, 2 (2000): 263–93. A shorter version of chapter six appeared in *Middle East Report* 221 (November 2001).

Each of the texts benefited from the insightful commentary of anonymous reviewers. The text as a whole benefited from Anna Enayat's critical reading, comments and careful editing.

My family, and my mother in particular, have been sources of inspiration and sustenance throughout my research and writing endeavours. My greatest debt is to Brian Aboud who is always my first reader. His support and sustained encouragement made it possible for me to complete this work. I am forever heartened by his generosity of spirit.

                                                                S.I.

1

The Study of Islamism Revisited

During the 1980s and 1990s, Islamist movements and ideologies emerged as important subjects of scholarly investigation in the fields of politics, sociology, anthropology, history and religious studies. Interest in the subject grew in conjunction with such events as the Iranian revolution (1978–79), the assassination of President Sadat (1981), the Hama uprising in Syria (1982) and the World Trade Centre bombing (1993). Although they are not of the same order, these events have come to form part of a discursive phenomenon carrying the labels of 'Islamic fundamentalism,' 'Islamic revivalism' and 'Islamism' – labels which soon acquired the qualifiers 'radical,' 'traditional,' 'militant,' 'conservative' and so on.[1] These labels, qualifications and classifications have been devised in order to account for spectacular events involving groups and individuals who invoke signs and symbols associated with Islamic traditions to justify their activities. They were developed within particular frameworks of understanding and in relation to particular modes of social, political and historical inquiry into the subject of study as constituted. We now have a rather large body of literature designed to help us comprehend the varied events, actors and activities having an Islamic point of reference. The task at hand is to reflect on the tools, concepts and categories of analysis that this literature offers. In this introductory chapter, I begin with a critical survey of the most influential of the various approaches used in the study of contemporary Islamist politics: the historical master-narratives, the Durkheimian-inspired sociological models and the statist/political economy perspectives. I then outline the elements of an alternative approach; one that is both historically informed and empirically grounded.

Before proceeding further, a note on two key terms used throughout this text. The term 'Islamist politics' is used here to refer to the activities of organisations and movements that mobilise and agitate in the political sphere while deploying signs and symbols from Islamic traditions. It is also used to refer to political activism involving informal groupings that (re)construct repertoires and frames of reference from Islamic traditions.[2] The term 'Islamism' is used to encompass both Islamist politics as well as re-Islamisation, the process whereby various domains of social life are invested with signs and symbols associated with Islamic cultural traditions. Examples of this process include the wearing of the *hijab* (veil), the consumption of religious literature and other religious commodities, the publicising of symbols of religious identity, the reframing of economic activity in Islamic terms. In much of the recent literature, re-Islamisation is considered to be broader and, in some ways, distinct from 'Islamism.' The distinction is not used in this book. Islamism, as I conceive it, is not just the expression of a political project; it also covers the invocation of frames with an Islamic referent in social and cultural spheres.[3]

How, then, has Islamism been constituted as a particular subject of study? Which traditions of inquiry frame the formulation of the *problématique* of Islamism? To answer these questions, I begin by looking at the constitution of Islam as a domain of study and the wider analytical frames that have been used to explain the role of religion in society. A reader of the recent literature on 'Islam and Politics' or 'Islam and the modern age' is likely to encounter a set of propositions which generalise about the role of the religion in history, and place 'Islam' within an established narrative of world history. In this narrative, a major preoccupation is to account for Western modernity. More particularly, its aim is to affirm the factors that lie behind the rise of modernity in the West and thereby confirm Western exceptionalism.[4] This account of modernity articulates the self-identity of the West by abstracting features found in the West as the essence of modernity.[5] Integral to this enterprise is to draw contrasts between the West and Islam, wherein the latter emerges as a series of historical gaps.[6] It is in this tradition of counterposing Islam and modernity that much contemporary analysis of Islamism develops. Islamism's relation to modernity becomes the main line of inquiry, hinging, essentially, on how the relation between Islam and modernity is conceived. If Islam is seen as incompatible with modernity, then Islamism expresses a rejection of modernity. If, on the other hand, Islam is not viewed as antithetical to modernity, then Islamism is a way of embracing it 'authentically.'[7]

The view of Islamism as anti-modern rests on the assumption that modernisation is associated with secularisation and the retreat of religion from the public sphere. Islamism thus appears as an expression of an anti-modern strand that, for some, is inherent in the religion. A more interesting proposition is found in Ernest Gellner's model of Muslim societies, which purports to uncover the internal logic and mechanisms of Islam. The model sets up a dualistic structure of Islam: the High Islam of the city dwellers and the Low Islam of the tribes. The former is scripturalist and ascetic, suitable to the temperament of the city entrepreneurs, while the latter is ecstatic, meeting the needs of the tribes. These two forms of Islam are in perpetual struggle. According to Gellner, with greater urbanisation and the consolidation of the central state in the modern period, Low Islam declines and High Islam becomes ascendant. This occurs because High Islam captures the urban strata's desire for learning and upward mobility. This desire is frustrated, however, by the laxity of the rulers and their failure to modernise their countries. In this scheme of scriptural High Islam versus ecstatic Low Islam, Islamism is viewed as an affirmation of the scriptural-based egalitarian spirit expressing frustration with the blocked road to modernisation.[8] In some other accounts, Islamism is a variant of religious fundamentalism that emerges in a normative clash with modernity.[9]

A different understanding of the relation between Islamism and modernity may be found in critical readings of the Western discourse of modernity. In line with post-modernist thought, these readings identify the Western discourse on modernity as a meta-narrative asserting Western hegemony. Islamism's anti-Western posture is a rejection of that hegemony and the meta-narrative that sustains it.

It is not essentially an anti-modern movement, but an effort at dis-
lodging the West from the position of centrality that it claims.[10]
Islamism is located in the space that is freed through the deconstruction of the relationship between the West and modernity. These
readings situate Islamism in a dialogue with post-modernity defined,
following Jean-François Lyotard, as expressing 'incredulity towards
meta-narratives.' This in turn displaces the issue of the relationship
between Islam and modernity, bringing into focus the politics of identity and power relations at the global level. This perspective opens up
new ways of looking at Islamism without placing the West as the
ultimate referential frame and the supreme global authority. Yet, although the Western discourse on modernity has been subject to a
critical reading, the construct of Islam conceived in the production of
Western identity continues to animate discussions of Islamism, finding parallels and reinforcement in the discourses of the Islamists
themselves.

Historical Master-narratives of Islamist Movements

A number of influential studies of contemporary Islamist movements
take the history of Islam as a point of departure. This is a history
constructed in particular terms. Before examining them, it should be
noted that this construction serves a methodological objective. It is
essential for the enterprise of 'slotting' Islamist movements into a
known chronological narrative. The sequence of events or the chronological unfolding of developments appears to be self-explanatory by
virtue of basic patterns that they are presumed to embody. Several
prominent scholars of 'Islam in the modern period' employ these
types of explanatory strategies in their work on Islamist movements.
To illustrate, I will focus on two of these works: *Islam and Politics* by
John Esposito (1983) and *Islam: Continuity and Change in the Modern World* by John O. Voll (1982).[11] The perspectives outlined by
Esposito and Voll have their echoes in many other writings dealing
with Islamist politics.[12]

In *Islam and Politics*, Esposito anchors his explanation of Islamist
movements in a unitary understanding of the religion. Although he
acknowledges the specificity of the socio-political contexts in which

these movements emerged, his underlying premise is the idea of a totality called Islam explained as the basic beliefs of Muslims and the ideas they all share. Thus, in his introduction, Esposito highlights 'shared Muslim beliefs': in God's revelations, in Muhammad's prophethood and so on. Most important is the belief in the unity of religion and politics. This is 'the Islamic imperative' (p. 4) which functions as the basic belief that motivates Muslims with regard to state and government and guides their assessment of whether or not their government is mandated by God.

The underlying assumptions of these simple propositions need to be spelled out in order to signal the reification and objectification that follow from them. One such assumption holds that social and national collectivities whose members adhere to the Islamic religion share a primary identification as Muslims with common beliefs, and belong to a totality called the Muslim World. In this World, a primacy of religious beliefs in guiding individual and collective action is attributed to those who profess the religion. Esposito pays no attention to how beliefs interact with the sociality of everyday life in various settings. Hence the substantive content of the beliefs that are thought to be determinant of much of Muslims' lives is not dealt with either.

The assignment of primacy to religious beliefs is questionable on two main grounds. The first is by now somewhat axiomatic. It points out that Muslims occupy differing and multiple positions in various social and national formations that shape how they relate to each other and to their government. Second, beliefs are not transhistorical, but historically and materially grounded. The belief in God in seventh-century Arabia and the belief in God at the end of the twentieth century have to be understood in relation to their material contexts. What the belief represents or signifies is part of a system of meanings that interacts with systems of meaning articulated in other fields of social life. The idea of God may not just differ from one religion to another, but from one group of practitioners to another and from one historical period to another. Islam, as a religion, developed different ideas of God and in this respect is not unlike other religions. For instance, in seventh-century Arabia, notions of agnosticism or atheism did not exist and were therefore not dealt with in the sacred text.[13] It was thus in relation to other notions that the criteria of belief and un-belief were formulated. It follows from these two contentions that if we are to take account of the role of religious beliefs, we must view them as components of historically produced systems of meanings.

Having assumed the unity of Muslims in the totality of Islam, Esposito develops his discussion around the idea of the continuity of their history conceived as the extension, into the present, of ideas and beliefs from the religion's formative period. In the early period, the Islamic community was both temporal and spiritual, embodying the unity of religion and politics. According to Esposito, '[r]eligion provided the worldview, the framework of meaning for both individual and corporate life.' (p.30) This shared view, translated into a public commitment to the Shari'a (law based on the scripture), is a primary principle (p.31). In turn, this commitment, and the ideal of the early community, inspired pre-modern revivalist movements. In his view, it is this commitment both to the Shari'a and the model of the early community that motivates Muslims, in a variety of contexts, to engage in restorative or corrective activity. Esposito, therefore, develops his analysis within the framework of Islamic revival and reform so methodically constructed (as we will see below) by John O. Voll. It emerges that the character and legacy of both pre-modern and modern Muslim societies as well as Islamic modernism responded to 'the Islamic imperative' of uniting politics and religion. The need to do so was particularly felt because of the challenge of Western colonialism (p. 32). According to Esposito, 'pre-modern revivalism' is a response to the socio-moral decline and reveals much of the patterns of modern Islamic movements, in their worldviews, their ideology, their language and methods' (p. 32). Subsequently, Esposito postulates a continuity and recurrence of basic patterns. For instance, he asserts that Islamic modernism built on and broadened the pre-modern revivalist legacy (p.32).

Situated within this continuity, contemporary Islamist movements represent basic responses and express modes of action which have been patterned in earlier historical periods. Although Esposito sketches the variety of specific socio-political contexts in which the movements emerge, he does not accord these contexts adequate explanatory weight. Consequently, contextual specificities are superseded by the shared drive among Muslims to reunite religion and politics: regardless of the differences in conjunctures, all contexts are bound to elicit the same type of response from Muslims. The formation of Islamist groups in various settings is presented as the expression of a mood of discontent towards what they perceive as generalised conditions of decay. The Muslims' assessment of decay is itself undertaken in relation to the ideal. One may then ask in what way the context influences the positions of the actors and their relations to government and state. Based on Esposito's analysis, one is led to conclude that the impact of the ideal to which Muslims aspire overrides the effects of the actual conditions in which they live. In other words, regardless of prevailing conditions, as long as the ideal society is not established, Muslims will agitate and engage in reform action.

The notion of recurrence with respect to movements, their symbols and ideas, results in a static vision of Muslim societies. From an empirical point of view, there is no evidence that Muslims have assessed their states and societies as being decayed whenever the Shari'a was not applied or when rules of moral propriety were transgressed.[14] However, it is not only on empirical grounds that I take issue with the conception of Islamist movements as reformist organisations seeking moral reconstruction. Rather, as I will elaborate below, I contest the assumption that the moral and moralising discourses articulated by the various Islamist groups express some agreement on unchanging core ideas and beliefs.

The idea that the continuity of Islamic history provides the basic framework for understanding Islamist movements is best articulated by J.O. Voll. Criticising the view that Islamic activism expresses social, economic or nationalist interests, Voll argues that '[it] is possible to see the current resurgence as a continuation of basic themes, even though those themes may be expressed in new ways' (p. 4). Two points are central to Voll's position: religious motivation lies behind the 're-vival,' and the past plays an important role in guiding action in the present (p. 4). 'Islamic resurgence,' in his view, '... involves the creation of new and effective forms of continuing the vitality of the Islamic message' (p. 4). Voll's reading of Islamic history aims to construct ideal type categories of Muslim action, what he terms 'styles of action.'

Four such styles are characteristic of Muslim activism in relation to government: adaptationist, conservative, fundamentalist and individualist.

In what way do these four styles serve as a framework for comprehending the entirety of Islamic history in general and the experience of 'revivalism' in particular? First, it should be noted that Voll posits action as a response to events and actual conditions – it is more of a reaction. In this sense, the four styles are conceived as particular ways of responding to given challenges. To illustrate, Voll sees the emergence of a fundamentalist style of action embodied in eighteenth-century revivalism – an archetype of modern revivalism – in the following manner:

> Just before the time of European dominance, a reformist-revivalist tradi-
> tion had been established in the mould of the fundamentalist experience.
> Social groups and associations had been created to meet the issues raised
> by the adaptationists within the Islamic community, and those groups
> had a fundamentalist mood, which has always been close to the surface
> over the last two centuries. Thus, the style of the eighteenth-century
> spirit of socio-moral reconstruction has provided the counterpoint to the
> adaptationists' secularising reforms. When the latter weaken or appear
> to have failed, as was frequently the case by the 1970s, the more funda-
> mentalist style emerges into full view (p. 30).

In this framework of constructing and understanding Islamic history, modes of action identified with 'the Islamic experience' appear in cyclical or recurrent patterns. These modes of action are posited as responses to challenges unleashed by changes at the local and global levels, in particular, the challenge of modernity. Voll contends that different styles of action predominate at different historical periods. For instance, adaptationist reformers prevailed under eighteenth-century Ottoman rule while fundamentalism and conservatism were in minority positions. In the nineteenth and twentieth centuries, reform continued to be the major issue for Muslims but came to involve adaptation to Western techniques and ideas (p. 92). Adaptationism in the twentieth century took the form of Islamic modernism, secular reformism and radical reformism (p. 158). Other styles, namely fundamentalism and conservatism, were present but only at the level of everyday life or at moments of contestation. While adaptationism was the main response to the challenge of modernisation and Western dominance during the first three-quarters of the twentieth century, fundamentalism re-emerged during the last quarter. This resurgence has come about with the westernisers' loss of control over the process of popular mobilisation (p. 159). Given the religiosity of the popular sector, and its mobilisation through mass communication, fundamentalism was adopted as the only style capable of appealing to the religious sub-stratum in Muslim societies (p. 159). It turns out, then, that adaptationism was no more than an elitist style that failed to achieve modernisation (p. 290), while fundamentalism was an expression of the desire for authentic modernisation as opposed to westernisation (p. 332).

The four styles of action in Voll's narrative are too general to capture any specific process or to be seen as particularly unique and defining of Muslim societies. Voll's effort to provide substantive definitions of the four styles proceeds by describing events, actions and phenomena and then assigning them to the respective categories. In this way, a wide variety of developments and events from different periods and places are slotted into pre-conceived categories under common labels. This methodology allows for a classification of events, responses, actions and so on, but it compromises their historicity. Moreover, the labels used to classify Muslim responses and actions amount to characterisations that do not permit analysis or explanation of what is being characterised. By adding the qualifier 'Islamic,' the labels are rendered simplistic and reductive. They are so not just by virtue of parallels drawn between various historical periods – affirming their repetitive occurrence – but also because the underlying logic of the narrative is that 'things are Islamic because they are constituted by Islam.'[15] Thus, policies of modernisation are labelled Islamic adaptationism – a style which developed in the early period of the religion and was repeated in later periods. No clarification is offered of the parallelism or isomorphism between the different historical contexts in which this style was adopted. We cannot, therefore, know under what historical conditions adaptationism or any of the other styles is likely to be favoured by Muslims. Ultimately, Voll's enumerative exercise depends on a notion of Islam as an agent that imprints its essence on all particulars subsumed under it. As Aziz Al-

Azmeh puts it, in this mode of conceptualisation Islam arises as 'the self-explanatory, self sufficient and utterly *sui generis* nature and reality whose vicissitudes are internally propelled by 'the community' in its successive generations, responding to 'their vision' under different external circumstances. But these circumstances are sheer accidentals in connection with the solidity of trans-historicity.'[16]

It should be noted that while Voll finds it necessary to devise four categories to classify the actions of Muslims across the multitude of Muslim societies and across varied historical periods, his account is developed around the organising principle of revivalism. The idea that a revival mode of action is always close to the surface, about to erupt on the scene, is used to substantiate the claim that the revival spirit is a constant in Islamic history. This narrative of reform and revival is problematic in several respects. Although it makes reference to the variety of Muslim settings and different historical junctures, it elaborates an Islamic history totalised in terms of an episodic recurrence of movements of reform and renewal that embody some inherent modes of responding to general socio-political conditions. Further, these conditions are characterised in abstract terms as representing decay. Built into the revival perspective is the view that Muslims are bound to be unhappy with their societies as long as they judge them as having strayed from the ideal model of the early period. This ideal is an enduring and ubiquitous thought occupying the minds of Muslims everywhere, at all times and manifested in ideas of reform that have developed historically and that are seen to lend continuity to Islamic history.

Continuity is often conceptualised by Voll in terms of intellectual lineage. Voll speaks of conceptual continuity, affirming that contemporary discourse taps into the legacy of revival as a dominant and recurring theme.[17] As Eric Davis points out, this idea of continuity creates an intellectual bridge between the Islamic reform of the nineteenth century and the 'revival' of the late twentieth century. In his critique of the revival and continuity framework, Davis questions this historical link given the differences in social background, ontological views and modes of action of the participants in the various movements.[18] Indeed, the reception of ideas and discourses is contingent on context. Contemporary Islamist movements cannot be understood simply through the slogans they brandish. Indeed, the call for the application of the Shari'a, the claim that 'Islam is the solution' and the denunciation of society as *jahiliya* all enter into the constitution of particular systems of meaning that are themselves historically and materially inscribed.

Sociological and Political Economy Approaches

Sociological and political economy approaches offer alternatives to the understanding of contemporary Islamist movements and to the essentialist views of Islam found in the master-narrative accounts discussed above. Sociological analyses of the movements have, on the whole, developed within a conceptual apparatus inspired by Durkheimian views of social change. These analyses interpret the social reality of Islamist action in terms of the actors' backgrounds and socio-psychological states. Thus, studies by sociologists such as Saad Eddin Ibrahim examine the social characteristics of Islamist activists, sketching a profile of group membership in terms of age, education and family conditions. This profile is set against a background of rapid social transformation marked by industrialisation, urbanisation and so on. Within this perspective, Islamist activism is understood as the expression of frustrated aspirations. Concepts such as uprootedness, disenchantment and disintegration are deployed to account for the socio-psychological states that lie behind decisions to join Islamist groups and to become active in them.

Based on case studies of two Islamist groups active in Egypt in the 1970s, Ibrahim has developed a profile of militant activists. He indicates that the members of these groups were of rural background and recently urbanised. For the first time, they were experiencing life in large cities where foreign influence was most visible and where impersonal relations characterised social interaction. The resulting psychological effects of this experience were intertwined with the prevailing national crisis. The weakening of adjustment mechanisms for these migrants resulted in alienation. Membership in Islamic groups fulfilled a de-alienating function.[19]

Although the conceptual problems associated with this model are raised in subsequent chapters, it is worth recalling here some of

Charles Tilly's objections to Durkheimian influences on analyses of social transformation. The most important of these relate to the idea, expressed in the Durkheimian model, that the social differentiation involved in processes of industrialisation and urbanisation is accompanied by societal disintegration.[20] Tilly questions the theoretical and empirical validity of the argument that integrative mechanisms dissolve during moments of social change and that anomie, violence and disorder express the disintegrative effects of urbanisation. He contends that processes of social transformation bring new forms of struggle based on new types of organisation in the urban setting.[21] His emphasis is on the solidarity of the actors and the resources of mobilisation.[22] Conflict and protest are not the products of uprooting, dissolution of controls and individual disorganisation. Rather, they build on organisation and strategies designed to achieve shared goals. Action is conceived as being shaped by the opportunities and the constraints of the city. In light of this, the study of social movements should be concerned not with the mental states of the actors but with 'infrastructures of action': resources, socially produced norms of interaction, and frames of social organisation and community formation.

Propositions about frustrated aspirations among the youth and members of the middle classes are also found in political economy explanations of Islamist movements.[23] Using data from the social profiles of the members of Islamist groups, some analysts have put the emphasis on social conflict and class struggle. Eric Davis has argued that the Islamist movements express the contradictory socio-economic positions and the psychological states of their members.[24] Arguing from a view of ideology as embodying an expressive relation to class interests, Davis contends that the radical Islamist discourse has had a greater appeal to a particular social strata, namely the petite bourgeoisie. Although Davis explicitly rejects the notion of ideology as false consciousness, it seems to underlie his reading of the discourse of the militants. Thus the articulation of an Islamic ideology '... can be understood in terms of social strains as Islamic militants do seek refuge in Islam to soothe the alienation stemming from deprivation. The transference of their hostility on to scapegoats such as liberals, imperialists, communists and Jews ... is a classic syndrome associated with social strains.'[25] According to Davis, this ideology is functional for the social groups that use it, offering them categories that can mediate their reality.[26] The particular appeal of Islamist ideologies to the petite bourgeoisie is also asserted by Michael Fischer in his analysis of the structural conditions of the revolution in Iran. In this instance, Islamic ideology expressed not only the petite bourgeoisie's discontent, resulting from frustrated aspirations for social mobility, but also its protest against the modern way of life.[27] However, it is not clear in what way 'Islam' contains a better reservoir of symbols of protest and in what way it offers 'reality-mediating' categories that are more suited to the interests of particular classes, especially the petite bourgeoisie.

What is important to note is that signs and symbols with an Islamic referent are functionalised and instrumentalised in a variety of competing and contiguous Islamist discourses. The position of these discourses in the ideological formation and their role in sustaining or transforming relations of domination cannot be determined a priori. Rather, discourses must be analysed in terms of their effects of meaning, and the subject positions they make available.

In a number of works, the analysis of Islamism as an expression of class interests develops against the backdrop of the idea of the crisis of the state in the Arab world. The crisis of the state is explained in terms of social, economic and national failures which are perceived by opponents as evidence of the bankruptcy of secular ideologies. Islamism thus develops as a counter-ideology appealing to disadvantaged social groups and allowing an expression of political and economic demands. This line of argument is elaborated by Nazih Ayubi in his book *Political Islam*. Simply put, modernising states have failed to deliver on their promises of prosperity. Financially exhausted, they are unable to meet social needs in areas of housing and employment. Comparing the Egyptian case with the Iranian experience, Ayubi argues that 'the same paradigm of frustrated expectations that explains the Iranian revolution would also explain, albeit on a smaller scale, the recruitment into militant organisations of political Islam.'[28]

Political economy analysis has, thus, placed an emphasis on certain economic and political conditions as representing the environment favouring the rise of Islamist groups. Lisa Anderson situates the growth in support for Islamist groups in North Africa at the juncture of two developments: state retreat from welfare and re-distributive policies and political liberalisation initiatives. Anderson highlights the fiscal crisis of the state, pointing to the rearrangement of the relations between rulers and ruled.[29] She sees the opening up of the political field as a strategy of the elite aimed not at wider popular participation but at a broadening of its base of power and a widening of the reach of state taxation.[30] However, an unintended consequence of this was that disenfranchised sectors became the constituents of Islamist organisations. In a context of state retreat, Islamists proved better and more efficient providers of social services.[31] The idiom of political Islam was used in a context that banished discussion of eve-ryday problems and economic discontent.[32] For Anderson, the Islamists are by-products of the environment created by their governments.

The change in the state's redistributive policies and capacities is important for understanding other structural transformations in the economic and political spheres, but does not, on its own, account for the development and workings of Islamist movements. Political economy and statist approaches highlight the macro transformations in economy and society that are part of the wider setting in which Islamist movements operate. However, they ignore symbolic and cultural issues and local specificities. The focus on the macro level comes at the expense of the micro level where the everyday-life communities wrestle with the effects of macro changes, initiate new forms of action, and struggle for and contribute to a reconfiguring of the political scene. The abstraction of Islamism as the idiom of disen-chanted youth and the blocked and disenfranchised middle classes fails to take account of the various modes of insertion of local actors into the national and international economies. In view of this, the link between macro and micro changes should be elucidated. For in-stance, macro changes in the labour market that accompanied economic liberalisation and privatisation policies are tied to the ex-pansion of informal economies. These are in turn connected to the development of community autonomy and practices of self-help. The analysis of these practices reveals the emergence of new forms of activism that recall practices of solidarity from earlier periods.

The political economy approach to Islamist movements is often presented as an alternative to culturalist interpretations. It emphasises structural and institutional conditions over cultural factors. It is in opposing essentialism that it presents a critique of works that attribute primacy to culture, conceived as unchanging views, attitudes and norms. However, cultural practices and cultural production should not be cast aside in the interests of structural analysis. The analytical alternatives are not limited to a choice between structure and culture. The materiality of culture and the mobilisation of cultural capital in all domains of life, including the economic, are important determinants that interact with the political-economy determinants. That the idiom of 'Islam' came to express the grievances and claims of oppositional groups could not simply be a matter of displacement or convenience. Rather, structural transformations in the areas of cultural and educational production made it possible to transfer and instrumentalise the language of religion in the public space.[33] The links between changes in cultural production and economic transformation are demonstrated in both the formal and informal spheres. Peter Gran shows how, in eighteenth-century Egypt, change in cultural production was tied to early capitalist transformation.[34] In the late twentieth century, the commodification of religious books and the aesthetic appeal of artefacts with religious inscription must be understood in relation to the circulation, in mass markets, of cultural symbols recycled and reinvented as part of a wider process of the commodification of identity and the consumption of religious referents.[35] Much like the field of morality, the investment of the economic field with referents drawn from religion constitutes the other facet of this development. The instrumentalisation of these referents involves both dominant and dominated strata. In other words, cultural production enters into the constitution of power relations – a dynamic process shaping the positions of the various actors.

Historical, Historicising and Critical Anthropological Approaches

How, then, may we treat cultural traditions without falling into essentialism and how may we remain attuned to the specificity of the various socio-historical contexts while integrating the cultural sphere

as a constitutive dimension? Culturalist approaches are often criticised as ahistorical. Political economy perspectives, on the other hand,
tend to neglect cultural processes and to focus their analysis at the
level of macro processes, neglecting the details of everyday life that
are determinant of action. In what follows, I draw on critical comparative-historical and anthropological perspectives on the social,
cultural and political role of Islam in Muslim societies in order to
elucidate the terms of a historicising approach to Islamist movements
and politics.

The critical perspective has subjected the arguments of culturalist
approaches to considerable scrutiny beginning with the construction
of Islam as an analytical category. As Sami Zubaida has succinctly
put it, the main problem with this construction is that it is based on
an idea of Islam as a coherent sociological and political entity.[36] Zubaida argues that there are many Muslim societies whose historical
variation cannot be unified in terms of common cultural items. Cultural themes referring to religious and historical traditions are
assigned different meanings in the different socio-political contexts.[37]
In Zubaida's view, '... cultural patterns are not fixed, but reproduced
at every generation in relation to different situations and conjunctures.'[38] It follows that these cultural themes should not be treated
as sociological or political constants. From this perspective, the
contemporary Islamist movements, much like other political developments, are not the expression of continuity and of persistent themes
of Islamic history. Rather, they are constituted as political forces
shaped by the socio-economic and political contexts in which they
operate.

If a homogeneous view of Islam, and the notion of 'Muslim society,' are found unacceptable from an analytical standpoint, how do
we approach the diversity of Muslim societies, or, as Talal Asad puts
it, how do we organise this diversity in terms of an adequate concept? Asad's insightful suggestion is to treat Islam as a discursive
tradition.[39] The concept of a discursive tradition as articulated by
Asad offers us the means of grasping the historicity of Islamic discourses. Key to this understanding is the idea that Muslim discourses
and the actors who articulate them are historically situated. Meanings and action are determined in relation to material conditions such

as institutional relations and the actors' positions of power. Just as actors are historically situated so too are discourses and frames of reference. The scripture should not be used to attribute homogeneity to Muslim societies since its interpretation is subject to contestation. The variation of interpretations and their insertion into particular contexts with varied meaning/power effects present us with a multitude of discourses that must be accounted for with reference to the power positions at stake.[40] It is the merit of Asad's conception of Islam as a discursive tradition that it underscores the dynamic processes of power and resistance involved in the production of practices and ideas authorised as Islamic. Claims to orthodoxy embody the power to authorise practices and ideas as Islamic. The processes and techniques through which this power is exercised, as well as the conditions which sustain it, are dimensions of the historicity of orthodoxy.[41]

Building on the concepts of discursive tradition and orthodoxy as a relation of power, it is possible to broaden our understanding of Islamist movements to incorporate both the strategies pursued by actors at the micro-social level, and the norms guiding action; the norms being articulated and defined in context and involving relations of power and struggles for hegemony. In other words, it is suggested here that the deployment of religious symbols and signs and the use of frames of reference derived from religious traditions belong to a power-laden field of action and practices. An important premise is that there are no inherent meanings to the text. Thus, to share or make use of the same frames of reference does not result in agreement on substantive meaning or positive content.[42] A clear case of the invocation of particular repertoires without agreement on content is the call for the application of the Shari'a.[43] In Egypt, advocates of the application of the Shari'a include both those who believe that it is not in place and those who assert that it is already applied. In substantive terms, there is no agreement on what the Shari'a and its application mean. For the Islamists, it has come to mean more than the implementation of personal status laws and the codification of the penal code to incorporate the *hudud* (religious ordinances). For them, the scope of the Shari'a covers the regulation of all aspects of life.[44] This view may be problematic in light of the fact that throughout its historical development, the Shari'a has covered a limited scope of social life. Objectors may point to the fact that the Qur'an and the Tradition do not address many of the questions arising in contemporary society. However, the key issue here is the practice of assigning an Islamic referent to the various forms of ordering and arranging society. This may involve the production of competing and multiple 'Islam' positions on disparate dimensions of the social order (as, for example, the 'Islam' position on nuclear proliferation, artificial insemination and space exploration). What would be the criteria for deciding the 'true' Islam position on these matters? How could the *ijtihad* (personal effort in interpretation) carried out be referred back to the scripture or the body of tradition? The invocation of these referents represents a discursive strategy, perhaps a rhetorical device. The 'Islam' position on any of these questions is more likely to be constructed outside the referent.[45]

If there are no inherent meanings, how do we account for religiosity and norms anchored in religious traditions? The situatedness and context-bound effects of all systems of meanings apply to norms articulated in reference to Islamic traditions. Examples of the socially constructed norms placed by actors within religious frames support this contention. The ambiguity involved in judging conformity and transgression in relation to everyday-life experiences demonstrates the contested nature of orthodoxy. This ambiguity is illustrated in the following cases of conformity with and transgression against socially and religiously sanctioned norms in Egypt and Morocco.

The first case features an Egyptian woman involved in an extramarital affair. She consults the Lajnat al-Fatwa (committee of religious rulings in al-Azhar) on how to deal with a neighbour's threat to publicly expose the affair.[46] The threat is accompanied by an offer to keep silent in exchange for the woman's sexual favours. The woman refuses to succumb to the neighbour's blackmail, but fears public exposure. The *fatwa* of the Lajnat advises that she end the illicit affair and not succumb to threats of publicity. In another case of adultery, a married couple in Egypt consults a Shaykh in Sayyida Zaynab.[47] The wife has confessed to an adulterous affair with the landlord of the house in which the couple lives. The shaykh advises that the husband forgive his wife and accept her repentance and that the marriage continue. The Lajnat's response in the first case, and the shaykh's advice in the second, both depart from the established norm of condemning adultery and seeking punishment following the transgressor's confession. Should the *fatwa* and the shaykh's opinion/advice be placed outside the realm of orthodoxy? In a case from Morocco, a Muslim woman helps an unmarried female friend get an abortion.[48] In undertaking this action, she viewed her support as private and not subject to societal rulings of morality. Instead, she considered herself to be answerable to God alone and the matter to be a strictly private affair.

In the adultery cases, we may note that the Lajnat and the shaykh drew on alternative traditions that discourage publicising transgressions and recommend clemency rather than punishment. In the case from Morocco, the exercise of individual morality superseded any notion of transcendental morality. Cases such as these abound and demonstrate the limited benefit of relying on scripture for apprehending societal norms even when they make explicit reference to religion, whether involving ordinary practising Muslims or individuals in positions of religious authority. The examples also confirm the idea that norms are constituted within alternative frames developed in reference to social situations and existing in public and semi-public spaces. Moreover, they may compete with dominant representations in the public sphere that are sustained by power relations. In the adultery cases, people sought to resolve their moral dilemma through the mediation of religion, by referral to the Lajnat and the shaykh. The resolution was framed in the language of religion. Yet, this did not amount simply to the following of the 'Rule.'[49] Nor was the resolution conditioned purely by religion. In the abortion case, the woman's mode of reasoning did not exclude the divine, but nor did it conform to religion as a set of rules. What is pertinent in these examples is that competing frames and situational logic shape the everyday-life experience of the interaction between religion and the social.

The cases serve as good entry points to the exploration of the relation between religiosity and Islamism. A number of studies assume implicitly that religiosity feeds into political engagement. Others present this link as a central hypothesis of inquiry. In her analysis of the conditions favouring the rise of what she terms the 'new religious politics' (NRP), of which Islamism is one example, Nikki Keddie contends the following:

> ... significant NRP movements thus far tend to occur *only* where in *recent decades* (whatever the distant past) religions with a supernatural and theistic content are believed in, or strongly identified with, by a large proportion of the population. In addition, either or both of the following must also be true in recent times: a high percentage of the population identifies with the basic tenets of its religious tradition regarding its god or gods, its scriptural text, and so forth. The only single word for this phenomenon is a term, normally used differently but recognizable – religiosity. Or else, or in addition, at least two strong communities exist.[50]

It should be pointed out that, for Keddie, religio-politics are determined by global trends but more centrally by 'religiosity,' understood as the belief in the basic tenets of a given religious tradition regarding its god, scripture and so on. But if we consider actual practices of conformity and transgression, as exemplified by the cases presented above, it becomes clear that a global world of religiosity totalising the practices of the believers does not exist.[51] As such, it may not be helpful to treat religiosity as a predisposition to religio-politics as does Keddie.[52] Nonetheless, it remains imperative to explore the nature of the relation between religiosity on one hand, and, on the other, an engagement in political activity that is justified using frames of reference drawn from religious traditions. As will be shown below, Jean-Noël Ferrié's work on practices associated with religiosity is instructive in this regard.

In exploring the relation between the social and religion, Ferrié demonstrates how the passage from one domain to the other is mediated by rituals that only acquire a substantive content through the individual's self-conception. It should be stressed that this self-conception is a social production involving processes of constituting meaning and producing norms. In his study of solicitation prayers, Ferrié shows that the practice of calling on God with specific demands is driven by a particular mode of life.[53] What the supplicant asks of the divine is conditioned by the social setting. In other words, reference to God does not equal transhistoricity of the referent.[54] Further, invoking the divine is not the same as submitting to the rule.[55] In its

relation to the social dynamic, religion ceases to be religion and becomes one dimension of social relations and interaction. Thus, if
religiosity is socially conditioned, we need to explore the links between particular expressions of religiosity and the advocacy of Islamist
politics. Two questions can be posed here:[56] (i) in what way do the
multiple inscriptions of religious reference in everyday life serve to
facilitate the acquiescence to Islamism? (ii) to what extent is the reference to motifs and themes from religion undertaken with regard
to activities without necessarily conforming to the religion as a set
of rules?

The link between religiosity and Islamism is also explored with
reference to the discursive practices of Islamist movements. There is
no doubt that repertoires and frames of reference reconstructed from
Islamic traditions are at work in the contemporary political scene in
a number of Muslim societies. As argued by Beaudoin Dupret and
Jean-Noël Ferrié, the invocation of these frames represents a strategy of action and a mode of insertion into the political scene.[57] This
is true of groups belonging to different social strata and occupying
varying positions in the social formation. The analysis of the strategies of action pursued by the Islamists in the cultural sphere in Egypt
reveals the simultaneous process of redefining old norms while framing the present in terms of those norms.

The deployment of frames and repertoires from Islamic traditions
in new forms is seen by some as a dilution of the Islamic referent.[58]
A correlate of this is the assessment that Islamism has failed and that
what we witness today is the advent of post-Islamism.[59] Thus, the
hybridity of symbols in the public sphere, noted above, is constructed
as a breakdown in the coherence of the Islamist alternative. Examples of this incoherence are the mixed attire of women (i.e. combining
the veil with jeans or tights), social solidarity with a Western philan-
thropic flair, or engagement in community organisation that betrays
patronage and clientelism rather than Islamic equality.[60] (This argument is subject to close scrutiny in chapter six). Based on the premise
of dilution, the registry of various Islamist manifestations and forms
of re-Islamisation attests to the ideological bankruptcy of Islamism.
However, this approach ignores the hegemonic practices that are at
the core of the production of orthodoxy. The deployment and

mobilisation of certain repertoires articulate relations to power. The structuring of the political field in terms of cultural invasion, authenticity and the licit and illicit is linked to power struggles, modes of domination and social control. This is demonstrated in my analysis of conservative Islamist discourse in chapter two and the Islamist strategies in the cultural sphere in chapter three.

Towards an Integrated Approach: A Comparative-Historical and Interpretative Understanding of Contemporary Islamist Movements

As pointed out by Edmund Burke III, the study of movements in their historical contexts emphasises their patterns and connections to structures of social action.[61] This kind of analysis looks at the institutions that organise social and political life, and the local economic and social structures that shape social movements. Of central importance is the linkage between changing social structures and patterns of action. Attention to context bridges the macro and micro levels of analysis to highlight the relationship between macro changes and micro everyday-life forms of social and political organisation. Infrastructures of action cannot be identified a priori – on the assumption that social actors necessarily react in particular ways to certain macro social and economic transformations. Rather, the formation of societal groupings during periods of change must be studied in relation to practices and strategies of action at the local level. Community organisation, cultural practices, spatial forms and other determinants of local-level action must be seen as part of a dynamic, ongoing interplay between the various levels of the social and the political.

In my examination of prevailing approaches to Islamist movements, I have noted the tendency to generalise about socio-historical conditions. These conditions, as found in the Middle East where most of the movements are active, are characterised in these approaches either by decline and decay or as expressing a national crisis in which the state fails to meet rising expectations. As a result, Islamist opposition emerges as the expression of social discontent. These features may be present in Islamist movements, but they do not equate to structures of action and change. It may be helpful to uphold the distinction between general socio-economic processes and specific historical conditions.[62] For the countries of the Middle East, the general socio-economic processes are those associated with the insertion of national economies/markets into the capitalist world economy. This took different forms during colonial and post-colonial times. In a number of Arab countries during the post-colonial period, the articulation of the national economies with the international economic system took the form of state capitalism sustained by corporatist structures and a degree of welfarism and populism. By the 1970s, the rentier economic activity that was predominant in the oil-producing states became a feature of most of the other Arab states. The structural changes accompanying the shift from state capitalism to rentier market economies, along with the socio-political processes that spanned both economic conjunctures (in particular, the crystallisation of the spheres of relative societal autonomy) constituted the background against which Islamist politics took shape. In what follows, I outline the contours of the development of these processes as they shaped the formation of Islamist movements in Egypt, Algeria and Tunisia.[63]

In Egypt, a dynamic process of constituting multiple social and political forces has occurred. Interaction among these forces, and between them and the state, contributes to further shifts and transformations in the political field. The present configuration of Islamist politics points to the various processes that are at work in the rise of Islamism and that are transformative of state-society relations. There is no need to search for an original first cause or a triggering event behind Islamism. Instead, we should note the transformative processes that reorient the political field. The end of the ideological hegemony of the nationalist discourse in Egypt, in conjunction with the socio-political developments of the 1960s, represents one dimension of changing state-society relations. Another is the expansion of the arena of informal politics. This occurred through processes of community organisation and network formation in the semi-autonomous communities that emerged as distinctive urban spaces in Cairo. Key features of these communities were the presence of the informal economy and informal (unregulated) housing. Islamism, as an oppositional movement, linked up with these new

autonomous urban spaces. Islamist activism in urban neighbourhoods
became intermeshed with the societal modes of organisation and with
local power struggles. However, opposition to government is not the
only form that Islamist politics has taken. Islamist discourses have
been articulated within state structures and by dominant social forces
tied to the rentier economic activities and non-productive capitalist
economy of the 1980s and 90s. What has emerged in Egypt is a multitude of actors who articulate competing Islamist discourses and who
structure the political field in particular terms through their
interaction.

The analysis of the micro contexts of Islamist movements in Egypt,
Algeria and Tunisia indicates that structural transformations, beginning in the 1970s, have contributed to the development of particular
forms of organisation at the local level. In Algeria, much like Egypt,
semi-autonomous spheres emerged in the urban setting where the
informal economy thrived. The social groupings constituted in the
course of these transformations enjoyed a degree of autonomy and
occupied oppositional positions. The articulation of this oppositional
stance in Islamist terms was not inevitable. Local conditions, as determined by particular social relations and cultural practices, favoured
the organisation of this opposition in Islamist terms. Societal disengagement has unfolded gradually at the local level in popular quarters
and communities. Its nodal points are the urban neighbourhoods –
their mosques, economic enterprises, cultural and sporting associations and the web of social relations traversing them. In this
disengagement, the actors, whether entrepreneurs/contractors, small
merchants or *trabendistes* (smugglers/traffickers), are socially constituted through the expansion of the informal economy. The
engagement of these social forces in Islamist politics, and the strategies they pursue, are shaped by their positioning from the state and
their standing in the social hierarchy. For the entrepreneurs, support
of Islamist groups (FIS and Nahda for instance) reinforced their position of notability and enhanced their economic and political power.
For small merchants and *trabendistes*, their pursuit of Islamist politics
represented an affirmation of their autonomy or a protection of gains
achieved. Local activism linked up with national struggles involving
the various wings of the state, particularly the secularists and the

Islamists. At the national level, Islamist politics became imbricated in the historical divisions involving military cliques and state clans. The interaction among the multitude of actors and factions was shaped by the juncture of economic privatisation that took the form of the liquidation of state assets and their transfer into private hands.

Islamist politics develops in relation to existing political fields, building on, extending and modifying patterns of interaction. The political field, as Zubaida points out, does not refer merely to the state and the elites, but includes other actors and societal spheres of action. Politics is not restricted to the circumscribed formal sphere.[64] Even in countries like Tunisia, centralised state structures do not exhaust the political field and are not the only loci of power. Complex processes involving state and non-state actors and different forms of interaction are also productive of the political. A widening of the conception of politics to recognise the relations of power structuring everyday communities allows us to see the terms of Islamist insertion into the political field. In Tunisia, the Islamist intervention in urban neighbourhoods came at moments of loosened state control. The Islamists' ability to mobilise popular support was constrained by the historical structures of state-society incorporation at the local level and by societal forces' instrumentalisation of mediating spaces and agents.

The development of Islamist movements was conditioned by a particular micro-setting and specific processes tied up with changing social conditions. At the same time, these movements linked up with social and cultural practices of everyday life. Practices of societal control covered a wide range of relations and interaction such as gender relations, solidarity, arbitration and sociability. We should react guardedly to views holding that Islamists are ubiquitous or that Islamism is homogeneous and homogenising. Indeed, alternative lifestyles and hybridity stand as evidence that a more nuanced understanding is needed.

Conclusion

In revisiting the literature dealing with contemporary Islamist movements, I have discussed the conceptual difficulties that may be found in the dominant approaches. Essentialist perspectives are not only limited in terms of their explanatory power, but obscure the multiplicity and diversity characterising Islamist politics and Islamism. I suggest that this diversity can be understood in terms of power struggles, the patterns of insertion of micro-level actors into the political field, and everyday practices of social control. The invocation of repertoires and frames of reference developed in Islamic traditions involves a process of reworking these traditions, redefining norms and reconstructing signs and symbols. Hence, ideas of recurrence and revival, where Islamist movements are concerned, are mistaken and fail to capture the complexity and the dynamic nature of this process. There are no inherent meanings or persistent ideas continuing into the present and guaranteeing the unity of a totality called Islam. Notions of religion and religiosity as external to the setting and as determinant of action forsake comparative-historical and interpretative analysis for the comfort of a priori textual certainties.

Critical comparative-historical and anthropological approaches suggest the terms of analysis needed to break out of the mould of essentialism and the framework of revival and renewal. These approaches emphasise the historical situatedness of Islamist movements. This is not the same as viewing them as a moral reaction to a context of decay or a psychological response to conditions of economic strain. Islamist movements, like other social movements, develop within infrastructures of action and are geared toward particular political fields.

2

Confronting the Other:
Conservative Islamism in Egypt

The rise of Islamist groups in Egypt's polity and society is given force through the articulation of a set of competing yet inter-linked discourses that challenge the authority of the post-independence secular nationalist discourse and attempt to reconstitute the field of struggle and domination in religious terms. Concurrently, these discourses seek authoritative status over the scope of meanings related to questions of identity, history, and the place of Islam in the world. The interpretations and definitions elaborated in reference to these questions by radical Islamist forces (the Jihad groups and other militant Islamist elements) are often seen to dominate the entire field of meaning. However, claims to authority over issues of government, morality, identity, and Islam's relationship to the West are also made in and through a discourse that can appropriately be labelled 'conservative Islamist.' The discourse and political role of conservative Islamism are the subject of this essay.

Conservative Islamism in Contemporary Egyptian Politics

The conservative Islamist discourse is articulated by Islamist political forces working within legal channels such as the right-wing al-Ahrar (Liberal) Party and its ideologues.[1] The discourse is best represented in the al-Ahrar Party's two publications, *al-Ahrar* and *al-Nur*, but can be found in the al-'Amal (Labour) Party's press organ, *al-Sha'b*, and in a number of the Muslim Brotherhood's publications, including *al-Mukhtar* and *al-I'tisam*. As such, the discourse is tied to the forces of the Islamist alliance formed in 1987 and to the regrouping of al-Ahrar, al-'Amal, and the Brotherhood for electoral purposes. This does not mean that the conservative Islamist discourse is the cement that binds these forces. In fact, one finds various manifestations of Islamism within these groupings. However, conservative Islamism is not confined to an oppositional role in Egyptian politics. Rather, it can be located in state institutions in the words and personage of a number of shaykhs associated with the state. It also finds expression in the official media. State-affiliated conservative shaykhs such as Shaykh Sha'rawi and 'Abd al-Sabur Shahin are given a forum for their ideas in state-sponsored newspapers such as *al-Liwa' al-Islami* and *'Aqidati*. Further, they reach a wide audience through the extensive circulation of their polemics on cassette and video and their frequent television appearances. These forces are labelled "conservative" because of their willingness to work within the established order and because they promote hierarchical and patriarchal values reinforcing the status quo.

Before proceeding to an investigation of the terms of the conservative Islamist discourse and the role of conservative forces in shaping the political field in Egypt, it is important to note some of the lines of distinction between conservative and radical Islamists. The common denominator among the militants/radicals is their advocacy of and resort to violence in their effort to establish the Islamic state. A first distinction between radical Islamism and conservative Islamism, therefore, concerns their respective strategies and modes of action. The former adopts violent means to bring about social transformation, while the latter works within the existing institutions to Islamise society while preserving the political status quo.[2] A second distinction relates to the content of their respective ideologies. The radicals articulate a clear denunciation of society as *jahiliya* (state of ignorance before Islam) and of government as un-Islamic. The concept of *hakimiya* (God's sovereignty) is central to their doctrine and to their call for jihad.[3] The conservatives anchor their discourse in popular traditions with concerns about the afterlife, the spirits and rituals. Morality is an area of convergence between the two groups, although conservatives do not dwell on the issue of the legality of present-day government. A more comprehensive basis of differentiation must include the socio-economic positions occupied by these groupings. This is captured in the categories of *Islam al-thawra* and *Islam al-tharwa* (Islam of revolution and Islam of riches), which underscore the class affiliation of the two lines of Islamism. Conservative Islamism is identified with petro-dollars, while radical Islamism draws support from the less well off segments of society.[4] Finally, there is a need to emphasise the location of both in the overall political configuration by looking at their relations to the state, to other political groups and to one another.[5]

It should be noted that the two categories of conservative Islamism and radical Islamism do not exhaust the whole range of Islamist ideas and activities. Islamist politics in Egypt extends from organised groups such as the Muslim Brotherhood organisation to informal groupings such as the 'Islamist lawyers.'[6] The Muslim Brotherhood itself is associated with positions and individuals who are seen to represent various lines of Islamism. In fact, the attempt to establish the al-Wasat Party in 1996 by individuals from the new generation of the Muslim Brotherhood reflects divisions within the organisation. There was dissension in the ranks over both the idea of establishing a party and the route to be taken. These divisions are seen as generational – between the old guard and a new vanguard – as well as representing differences over procedures and ways of thinking.[7]

Islamists pursue a variety of strategies aimed at the Islamisation of social arenas and the appropriation of the public sphere. The Islamisation of the professional syndicates along with social service networks set up by the Islamists are differing facets of their struggle for power.[8] Conforming to its strategy of working within existing institutions, the Muslim Brotherhood found in the professional syndicates an arena to expand its ranks and develop a strong base among an important segment of society. In running candidates for executive-board positions in the syndicates, the Brotherhood presented an alternative to the government-controlled leadership as well as to the secular liberals and leftist activists. Meanwhile, social service networks have emerged, some of which are set up by Islamic charitable organisations with no particular political affiliation; others are controlled by the Muslim Brotherhood and the militant groups. Private voluntary organisations, which are usually connected to mosques, have been established by the Brotherhood and the al-Jama'a al-Islamiya.[9] The development of these kinds of organisations is of strategic importance to the Islamist groups. For instance, structures such as 'the mosque complex' are engaged in expanded activities ranging from preaching and gathering believers to the provision of social services. Mosques have also served as headquarters for militant groups.[10] Naturally, the mosque is a space of activity for the conservatives. The 1980s and 1990s saw a reassertion of the phenomenon of popular preachers claiming their own followers or devotees and effectively mobilising public opinion. In this regard, the pulpit is used by conservative shaykhs to wage battle on questions of morality with secular intellectuals.[11]

In an earlier study dealing with contemporary Islamism, conservatives are viewed as a part of a wider fundamentalist trend and a return to religiosity.[12] According to this view, a commonality of ideas and beliefs characterises the various manifestations of Islam across time and space. Thus, in surveying the signs of the 'conservative periphery' in Egypt, Emmanuel Sivan puts forward the following thesis: 'Fundamentalism – in the sense of a world view harking back to the essential verities of the faith – thus seems not to be restricted to the militants alone: it permeates conservative circles as well.'[13] This underlying essentialism projects a disembodied view of Islamist groups and movements, failing to appreciate the nature of the interplay among the various groups and their socio-political setting.

In contrast, conservative Islamism is seen here as being shaped by the socio-economic context of contemporary Egypt. It is articulated in relation to power positions, and in turn shapes power relations in society. Central to this approach is the concept of ideology understood as a relation to power.[14] As such, in examining the operation of ideology through language, the purpose is to evaluate its impact on the dominant relations of power in society. In other words, our interest is to assess the role of the conservative Islamist ideology in strengthening or transforming these relations. In studying movements and ideologies that ground themselves in Islam, it is important to take account of the traditions that are called upon and inserted into the contemporary Islamist discourses.[15] However, invoking particular traditions is not viewed as the expression of a revival or recurrence of some fundamental ideas and principles. Instead, Islamist movements and ideologies are placed in their socio-historical conjuncture.[16] In other words, Islamist discourses are understood by examining how they shape and are shaped by their socio-political setting.

Conservative Islamism operates in a context of socio-political transformation, marked by the rising challenge of militant Islamists. The confrontation between the militants and the state that spanned the 1980s and has continued into the 1990s took the form of assassination attempts on state officials, an escalation of Jihad activities with a campaign against tourism, and a heightening of social warfare with attacks aimed at the symbols of *jahiliya* in society.[17] This period also witnessed the proliferation of Islamist groups, although the two main contestants remain the Jihad and the al-Jama'a al-Islamiya.[18] These groups are most active in upper Egypt and in the peripheral areas of Cairo, particularly in the informal housing communities. The militants have virtually declared war on the state, turning certain upper Egyptian governorates and cities into war zones. Places such as Mallawi and Abu Qurqas in Minya have become contested territories. The state responded with, and at times initiated, crackdown campaigns aimed at extricating the Islamists from their stronghold.[19] Under the state emergency rules, trials of the militants went before military courts in order to speed up and control the process. In its confrontation with the militants, the state also called on its official *'ulama* and was able to gather support in the form of al-Mufti's report in 1981, the al-Azhar statement in 1987, and various other documents condemning the Islamists as religious extremists.[20] In addition, the state has been engaged in propagating its own brand of Islam, sponsoring religious newspapers and television programmes, and expanding the powers of al-Azhar in censoring un-Islamic intellectual and artistic productions.[21]

Conservative Islamism is closely associated with this state-sponsored religiosity and morality. It is precisely the insertion of the conservatives into this context that should be stressed. Conservatives put forward an alternative frame of ordering the world. As guardians of 'orthodox' and 'moderate' Islam, they contain the radicals while Islamising the state at the cultural level and setting the boundaries of public discourse. Culture and morality constitute the grounds upon which the *problématique* of the time is articulated: a cultural conflict with the outside and the struggle for the preservation of public morality inside. The convergence between the conservatives and the state puts limits on the positions available, not only neutralising the militants but also containing the Islamic left and circumventing the secularists.

The theme of cultural conflict constitutes common ground among a number of Islamist discourses and movements. This does not, however, imply unity among them, as is suggested in some studies which view Islamic thought as embodying the fundamental principles shaping the Muslims' action. Such an approach tends to attribute continuity to Islamic movements. Its underlying view, as Eric Davis has noted, is that these movements emerge as a response to the West.[22] This perspective guides William Shepard's typologies of Islamic groups, which are classified according to their position from modernity and the role they attribute to Islam in politics.[23] In a similar fashion, Hrair Dekmejian sees Islamism as an expression of a revivalist tradition in Islam and as a response to internal decay. As such, it is a cyclical occurrence.[24] These studies are instructive in terms of noting the positioning of particular groups in relation to Western material progress and values. However, they tell us little of local contexts, social groups, dynamics of interaction, and power struggles. Yet it is precisely by examining the dynamics of the insertion of Islamism into the overall political and socio-historical context that we can acquire a better understanding of the nature of contemporary Islamism. Key questions centre on how a particular Islamist force interacts with other actors, and how the interplay among the various groups shapes their positioning.

In examining the discourse and political role of conservative Islamism, this chapter integrates these questions by looking at how conservative Islamism is constituted as a political and ideological force in the contemporary Egyptian socio-political setting. In trying to locate conservative Islamism in relation to other Islamist groupings, the chapter goes beyond providing a classification of a particular brand of Islamism. Rather, it maps out the various positions occupied by Islamist actors on the political scene, drawing attention to their relationship to the state and to militant Islamism. In this regard, the analysis is focused on the configuration of the political scene that emerges out of the actors' positions and the dynamics of their interaction.

The chapter puts forward the argument that conservative Islamism occupies a key position in shaping the structure of the political field. This is done in a manner that serves to maintain a political balance, allowing a neutralisation of the tensions caused by Islamist militancy. The ascendancy of conservative Islamism is also situated in relation to the material conditions of Egypt's social formation. In placing the conservative Islamist discourse in this context, the analysis demonstrates how, in constructing the *problématique* of cultural confrontation, it displaces the social and national struggle and produces an identity totalised in religious and moral terms. In so doing, it serves to sustain the dominant relations of power.

In the following three sections, I examine the discourse of conservative Islamist forces in Egypt; point to its links to other discourses – namely, the discourses on morals and rituals and on usury; and elucidate some aspects of its relation to the material conditions in which it is inscribed. In section two, an analysis of various texts representative of these forces looks at the meanings and concepts articulated by the conservative Islamist discourse, as well as the main themes that unfold through it. In this regard, the analysis focuses on the narratives that structure the discourse, highlighting two principal narratives: confrontation with the Other and superiority of the Self. It also examines the discursive mechanisms used to validate these narratives, mainly the use of history as a tool of validation and argumentative strategies deployed against its opponents. Section three, presents the key features of two discourses, complementary to the conservative Islamist discourse, which are active in articulating definitions and restrictions in the domains of morality, culture, and commerce.[25] In their aim to circumscribe the bounds of 'correct' practice in the private and public spheres, and thus construct a religious orthodoxy, these discourses are supported by actions that seek, on the grounds of morality, to challenge cultural productions. Finally, the essay analyses the discourse's position in relation to the political field and the forces that are active in it, particularly the secularists and the Islamic left.

The Conservative Islamist Discourse

The narrative organisation

The writings considered here are articles from official publications of the right-wing Islamist opposition party, al-Ahrar, and from independent magazines and newspapers in association with the right-wing Islamist opposition. Also included are a number of essays by Anwar al-Jindi, who has links with the Muslim Brotherhood and is associated with al-Ahrar publications.[26] Two simple but central narratives emerge from an analysis of these writings.[27] One announces the confrontation with the Other (the West); and the other asserts the superiority of Islam. These narratives serve as organising principles of the discourse. In a sense, they represent the worldview of the conservatives – their vision of the present state of society and religion and how the world is ordered. These narratives are analysed with a view to outlining their recurrent themes as well as the elements that give them a certain coherence and orientation.

Narrative of confrontation with the Other

The narrative of confrontation with the Other is articulated in terms of the threat of a cultural attack on Islam. This attack takes various forms, including proselytisation, intellectual invasion and the subjugation of Islamic concepts to Western ideas. The attack is aimed at Islam as understood as a cultural system that encompasses all aspects of the Muslim's identity. In one rendering, the 'assault' by the Other is cast as 'an attempt to encircle and destroy the make-up of Muslims and Arabs and denigrate their thought.'[28] A number of themes signal the assault and describe its features. These are: the pervasiveness of the attack; interaction with the Other as a cause of corruption; infiltration and distortion; and danger of annihilation.

The threat of cultural attack finds signs in the pervasive presence of the Other. The cultural assault has, in fact, penetrated an extensive range of institutions and socio-cultural realms, such as schools, the media, the arts, and popular tastes. These institutions figure as targets of the attack, and by virtue of their association with the secular state have come to signify the attack itself. Thus, 'school curriculum' is a target but also bears the marks of the assault in the form of 'Western concepts [:] ... Darwin's theory of creation, Freud's theory of the psyche, Durkheim's theory of society.'[29] The attack itself is likened to a 'tempest' (a sign of englobing and immersion), which carries 'poison through education, the press, theatre, film, fashion and clothes.'[30]

A second theme that is repeated within the frame of the narrative of cultural invasion points to the corrupting effects of interaction with the Other. Contact with or opening onto the outside are presented as dangers to the Islamic identity. These contacts may take the form of 'cultural exchange programmes,' 'scientific and educational missions,' 'visiting professors,' and 'foreign training experts,' all of which are identified as means and agents of proselytisation. Interaction with the Other is viewed as a process of transformation causing atheism, immorality (exemplified by the casting away of the veil), and a threat to Islam. A relation of cause and effect between contact with the Other and corruption is implied, giving rise to the ideological claim that the Other is morally corrupt.

In a third theme, the infiltration, distortion, and misrepresentation of Islam are articulated as features of the cultural attack and as part of an ongoing conspiracy against Islam. The attack is achieved through infiltration, implying the presence of hidden or disguised forces that are, in turn, projected as elements of distortion. Examples of disguised attacks are drawn from contemporary developments. A case in point is Salman Rushdie's *The Satanic Verses*, which serves as a symbol of distortive works against Islam. It is compared, by way of analogy, to the insertion of Israelite works into the body of the Islamic tradition. In the tradition, these latter represent both distortion and infiltration. Rushdie himself is an infiltrator 'who claimed entry to Islam,' an act that is described as 'an old Jewish trick used during the early age of Islam.'[31]

Efforts to distort Islam have also been undertaken by internal intellectual forces working in conjunction with the Other. Writings by these intellectuals dealing with the Islamic heritage are described as an 'infiltration' carried out in disguise. As indicated in the following, they constitute 'the presentation of Marxist thought … in an Islamic dress to deceive the reader.'[32]

Infiltration and distortion are articulated around the opposition between the hidden and the revealed or exposed. Thus, behind Rushdie's 'satanic work,' there is 'a hidden Jewish hand,'[33] while supporters of secularism have 'resorted to infiltration through the back door.'[34] The presence of infiltrators has been exposed and revealed by al-Azhar students who 'unmasked the face of the proselytisers,'[35] and by researchers who 'have revealed the Judaic roots in Western concepts.'[36] The hidden is associated with deception: 'Proselytisers and Orientalists slip the poison into the honey;'[37] 'these conspiracies do not come in an explicit fashion but in deception.'[38] Disguise and deception are further evoked in: '[Proselytisation messages] come on paper decorated with an Islamic motif with the name of God the most merciful in the middle, and, on the sides, commandments from the Old and New Testaments;'[39] 'Marxism infiltrated into our countries carrying the banner of progress and security.'[40] These cautionary messages about infiltration and deception serve as a pretext for an inquisition into the background of thinkers and writers, and for classifying them as either 'true' Muslims or infiltrators and *kafirun* (infidels).

A final theme is constructed around the notion of danger of annihilation. Specifically, the cultural assault threatens Islam with destruction. This underlines the dangers of absorption, or 'melting away,' faced by the entire nation, region, or civilisation. These images appear over and over in the discourse, as in the following: 'The Orient … will dissolve in the wide furnace which will melt it and destroy its existence;' 'Resistance to the intellectual invasion is a necessary and grave task to protect the nation from annihilation and melting away.'[41] The fatality of the threat is signified in: 'only Islam is the target of the swords of … the Crusades, Zionism and atheism.'[42] The same signification is found in: 'Egypt, country of al-Azhar, Mecca, 'the honest country,' are among the targeted countries.'[43] Here, the signs used to designate the targets are substantive symbols of Islam. Mecca is the birthplace of the religion and is its guardian, while Egypt is 'the true Islamic force,' 'the primary state in the Islamic East.' Thus, because Egypt is conceived as the heart of Islam, an attack upon the country is fatal. All signs of the presence of the Other (invasion) are associated with such terms as 'destructive,' 'dissolution,' and 'tearing down.' The assault is also represented as 'the attempt to destroy society and turn it into rubble via vulgarity of the novel and existential philosophy.'[44] It should be stressed that the 'grave' attack is conceived as a cultural invasion, thus constructing culture as the defining character of the Self and the Other.

The multi-faceted Other

Having indicated the terms by which the discourse represents the cultural confrontation, we should focus on who or what is designated as the Other in the discourse. A multiplicity of signs denominate the Other – the Crusaders, the proselytisers (i.e., the Christian West), the Orientalists (the West), the Westernisers, Zionism, secularists, Marxists, communists, and atheists – suggesting the existence of a number of different and distinct entities. This also gives the appearance that more than one opponent exists, or that from one text to another the opponent changes, and thus it is not a unitary identity. However, all of these actors are manifested in association with the West. Secularism, for instance, is produced in total identity with the West, while Zionism is presented in conjunction with both the Crusaders and secularism. Marxists, atheists, and communists seem to belong to a different entity – the atheist world in opposition to the Christian world – yet they slide back to and acquire an association with the West, which appears as a whole of which they are a part (French Marxists, for example). They also appear in conjunction with the Orientalists and the proselytisers. Some actors, such as the Crusaders, proselytisers, and Orientalists, are presented in virtual synonymy with the West. In sum, all the signs designating the Other slide back as 'the West.' In a sense, the many others coalesce into a singular unit – the West – which also unfolds as the non-Islamic. The same is true of internal forces that are conceived as the enemies of

Islam. Arab Marxists, nationalists, and secularists are identified with the West in statements such as: 'Preachers of secularism are those who are immersed in Western culture,'[45] signifying their foreign character and association.

The distinctive properties of Islam

The confrontation with the Other is articulated in terms of opposing systems of values. This opposition finds expression within two notional indexes: the first, an index of 'completeness' whereby Islam is presented as 'comprehensive' and 'unitary' versus the fragmented and divided Other; and the second, an index of 'mutability' in which stability has a higher value and is associated with Islam, whereas the Other is associated with absolute change and progress – values that are constituted as negative. The use of these indexes invests Islam with the properties of multi-dimensionality and unity, and confers on the West the properties of 'fragmentation' and 'unidimensionality.' Progress is constituted as a negative value, particularly when it is associated with ethics.

Islam as a comprehensive message does, however, account for change, albeit a change founded on the permanent and the unchangeable. Change and movement are conceived as grounded in order and stability, an order that is rooted in the religion and that sets the boundaries of change: 'Change is movement within the frame of the fundamentals of religion.'[46] It is important to note that ethics and instinct are produced in positive association with each other, both being immutable and stable in character and valorised due to their relation to religion. The various associations between these concepts has the effect of investing stability with a high normative content; it is instituted as part of the natural order and hence a defining aspect of instinct and ethics.[47]

In this context, the notion of 'absolute change' associated with the West appears as a transgression against the norm and order of the universe and is explained as an element of Western atomism: 'Atomism ... called for the relativity of ethics and absolute progress which is not based on a fixed orbit.'[48] Western concepts of change are found to inhabit the realm of the unnatural and are made contrary to instinct and belief: 'The theory of evolution is in opposition to instinct and the Islamic system of thought which dictates that the universe is constant and evolving.'[49] Thus, two conceptions of change emerge: one associated with order and restraint and sanctioned by the religion and instinct, the other absolute and standing in opposition to nature and the rules of the universe.

It should be noted that the conceptualisation of stability as the character of ethics and instinct is developed in a space of conflict with the secular discourse which posits change as the defining property of the human being. Egyptian secularists have argued that the human being is a changing creature and, therefore, the laws which govern him or her must change. The human being undergoes fundamental changes from one time to another and from one space to another. Change is also the defining character of values and ethics. In effect, there are no constants in the human field. This is carried to the conclusion that there are no laws which are valid for all space and time.[50] It is this conception of change that the conservative Islamist discourse attempts to refute through the inscription of absolute change in the realm of the unnatural.

The narrative of sanction: the superiority of Islam

Out of the distinction between Islam and the West, there emerges in the discourse a thematic defined here as 'the superiority of Islam' and corresponding, in our analysis, to the narrative of sanction. Its two major aspects – Islam's role as the leader of humanity and the collapse of the Other – were in fact part of the turn-of-the-century discourse of *Nahda* (Renaissance). In his critique of the Arab and Islamic discourse of Renaissance, the contemporary Arab intellectual Muhammad 'Abid al-Jabiri points out that the tensions that underlie articulations regarding Islam's superiority develop out of the perceived difference between the lived reality and the reality that is formed from the model of Islamic resurgence.[51] These tensions appear in the conservative Islamist discourse under study, wherein the announced success of Islam is oriented toward the future – a time of uncertainty. History is called on to overcome these tensions by guaranteeing the truth of Islam's inevitable success.

The particular ideological significance of the 'superiority of Islam' theme depends on the context within which it is inserted. For example, the Egyptian radical Islamic thinker Sayyid Qutb, writing in the 1950s when socialist principles were part of the opposition groups' discourses, developed a notion of Islam's superiority that was tied to values of equality and social justice. In Qutb's *The Battle of Islam and Capitalism*, the theme enters into a complex network of meanings in which the Other is both the Christian West and the imperialist West. The crusaders and the imperialists belong to the same entity. The war on Islam is caused by the latter's commitment to absolute equality.[52] In this context, Islam as a threat to the West is conceived as an obstacle in the way of imperialism and exploitation.[53] The reasons behind the Western assault have to do with the challenge represented by the social values of Islam. For Qutb, Islam's superiority is tied to its values of equality and justice.

When we turn to the manifestation of this theme in the conservative Islamist discourse, we find that the superiority of Islam is presented as a given or as an element of the religious truth. This bestows on the faith a higher duty – that of leading humanity: 'Only Islam possesses a superior capacity and assets to lead the whole of humanity.'[54] This duty is represented as a universal fact that is known to everyone: 'The whole world recognises the power of Islam and its capacity of expansion and good leadership and guidance of humanity;'[55] 'International circles have declared ...the longing of humanity for a merciful, just system which only Islam can offer.'[56] In effect, Islam's role becomes messianic, as the religion and its followers are perceived as predestined to lead: 'They [the Muslims] are the ones chosen by God to deliver his message to the Universe;' 'They are the superiors, they carry the noblest system and the most generous and dignified message – the greatest call;'[57] 'The world looks to Islam as the saviour from the siege of the Western system.' Moreover, the Other appears as cognisant of its inevitable demise: 'People in the West are searching for a religion and a creator – only Islam can provide an alternative.'[58]

As the narrative proceeds, recognition of the superiority of the Self is made concomitant with the demise of the Other.[59] In other words, the sanctioning of Islam as the leader of humanity is predicated on the collapse of the West. This is presented as a process of decay that is already taking place, with the actual collapse about to happen: 'Western society reveals the crises which face contemporary man, society and social life;' 'The Western civilisation offered to Muslims has reached a stage of deterioration and collapse;'[60] 'The secular experiment and most of what the West proposes today has failed to achieve its goal in its own environment.'[61] The inevitable death of the Other is announced in: 'Islam is the heir to these systems [capitalist and communist];'[62] '[This] behaviour demonstrates the bankruptcy of the enemies of Islam and their despair.'[63] The subject of the discourse, the Muslim, is used to further support the idea of the Other's failure: 'Muslims have realised that their experiment with liberalism has failed;'[64] 'It has been revealed that both Marxist and Western ideologies have failed to provide the Muslim soul with its ambition and their experience has failed.'[65] In this context, all opposing ideologies and value systems are classified as discredited remnants of the past, including secularism, which is dismissed as a failure.

Discursive organisation

In the following section, the main elements of the discourse's organisation are presented.[66] As indicated, the main message of the conservative Islamist discourse revolves around the announcement of the cultural attack and the assertion of Islam's superiority. The truth of this message is established through certain discursive mechanisms – namely, the use of history as a tool of validation and the articulation of counter-arguments to refute the position of opponents (i.e. the secularists). These mechanisms serve to validate the narratives described above.

History: A tool of validation

In the unfolding of the narrative of confrontation, history is used as a tool to establish the truth of various propositions about the present. Symbols of the confrontation, as it occurs today, are made analogous to earlier symbols, signifying not only the similarities between the past and present confrontation, but also its permanence. The extension of historical events into the present and future thus functions as a sign of the confrontation's continuity: 'The role of Salah al-Din during the Crusade wars was not and will not be forgotten by history – especially [in] Europe where the name of Salah al-Din still evokes resentment and hatred.'[67] Historical continuity is further manifested in: 'since the dawn of Islam;' 'from the time of revelation.'[68]

History also serves to validate the narrative of sanction. Here, the force and resilience of Islam are expressed in terms of the continuity of its tradition: 'The deep-rooted presence of Islam in this nation for fourteen centuries. ..was always capable of protecting it from collapse.'[69] This construction is made all the more effective as a means of validation by evoking the ephemeral nature of the interruption caused by colonialism. In one instance, the colonial interruption is likened to a 'raid' that was a short-lived experience. In this sense, historical continuity constructs a semantic space of authenticity and truth: 'The Islamic current is not a recent phenomenon but a rooted authentic reality encompassing all of society and representing its entirety, originating from its depths, soul and roots.'[70]

Argumentative discourse: Secularism as foreign and alien

The arguments articulated in the conservative Islamist discourse are developed in response to the secular discourse. One of the main objectives of the argumentation is to establish that secularism is alien to Islam. This conclusion is arrived at by first defining secularism in terms that render it specific to the Western experience. In this respect, secularism is defined as a historical development that emerged out of the conditions of the Middle Ages in Europe. The most salient feature is the polemical confrontation over the definitions of secularism, the religious state, and the Islamic state.[71] The definition of secularism enters into the arguments deployed against secularists by setting forth the idea that, as a concept and as a principle of social organisation, it can be upheld only under a particular set of circumstances. The definition produces a contextual restriction that acts as a premise for arguing that secularism is valid for Europe, but not for Islamic countries.

The specificity of secularism is established in the account of its development in the West. According to this account, secularism is a response to the religious state, which is specific to medieval Europe and has no counterpart in Islam: 'Secularism finds its justification in the conditions of theocratic governments.'[72] That is, Christian theocracy is viewed as producing the conditions that gave rise to secularism: '[Secularism] was a natural result of the Church's intervention in the process of life and of its opposition to science.'[73] As such, the definitions given to 'the religious state,' 'secularism,' and 'theocracy' aim at dissociating them from Islam. In this way, the discourse refutes Egyptian secularists who warn of the dangers of religious absolutism and the abuse of religious rule.

Islam's distinct identity is also developed in relation to Christianity. In the tradition, Islam's relationship to other divine religions is complementary in that it is conceived as a message that completes and perfects the previous messages. However, the conservative Islamist discourse constructs Islam in a relationship of antinomy with Christianity. It affirms that Christianity 'did not come to order the movement of life,'[74] but that Islam did. A correlation is established between the temporal order of the religion and the nature of its message. In this order, Islam is presented as a complete message and superior to the preceding religion: 'Christianity came to provide the missing normative factor in Judaism and did not deal with aspects of life.'[75] Islam, on the other hand, 'brought a system for the movement of life with values devoid of rigidity.'[76] The signification of Islam as complete and of Christianity as incomplete is manifested in: 'the religion of the West is only a belief system, while Islam is a religion and a system of life.'[77] According to this distinction, Islam is both religion and temporal, or secular (*din wa dunya*). In this context, we note that by qualifying Islam as comprehensive, it is endowed, at its most basic level of meaning, with the quality of superiority.

Secularism in this sense (separation of state and religion) is established as alien and threatening and is inserted into the narrative of confrontation with the Other: 'Secularism has succeeded in transposing its philosophy to Arab and Islamic countries via foreign occupation;' 'Colonialism succeeded in imposing secularism on our societies which was a cause behind the current retardation and continuing re-gression.'[78] As mentioned earlier, all signs of the secular state signify the 'Western cultural attack.' Secularisation is presented as the object of westernisation: 'westernisation efforts aimed at removing the power of Islam from the centres of influence in society ... the school, the court, and the bank.'[79]

The confrontation with the Other: From contrariety to contradiction

It is important at this juncture to point out the distinction between the polemic against the West articulated in the conservative Islamist discourse and that articulated at the turn of the century, when the first long, drawn-out encounter with the West took place. The early polemic sought to prove that Islam was compatible with modern civilisation and culture, as in the case of Muhammad 'Abduh's exchange with Western thinkers.[80] 'Abduh was critical of Western intervention in the Muslim world and opposed the British presence in Egypt. He also saw dangers in certain strands of Western thought, particularly metaphysical doctrines that could undermine the faith necessary for the foundation of society.[81] At the same time, 'Abduh and his disciples perceived that the Muslim community was in a state of decay and, therefore, in need of reform. The perspective underlying the early Arab Renaissance movement held that the decaying Islamic society could benefit from certain aspects of modern civilisation. It was possible to adopt this view because the relationship between Islam and the West was articulated in terms of difference, where each existed as a positive entity in a relation of contrariety. This stands in sharp contrast to the conservative Islamist discourse's construction of a pole of negativity between Islam and the West, casting them in a relation of contradiction with each other. It should also be noted that while the early reformers sought to reconcile Islam with modern civilisation, they upheld the need for their society's political and economic independence from the West.[82]

Islam is constituted in the conservative Islamist discourse as a totalised entity encompassing the people (Muslims), the civilisation, history, culture and the intellect. The focus of identity shifts from the nation and society to religion. The main thrust of the discourse is summed up in Anwar al-Jindi's proposition that: 'There is a fact which cannot be transcended, the world is two cultures – Islamic and non-

Islamic – and they cannot meet in a single frame.'[83] This confirms a conception of Islam as a cultural system that defines all aspects of the Muslim's identity. The category of the non-Islamic is a residual one that emerges by exclusion.

Islamic identity and the discourses on morals, rituals, and usury

The conservative ideological Islamist discourse is closely tied to an ethical and moral discourse articulated by conservative shaykhs such as Shaykh 'Abd al-Hamid Kishk and Shaykh Muhammad Mutawalli al-Sha'rawi. Both shaykhs became important figures of conservatism in the 1970s. Shaykh Kishk was a mosque preacher whose influence was felt at the popular level.[84] His sermons dealt with ethics and morality. Shaykh Sha'rawi is a leading conservative figure who is considered an Islamic authority and a point of reference for the public.[85]

As shown in the previous section, conservative Islamists have framed the *problématique* of the present era in terms of cultural invasion. Concurrently, there have been growing efforts to frame the daily concerns of Muslims in terms of rituals and metaphysical issues. This discourse, which has become an essential component of the popular culture, focuses on rituals and religious symbolism and on the hereafter. It expounds on ethics and morals and explains how to perform rituals 'the correct way.' Moreover, it is framed in terms of the permissible and the forbidden and is presented as a legal ruling (*fatwa*) on a variety of subjects related to morality and religious practice. Although it is true that these concerns are found in all moral and religious discourses, it is important to take account of how this discourse is articulated and how widely it is circulated. In Egypt, it has gained popularity, commands a vast audience, and has become part of the everyday life of the 'believers.' It is disseminated in books and on a daily basis in the official newspapers and on television. It pronounces on the body, sexuality, and the permissible in thought, and a large part of it is devoted to issues of the afterlife. For example, it informs its 'subjects' about the maidens in heaven and conjugal relations in the afterlife. That these issues are discussed by Shaykh Sha'rawi in a book entitled *al-Shaykh al-Sha'rawi wa Qadaya al-*

'Asr (Shaykh Sha'rawi and the Problems of the Age) is indicative of what has been elevated to an issue of great concern to the public.

The discourse on the body and sexuality reproduces relations of domination based on gender. The instructions about physical cleanliness are articulated in terms of purity; women, in this respect, appear as less pure or as impure due to their biological make up. Pregnancy, childbirth and menstruation are impurities that constrain the woman's access to worship. Sexuality is also inscribed in the realm of the impure. In this context, the discourse instructs its 'subjects' on the Islamic rules of sexual relations. All of this has the effect of controlling the body (if not the mind).

Torture in the grave is also paid considerable attention by many of the popular preachers. Shaykh 'Umar 'Abd al-Kafi's cassette recordings include speeches warning of the torture that awaits disobedient Muslims.[86] The increased concern with the afterlife is read by one politically engaged intellectual as a sign of the absence or banishment of reason.[87] However, given the nature of Egypt's social and ideological formation, the discourse on morals and rituals coheres well and contains its self-rationale. It acts in conjunction with the conservative Islamist ideological discourse to produce an 'Islamic identity.' It also produces 'Muslim subjects' with 'Islamic bodies' and 'Islamic sexuality' and outlines in detail how the 'Muslim' should cleanse himself or herself of impurities, particularly the 'Muslim' woman. The disappearance of boundaries between the public and private is manifested in the fact that individuals believe that they must refer to an Islamic authority for advice on washing their bodies or on the 'Islamic' tradition regarding sexual relations. Private thoughts also come under the realm of the permissible and the forbidden. This indicates that the subjects of the discourse are active in reproducing it. The discourse presupposes that these areas of the individual's life belong to the fundamentals of religion and, therefore, do not change. In effect, these areas of the 'Muslim's' life are ritualised.

In its attempt to construct a 'religious orthodoxy' through the articulation of public morality, conservative Islamism is active in appropriating the domain of culture. In this regard, it seeks to claim authority by using the categories of the licit and illicit in reference to cultural production, investing its moral outlook into the public sphere.

Court challenges and intellectual censorship are key aspects of its mode of action for imposing 'orthodoxy.' Recent examples of these manoeuvres are the legal cases brought against Yusuf Shahin's film *al-Muhajir* and against the movie bill-boards.[88] In similar fashion, *hisba*[89] has been used as a basis for initiating a lawsuit aimed at forcing the separation of the scholar Hamid Nasr Abu Zayd from his wife. The court action followed pronouncements by the conservative Shaykh 'Abd al-Sabur Shahin to the effect that Abu Zayd's intellectual writings were blasphemous and represented *kufr* (infidelity to Islam).[90] In the People's Assembly, questions put to Minister of Culture Faruq Husni by Member of Parliament Galal Gharib regarding the moral propriety of certain cultural products funded by the ministry brought the confrontation, and the conservatives' moral challenge over culture, directly into the political sphere.

The state's positioning in the cultural battle converges with that of the conservatives while manoeuvring to manage the challenge of radical Islamism. The state's Islamic image is increasingly being invested in the cultural realm as a strategy of neutralising the radicals. The state pursues this aim on the grounds of morality, using cultural productions and the media as weapons for discrediting militant Islam. In the convergence of forces, official Islam and conservative Islam close ranks. The positions that al-Azhar has taken on a number of issues demonstrate the links developing between the two. Al-Azhar's involvement in court cases brought against artistic and intellectual productions has lined up on the side of the conservatives.[91] The state courts have come to represent another area of convergence between the conservatives and the state on one hand, and between the conservatives and radicals on the other. With the verdict upholding the Islamist lawyers' case for the separation of Abu Zayd from his wife, the state adopted the discourse, ethic and mode of action of the Islamists.[92] *Takfir* (the charge of apostasy) is now wielded by representatives of the state and official Islam.[93]

Occupying an equally important position in the complex discursive formation that is active in producing Muslim subjects is the discourse on usury. Its significance lies in the fact that it is directly linked to the material conditions of the social formation, particularly the 'Islamic sector' of the economy. It purports to designate what an

Islamic economy is by defining the permissible and forbidden modes of economic transaction, with a focus on the question of usury. The issue of usury (*riba*) is articulated around the axis of the legal (*shar'i*) and the illegal (*ghayr shar'i*) in the 'literal' Islamic sense, while the issue of the national economy is displaced from the debate. *Riba*, according to the tradition, is conceived as the exploitation of the poor by the rich in moneylending transactions, and its prohibition is tied to the Islamic concept of justice. Yet it is not this sense of *riba* that is re-activated but, rather, the literal sense of the licit and the illicit. Thus, at the second congress of the Islamic Research Group, it was stipulated, in one of the recommendations, that 'interest on all kinds of loans is illegal without distinction between a loan for consumption or a loan for production. ... A loan with *riba* at a low rate is as illegal as one at a higher rate. ...[A]ll forms of credit providing interest are illegal.'[94]

Such directives displace the question of exploitation, which was behind the original prohibition of *riba*, by emphasising the literal interpretation centring on the permissible and the forbidden (*halal* versus *haram*). These formulations make no mention of national interest or of the constraints placed on national economies by virtue of their position in the international system. Instead, the Secretariat of the Organisation of the Grand Ulema and the directorate of the House of Advanced Research for Exhortation and Spiritual Direction call on Muslims 'to protect their societies from the practice of *riba* which will subject them to a war on the part of God.'[95] As mentioned earlier, this discourse finds its support in the production of an Islamic identity in religious terms devoid of national and social content.

The anti-*riba* utterances should not be viewed as an expression of an anti-capitalist position. Rather, they are better understood in relation to Egypt's rentier capitalist economy. The discourse is articulated by groups which are engaged in rentier activities and which seek to transform the rules governing economic investment in a manner benefiting their commercial interests. Along with the conservative ideological discourse, the discourse on *riba* is engaged in the production of an Islamic identity understood in a limited religious sense. This is achieved through the construction of contradiction with the West in religious terms. That is, the Other, as the Christian West, inverts the capitalist West and displaces social and economic contradictions. This Islamic identity coheres with the parasitic economic activity that has been the dominant feature of the social formation.

The Islamic identity constructed through the conservative Islamist discourse rejects and opposes the secular state and its institutions, including the banking system based on usury. The alternative was found in the Islamic banks and the Islamic Societies for the Placement of Funds (ISPF) which absorbed the influx of capital from the Gulf. These societies operated outside government control and legal regulations. They did not conform to the structure of shareholding societies or that of financial institutions. The ISPF diverted capital from the national economy and invested it in speculative and nonproductive commercial activity.[96] The main areas of placement were in the importation of consumer goods and speculation on foreign currency. However, the ISPF were legitimised as Islamic. This notwithstanding the fact that speculation and commercial transactions took place in the West, and that this segment of the economy is tied to the West and to the bureaucratic elite. In the confrontation with the Christian West, the issues of exploitation and dependence do not figure in the discourse. As such, the discourse coheres with the interests of a parasitic class and petite bourgeois strata associated with petro-dollars. In this respect, state 'ulama and independent shaykhs such as Sha'rawi and 'Abd al-Sabur Shahin provided the ideological support for this sector. In fact, many of these religious figures, including Sha'rawi and Shahin, acted as consultants to the ISPF.[97]

The parasitic economic activities of the early years of infitah took on an Islamic identity with the advent of the Islamic societies and banks. Publicity for the 'Islamic sector' of the economy (mainly finance and commerce) used the following Qur'anic verse as a slogan: 'God permitted commerce and forbade usury' (Ahlalla Allah al-bay' wa harrama al-riba). Commerce was represented as an Islamic activity par excellence anchored in the image of the Prophet as a merchant. In this context, all commercial activities were considered licit, including trading in foreign currency on the black market, which was declared legal by a prominent shaykh of the Islamist movement, who happened also to be a member of the al-Ahrar Party and a representative in the National Assembly.[98]

There has also been a blurring of the difference between *mudaraba*, or speculation in the traditional Islamic sense (partnership in trust), and *muqamara*, market speculation in the contemporary sense (which implies risk and is prohibited by Islamic legal rulings). Thus, when a founder of one of the main Islamic societies was asked about its speculative activity on the international stock market, he answered that speculation is found in all forms of commerce and, therefore, the word 'speculation' applies to any type of buying and selling.[99]

All aspects of the Islamic societies' operations were articulated in Islamic terms, including commercial operations (which were classified according to Islamic concepts); and their corporate names were Islamic or had Islamic connotations – such as, for example, *al-Huda*, *al-Nur, Sa'udiya* . Furthermore, the products they sold were labelled 'Islamic.' Thus, advertising campaigns marketed the 'Islamic' refrigerator and washing machine. The fact that the appliances were produced in the West and merely assembled in Egypt was irrelevant to those who sought to confer an Islamic identity on inanimate objects. Indeed, inanimate 'Islamic' objects are more marketable in a society of 'Muslim' subjects who are invested with 'Islamic' bodies and minds.

The Conservative Islamist Discourse and the Structuring of the Political Field

The conservative Islamist discourse articulates social categories and political positions that draw on different discourses and practices. For instance, the articulations concerning such questions as the wearing of the *hijab* (veil) and the segregation of the sexes call on the practices of male domination in patriarchal society and are embedded in the system of social values. In this way, the code of female chastity and honour is brought into play, and restrictions are imposed on the whole field of interaction between the sexes. Ideology, understood as a relation to power, functions at two levels: as a universal system whose categories are not bound by class, and as a particular position appropriated by the dominant group.[100] The conservative Islamist discourse cannot be identified as a bourgeois ideology; rather, it is a universalising discourse that produces totalising positions (the

Muslim, the Islamic). These positions are appropriated for tactical purposes by the dominant power bloc, which comprises various class fractions involved in rentier activities, including a state bourgeoisie in conjunction with parasitic private capital (financial, commercial, industrial).[101] Its hegemonic strategy consists not only in yielding ground to popular tradition and allowing the articulation of autonomous discursive positions, but also of totalising or universalising these positions and expanding them beyond their particular domain, from religion to culture and ethics. The conservative Islamist discourse is also the ideology that mediates the role of the dominant bloc as a force in the political field, although the components of the bloc do not necessarily assume a homogeneous position. As a result of the interplay of the conservative Islamist discourse with radical Islam, the field of struggle is defined in terms of a contradiction between a correct understanding of Islam and a mistaken and misguided one. Both sets of representations belong to the religious domain, where categories draw upon the discourses of culture and ethics.

The roles of the state and the political forces constituted through the conservative Islamist discourse represent a division of labour in the production and dissemination of the ideology. The state through its ideological apparatuses – the media in particular – is active in producing and spreading the discourse. Meanwhile, the most prominent agents of production are located outside the state and thus appear independent of it (Shaykh Sha'rawi for example). The conservative Islamist discourse is also produced by 'oppositional' forces represented in the al-Ahrar Party and by segments within the Muslim Brotherhood.

The convergence of forces that arises in the political field is mediated by two inter-related factors: first, the constitution of the Muslim subject in ethical and cultural terms; and second, the divergent and convergent positions assumed by the state and the 'moderate' oppositional forces in relation to radical Islam. These two factors enter into the production of a 'state of balance,'[102] where the state deploys a strategy of co-optation and coercion, while the 'oppositional' forces assume the role of guardianship and arbitration. On one hand, the state uses dialogue and repression to contain the resistance positions articulated by radical Islamist groups such as the Jihad. On the other, the 'oppositional' forces of 'moderate' Islam act as defenders or guardians of *al-Shabab al-Salih* (the good youth) and as mediators between them and the state. Hence, the 'moderates' condemn violence,[103] while faulting the government for allowing transgressions against Islam.[104] Structuring the political field in terms of the positions mapped by these political forces (Muslim identity totalised in cultural and ethical terms and a contained position of resistance) maintains a 'state of balanced tension.'

The conservative Islamist discourse plays a key role in structuring the political field by the manner in which it positions itself in relation to militant Islam, the government, and the secularists. A regrouping in the political field takes place with a polarisation of positions whereby secularists face off with various lines of Islamism.[105] Positions of resistance and confrontation revolve around the two poles. As noted, different points of convergence have emerged between the conservatives and the militants and between the conservatives and the state. This convergence puts limits on the positions available to other actors and, as such, attempts to break down the ideological dominance are contained. This is the case of the secularist position as well as that of the 'Islamic left.' The secularists develop a position of 'counter-identification' taking the form of 'your Islam versus my Islam,' best exemplified by Faraj Fuda's text *al-Haqiqa al-Gha'iba* (The Missing Truth).[106] The Islamic left, while attempting a subversion from within, is itself absorbed into the dominant ideology. Following is a brief discussion of these two positions.

The insertion of *al-Haqiqa al-Gha'iba* into the debate illustrates the confrontational space in which secularists operate. The text is representative of the secularist position and, at the time of its publication, was viewed as the strongest secularist challenge to the Islamists. Its author, assassinated by militant Islamists in 1992, was a member of the National Unity Committee, an umbrella organisation established in 1990 that comprised both leftist and liberal secularists. *Al-Haqiqa* was produced as a response to *al-Farida al-Gha'iba* (The Missing Precept), by the militant Islamist leader 'Abd al-Salam Faraj.[107] Its objective was to provide an evaluation of the truth value of the opponent's (Islamists') discourse. However, the text's search for the truth is carried out on the same ground of history as its adversary. Arguments draw on the referential discourse of early Islamic history, itself a weapon in the hands of the conservative and radical Islamists. The narrative structure of Fuda's text is developed around the opposition between 'what they say' and 'what actually happened.' In other words, history is called upon to invalidate the assertions of the Islamists. The narrative episodes serve as the premises for the refutation of the two main propositions in the Islamist discourse: one asserting the unity of politics and religion in Islam; the other asserting that 'the application of the Shari'a will be followed by an immediate reform of society.'[108] The episodes are presented as proof for the dissociation of Islam and government (as in the recounting of the Saqifa meeting and the murder of 'Uthman) and the dissociation of justice from piety and from the application of the Shari'a. The objective is to demonstrate that the Islamists' model of the early period does not correspond to the historical record of that period. The values they invest in the example of the Companions and rulers of the Golden Age were in fact absent. In other words, the claims of the Islamists are illusory. Furthermore, by the standards of morality that they propagate, the early Islamic history is found lacking.[109]

Much of the text is dedicated to negating affirmations about the Islamic character of the caliphate, using the moral and ethical code as a basis of proof. The validation of the proposition that the caliphate was not an Islamic state is undertaken in chapters three and four of the text, which are advanced as a new reading of the Umayyad and Abbasid dynasties. The episodes recounted in these chapters aim to demonstrate the profanity of government and the moral laxity of the ruler. The themes of sexual promiscuity and permissiveness, treachery and barbarity are developed in different stories advanced as proof.

In recounting events from the period of the Umayyads, Fuda underscores the brutality of caliphs such as Yazid ibn Mu'awiya and Yazid ibn 'Abd al-Malik. Both caliphs are referred to as *zanadiqa* (transgressors) whose rule serves as 'proof against those who claimed that the state is not separate from religion.'[110] The new reading of the Abbasid dynasty calls on fragments of that historical period that are designed to invalidate the opponents' claim that the caliphate was an Islamic institution. The founder of the Abbasid caliphate, al-Saffah, is projected as the embodiment of the religious state. Fuda starts his reading of that period with an account of two actions by al-Saffah: the desecration of the Umayyad tombs and the assassination of his opponents at a dinner party. The account of these two events articulates the theme of barbarity and treachery. The latter event is posited by Fuda as a revealing knowledge, which confronts the author and his readers with a question on the nature of the caliphate:

> The event poses a question ... about the nature of the Caliphate which they [the Islamists] claimed was Islamic and we proved was not. ... [I]t was an absolutist government covered in the garb of religion ...; we demonstrate to them the difference between the absolutism of religious government in the Middle Ages, the ages of torture ... and the secularism of the contemporary age -- the age of democracy and human rights.[111]

Fuda ends his journey into history with anecdotal accounts of al-Wathiq's (the last caliph of the early Abbasid era) and al-Amin's sexual relations with young men in their courts, thus bringing back into focus the violation of the moral code by the caliphs. It is, in fact, on the ground of morality that Fuda positions himself in combat against the Islamists. His counter-arguments in this regard map the field into two positions: the upholders of the moral code and the violators. The latter are identified as the caliphs and, by association, as those calling for the establishment of the caliphate, while the contemporary government occupies the former position. In effect, the combative strategy of Fuda's text is that of 'your Islam versus my Islam.' In commenting on al-Wathiq's and al-Amin's actions, Fuda concludes that the reader is likely to share his conviction that '[today's] rulers are better.'[112]

The political field has also been marked by the movement of the Labour Party into the arena of Islamic politics, a move viewed by some as an attempt at subversion from within. The shifts in the party's position and discourse can be dated to the mid-1980s. Prior to that, the themes covered in the party's newspaper al-Sha'b showed an emphasis on 'socialist' principles, while the party's relation to Gamal Abdel Nasser and Nasserism was stressed.[113]

A marked transformation in the terms of the Labour Party's discourse takes places in the mid-1980s with the arrival of 'Adil Husayn as editor of the party's paper (a position he held until the early 1990s). This does not mean that the shift in the party's ideological articulations is due to a change in personnel; rather, the transformation should be situated within the context of wider changes in the convergence of forces. 'Adil Husayn's own conversion to Islamic politics should be understood in this context. The instrumentalisation of Islamist articulations in the constitution of political forces started with the return of the Muslim Brothers, the manipulation of Islamic symbols by President Anwar Sadat, the rise of the Jihad group, and the Muslim Brothers' alliance with the Wafd in 1984. This brought about a rearrangement of forces, part of which is the Labour Party's alliance with the Muslim Brothers and al-Ahrar in 1987.

Whereas during the 1980–84 period the narrative of Young Egypt's[114] history emphasised the connection with Nasser, in the 1985–89 period these narratives recounted Young Egypt's relationship with the Muslim Brothers, stressing the similarities in their principles and programmes. The construction of the party's identity in religious terms was the new basis for its constitution as a political force. The tense balance achieved in the political arena as a whole can be seen in the party's positioning on particular issues. In a sense, the convergence of the 'Islam of riches' and the 'Islam of revolution' is crystallised in the party's defence of both the Islamic Societies for the Placement of Funds (ISPF) and the militant and sometimes violent activities of the Islamist groups. In his editorials, Husayn attacked the government for its treatment of the *al-Shabab al-Mustatd'af*[115] (oppressed youth), as well as for its new regulations concerning the ISPF. In this context, the antagonistic positions of these two groups are not articulated, because the *al-Shabab al-Mustatd'af* belong to the dominated class, while the ISPF has close links to the dominant bloc. An overlap with the conservatives can also be discerned in the increased concern with issues of morality.[116]

Some analysts see the Labour Party's movement into the Islamic camp as an attempt to capture the 'revolutionary' force of Islam.[117] Within this perspective, the party must provide an alternative to the readings of Islam advanced by 'the organisational Islamic current' (identified with the Muslim Brothers) and the radical Islamist groups.[118] Such an alternative reading is a third way lying between 'literal conservatism' and 'idealist radicalism,' and imposes a progressive understanding of Islamic values.[119] Yet the apparent takeover of the party by the conservative forces associated with the Muslim Brothers indicates that the potential for the left as a political force working within an Islamic alliance has been undermined. Between the rise of the alliance in 1987 and the party's Fifth National Conference in 1989, leftist forces, including those espousing the Islamic identity of the party, withdrew or were pushed out.[120] The Islamic current that emerged victorious in this internal power struggle is closely linked to the Muslim Brothers. Thus, rather than separating the 'Islam of riches,' or conservative Islam, from the 'Islam of revolution,' the party incorporates both, reinforcing the convergence of forces that maintains the political balance.

Conclusion

In the conservative Islamist discourse, the opponent is designated as either the Christian West or the West (secular) whose attack on the Self is carried out against an identity defined in solely religious terms. Little attention is paid to the different relationships in which this homogenised Self is engaged. This representation brings about an inversion of the nationalist articulations in which the opponent was cast as the capitalist West, with all that this involved in terms of relations of dependence and exploitation. In this respect, the conservative Islamist discourse expresses the 'opening to the outside world' as a cause of corruption in cultural terms (the dangers of conversion or secularisation) rather than in economic terms. Similarly, subjugation is presented as 'intellectual' (subjugation of Islamic concepts to Western concepts) instead of economic. In this way, the discourse displaces the image of the West as an imperialist force in opposition to the Third World, wherein the struggle is conceived as primarily a political and economic one. The national and social identity is reduced to a 'religious Self' in which social antagonisms are evacuated. The only contradiction that is conceptualised is between that religious Self and an undifferentiated Other – the West, subsuming both the left and the right, the religious and the secular. A similar inversion is noted in the articulation of the Arab-Israeli conflict in terms of an

Islamic-Judaic confrontation that displaces the question of the national identity and national rights of the Palestinians.

This inversion is clear in utterances that postulate the field of conflict and 'competition' with the West as that of values and principles: '[the enemies] do not *possess* the 'life' values and principles Islam possesses, if they did they would have depended on the quality of their *goods* in their competition and struggle. But their feeling of bankruptcy is what led them to ... vulgarity' (emphasis mine).[121] Here, the lexicon common to the domain of trade and finance is transposed to the field of ethics and morality, limiting the nature of the confrontation and superimposing morality on the whole field of exchange. Within this perspective, Islam's superiority is tied to the moral corruption of the West, itself a cause of its supposed deterioration, bankruptcy, and inevitable collapse. As such, the increased reliance on Western powers in matters of security, along with the deepening of dependency relations in the economic realm, is left out of the discussion of the relationship between the West and the Arab and Islamic countries.

The conservative Islamist discourse is articulated by the right-wing opposition party al-Ahrar and elements of the Muslim Brothers, as well as by segments of the state apparatus, the official newspapers, and the state-run mass media. It is produced in relation to a particular set of material conditions and finds support among various class fractions tied to the rentier economy (a parasitic bourgeois class, a fraction of the petite bourgeoisie, a transformed labour aristocracy, and professionals). Positions of individuals such as Shaykh Sha'rawi, a former cabinet minister who now occupies a central place in the ideological state apparatus, exemplify the links between the state and a bourgeoisie involved in parasitic economic activities.

The ideological significance of the notions and concepts developed in the conservative Islamist discourse can be grasped further in the way they function as a support for the discourse on usury and how they work in conjunction with a discourse on rituals and morality as articulated by Sha'rawi and Kishk for the production of 'Muslim' subjects.

3

Religious 'Orthodoxy' as Public Morality: *The State, Islamism and Cultural Politics in Egypt*

Since the late 1970s, Egypt has experienced a widening of the scope of Islamist activism and a proliferation of forms of contestation that base themselves in Islamic traditions. Islamist politics is not confined to the activities of militant groups such as the Jihad and al-Jama'a al-Islamiya or moderate organisations such as the Muslim Brotherhood. The web of actors engaged in Islamist politics includes the Islamist lawyers, who constitute an informal group actively 'enjoining good and forbidding evil' in the public space, and the dissident new vanguard of the Muslim Brotherhood seeking formal recognition of their political party, al-Wasat. The various elements within the Islamist movement adopt diverse strategies and occupy different positions in the political field.

Within the widening range of Islamist activism, lines of distinction may be drawn on the basis of varying modes of action, and differing religio-ideological principles and institutional locations. Thus, an advocacy of and resort to violence against both state and society have characterised militant groups such as the Jihad and the Jama'a al-Islamiya. In contrast, moderate groups such as the Muslim Brotherhood work within institutional channels – running candidates in parliamentary elections and organising within the professional syndicates. Other actors, such as the Islamist lawyers, have targeted state institutions in their Islamisation efforts. These lawyers are supported by conservative *shaykhs* within the religious establishment. Further, in terms of religio-ideological principles, the militants declare society to be *jahiliya* (the state of ignorance before the advent of Islam), and qualify the state as infidel. The moderates and conservatives avoid such blanket condemnation of society while being critical of the state for failing to implement Islamic laws.[1] However, a concern for the regulation of public morality has emerged as an area of convergence among the various groups.

With the proliferation of forms of Islamist activism in the 1990s, the realm of culture, as an arena for the articulation of public morality, has acquired a growing importance for Islamists belonging to various tendencies. Islamist discourses have attempted to appropriate culture, at once challenging and claiming authority over intellectual and artistic expression. To a great extent, Islamists justify their challenge in the cultural sphere in terms of a religious duty to reinstate the true understanding and proper practice of religion. In other words, a claim to 'orthodoxy' is at work in the discourses of the contemporary Islamist forces that adopt oppositional or critical stances toward government. Their oppositional practices ground themselves in the 'orthodox' Islamic tradition that, in their discourses, is constructed as being under threat from the moral and cultural symbols and images of the present socio-political juncture.

In its response to the Islamist challenge, official Islam, as represented by al-Azhar, the Mufti, the Ministry of al-Awqaf (Religious Endowments) and the state-affiliated *shaykhs*, has endeavoured to articulate the correct understanding of religion, producing the necessary support for the existing political structure. With the increased concern over issues of culture and morality, this state Islam has focused its attention on social mores and directed its attacks against 'un-Islamic' thoughts and cultural expressions. A cultural battle thus has ensued between the state (including the religious establishment) and its Islamist opponents.

This chapter investigates this battle over 'orthodoxy' constructed as public morality in an endeavour to suggest why culture is the preferred arena of contestation for the Islamists and why articulations

of morality in relation to cultural productions have provided organising and structuring principles for dealing with government and
society. There are two nodal points in the approach advanced here:
one is centred on the mechanisms of orthodoxy; the other on the
categories of popular traditions and social practices. The contemporary Islamist manoeuvres in the cultural sphere are located in the
area where the two points link up, encoding the mechanisms of 'orthodoxy' in social practices rooted in the popular culture.

The chapter is divided into three parts. The first looks briefly at
the principles and mechanisms of 'orthodoxy' with a view to understanding how they have been reinscribed in the contemporary
context. This review sets the background for the examination, in part
two, of the cultural politics of the Islamists and the positioning of the
state and the religious establishment. The focus is on the interplay
between the state and the Islamists in the cultural and political fields.
In this interplay, one sees criss-crossing lines between the state
institutions and the Islamists. These lines demarcate areas of convergence and divergence that do not correspond to the neat boundaries
dividing state and non-state actors. Finally, the interweaving of religious activism and popular practices in the Islamists' production of
public morality is highlighted. Within this process, differing yet associated mechanisms of social control, whether emerging from
profane or religious practices, fade into one another. By identifying
the workings of this *bricolage* one may explain why this kind of Islamist activism has found popular appeal while subverting other forms
of political activism whether grounded in social antagonisms or individual interest.

Religious 'Orthodoxy' as Public Morality

As noted above, much of the Islamist agitation around the preservation of proper Islamic practices and beliefs is focused on the area of
public morality. In Islamist articulations, public morality is cast as an
integral aspect of the faith and of conduct modelled after the example of the pious ancestors (*al-salaf al-salih*). In this respect, morality
is tied closely to the production of religious 'orthodoxy,' which is
defined as the true understanding of religion, the correct way of

performing rituals, and the right code of conduct.[2] In their opposition to contemporary social and cultural practices, Islamists draw upon the mechanisms and traditions associated with established orthodoxy. In the meantime, their opponents – the state and official Islam – operate on the same terrain, claiming adherence to and guardianship of orthodoxy. As Talal Asad points out, what constitutes orthodoxy in reference to a particular activity or belief is often subject to contestation.[3] Hence, orthodoxy is an outcome of power struggles, and while it represents a particular historical narrative with identifiable contours, it is subject to an ongoing process of reinterpretation and reworking. Below I outline the principles and mechanisms of orthodoxy which are recalled and reinvented in the present socio-political juncture in Egypt.

In the radical Islamist discourse, the notion of God's governance (*hakimiya*) restates the core principle of Islamic 'orthodoxy.' This principle is anchored in the consecration of the idea of God as the final arbiter in all worldly matters. As demonstrated by Muhammad Arkoun, this was achieved historically through a mode of reasoning and a set of principles of jurisprudence, enshrining the central proposition that the supreme authority is revealed in the Qur'an and expressed in the *hadith* (the Prophet's sayings).[4] If the first principle of orthodoxy has underpinned Islamist militancy over the last two decades, other supporting principles, such as the prophetic tradition (*sunna*), have come into play in more recent forms of Islamist activism focused in the cultural sphere. Observing the *sunna* in practice and imitating the pious ancestors have crystallised in the modern Islamist discourses and have been given a practical orientation in the application of the injunction 'to enjoin good and forbid evil' (*al-amr bil ma'ruf wa al-nahy 'an al-munkar*).

Devices established during the first two centuries of Islam for excluding and marginalising views that lay outside the boundaries of orthodoxy are part of the tradition within which the Islamists situate themselves. Thus, they use the categories of *kafir* (infidel) and *fasiq* (sinner) to designate individuals who are seen to challenge the fundamentals of the religion as laid down by the Prophet and his successors. They also position themselves on the ground of a legal-moral tradition that works on the supposition that rules of right and wrong are commanded by God and stipulated in the Text.[5] In this respect, they deploy key mechanisms of orthodoxy; in particular an evaluative grid whose main components are the ideas of truth and falsehood and the categories of *halal* (licit) and *haram* (illicit). As explained below, much contention revolves around the classification of behaviour, representations and ideas according to the categories of this tradition.

The juridical foundation of ethics and morality in religion guided the establishment of institutions of social control and regulation that served to oversee individual action and social interaction in public. Offices of control and regulation were created, chief among which were the offices of *qadi* (judge), *muhtasib* (inspector) and *mufti* (jurisconsult). The power reach of these offices was enlarged over time. For example, the functions of *muhtasib* expanded from the regulation of commercial transactions in the market to the monitoring of a wide range of social activity with an emphasis on the preservation of public morality as defined in orthodoxy.[6] In the present context, the powers of the *muhtasib* have been reactivated by the Islamist lawyers who seek to apply the grid of *halal* and *haram* to cultural products such as movie billboards, films and intellectual writings.

The mechanisms, practices of control, and claims to power briefly noted here have been fashioned and refashioned in a multitude of socio-historical contexts. As such, the deployment of the grid of orthodoxy should not be viewed as a reflection of essential and unchanging Islamic traditions. Rather, the grid, and the mode of reasoning that guides it, operate in new contexts which, as Talal Asad suggests, are reconceptualised to attain discursive coherence.[7] At the same time, in dealing with new situations norms are redefined. Thus contemporary Islamist activism in the area of public morality can be viewed as embodying the dynamics of reconceptualising the present in terms of orthodoxy while also redefining its norms. The greater attention given to public morality does not mean that religious orthodoxy is limited to this one sphere. As noted earlier, at the foundation of orthodoxy, there lie juridical and theological traditions which encompassed a wide range of issues dealing with the fundamentals of jurisprudence, the authenticity of the tradition, and providing an expanding body of rulings forming the branches of

Islamic law. These areas are subject to debate in the present. However, the articulation of orthodoxy and the deployment of its mechanisms increasingly are focused on public morality. In the militant discourse of the 1970s, the definition of orthodoxy centred on the notion of God's governance. In the 1990s, various Islamist forces have intensified their activities in the cultural sphere, reconstructing orthodoxy as public morality.

Cultural Islamism: Oppositional and Official

Concerns regarding morality have long been present in Islamist discourses of the modern period. Hasan al-Banna, the founder and first Supreme Guide of the Muslim Brotherhood, voiced much dissatisfaction over the importation of the Western lifestyle into Egyptian society. Radical Islamic thinker Sayyid Qutb's condemnation of society as *jahiliya* was motivated by his sense of dissonance between the ideal of Islamic morality and the practices of modern society,[8] a dissonance that extended to art and literature.[9] In the 1970s, the rehabilitated Muslim Brotherhood organisation focused its critique on the moral laxity of society. On university campuses, Islamist groups sought to enforce a brand of morality through gender segregation, censorship, and policing artistic expression.

In the juncture of the 1980s and 1990s, the modern battle over morality has intensified and has taken on new meanings. It is marked by a cycle of violence between the state and the militants who seek to undermine state power and respectability. The Egyptian government has attempted to contain the militants by providing an alternative Islamic position, one which also is grounded in 'orthodoxy.' A gradual process of Islamisation of state institutions and the public space has ensued, with the cultural arena located at the centre. In propagating its own brand of Islam, the government has sponsored religious newspapers and television programmes and has expanded al-Azhar's powers to censor artistic and intellectual productions.

The articulation of a moral code and the attempt to impose a vision of public morality is part and parcel of the Islamists' aim of controlling the public space. Defining and managing morality in public are linked intimately to the production of a religious 'orthodoxy.'

Applying the grid of the licit and illicit to the cultural sphere, invoking *hisba* (engagement in the defence of the Muslim community), and using charges of *takfir* are practices that claim orthodoxy and seek to preserve it. They form the ground of Islamist action and define the terms of negotiating relations with government and society. At stake here are positions and relations of power that are transformed in this public contestation.

Assuming the position of orthodoxy, the Islamist critique of a wide range of cultural products and practices attempts to set the standard of the Islamic and un-Islamic in relation to art, aesthetics, and creativity. It is from precisely this position that in 1994, Parliamentary deputy Galal Gharib questioned the minister of culture about state funding of 'immoral' and 'sinful' cultural products. The allegations concerned the publication of a poem, the reproduction of a nude painting by Gustav Klimt on the cover of an arts magazine, and the staging of a play dealing with the issue of homosexuality. Gharib argued that Islamic Egypt was in danger, and under threat of annihilation. In a statement in parliament, he criticised the Ministry of Culture for adopting a cultural policy that will 'estrange (Westernise) the national culture.'[10] The ensuing debate revealed the positions occupied by the protagonists in this conflict. For the advocates of cultural protectionism, the depiction of nudity stood outside the boundaries of art as defined in Islamic ethics. Gharib's supporters in the media argued against the proponents and defenders of freedom of thought and expression. They rejected the idea of relativism in ethics and morality and called for the preservation of virtuous values. From this perspective, art must contain the principles of order and coherence – principles that constitute a fixed or absolute premise.[11] They are set out in divine revelation and canonised in Islamic rules and regulations, and their violation threatens the natural order with destruction. Echoes of traditional theological views can be heard in these arguments and propositions. Yet, at the same time, the debate belongs to the popular construction of Islamic culture with its ideas of purity and taboos on sexuality.

Islamists identify transgressions against the rules of morality in the public space and set out to reinstitute the standards framed in and through orthodoxy. In this fight against the public symbols and signs of immorality, billboard advertisements have become a main target.[12] The offending ads are not attacked for their crude character and low artistic quality but for their 'erotic' content. The anti-bill-board campaigns provide a good illustration of the Islamist strategies employed in the cultural battle. Court proceedings against the ads, and other cultural products often are initiated on the pretext of ful-filling *hisba* obligations. The strategy and practice of invoking *hisba* makes the Muslims (Islamists) defenders of the faith and of the pub-lic good. It is carried out under the rubric of *al-amr bil ma'ruf wa al-nahy 'an al-munkar* (enjoining good and forbidding evil).

It was on this basis that a group of Islamist lawyers, together with Shaykh Yusuf al-Badri,[13] launched court cases against 'violators' of the moral code. Individual citizens, especially movie theatre owners, were targeted for ostensibly transgressing the strictures of public morality. However, the record of success on *hisba* challenges has been mixed. In a number of cases, judges dismissed the lawsuits, declaring that the Islamist lawyers could not establish their personal or imme-diate interest in the case.[14] For this reason, in launching legal action against a theatre owner who posted 'offensive' movie advertisements outside his establishment, the group, rather than taking the case di-rectly to court, filed a complaint with the public prosecutor of the Bab al-Shi'riya district of Cairo where the theatre is located. The complaint argued that the advertisements violated Law 430 of 1955, as well as Ministerial Decree 220 of 1976 regarding censorship. As a representative of the public, the prosecutor argued the case in court.

The advertisements in question were deemed by the group to be morally offensive because of their depiction of the film actors, particularly the female actors, in sexually suggestive poses. In con-junction with the legal action lodged in the court system, the lawyers requested that a *fatwa* (religious ruling) be issued on the matter by Dar al-Ifta' (The Office of Religious Rulings).[15] The latter obliged. The *fatwa* was published in the state-sponsored newspaper *'Aqidati* (My Conviction) and included an injunction that 'every concerned state official prohibit the posting of the scandalous pictures.'[16] The court decision supported the *fatwa*, and in a sense, was determined by it. Further, it had the effect of advancing the Islamist lawyers' strategy of extending morality laws. The theatre owner, meanwhile, was fined 500 Egyptian pounds and was sentenced to a three-month prison term.[17]

The case raises questions of jurisdiction, of who controls the public space, and of the basis upon which public morality is constructed. The evaluative grid deployed by the Islamists in this and other cases is that of the licit and illicit, drawing on the construction of sexual morality in religion and customs. It is important to note that, according to the report of the Censorship Board (named as co-defendant in the aforementioned case), most of the billboards did not violate the state laws of public morality (adab 'ama).[18] In fact, billboards are conventionally subject to administrative regulations governing advertising and publicity, not to morality laws.

The banner of morality and orthodoxy also was raised in the court case brought against the film al-Muhajir (The Emigrant), written and directed by Yusuf Shahin. In this instance, the idea of truth derived from a scriptural orthodoxy was deployed against the 'falsehood' of the imaginary. For his portrayal of an historical character inspired by the Biblical and Qur'anic story of the Prophet Joseph, Yusuf Shahin was accused of falsification and misrepresentation of religious history and of denigrating Islam. Invoking hisba, a Sufi lawyer sought a court injunction to ban the film from Egyptian cinemas on grounds that the portrayal of Joseph strayed from the Text and that the depiction of prophets is illicit. The lower court decision to impose a banning order was based on a report written by the General Directory of Research and Publication in the Islamic Research Academy of al-Azhar (Majma' al-Buhuth). This decision was overturned in the Court of Appeal. The appeal judge, drawing on articles from the civil code found that the plaintiffs had no immediate interest in the case, thus rejecting hisba as a basis of litigation. Further, within the current legal provisions, al-Azhar has no legal jurisdiction to censor or ban artistic products. This power lies with an administrative censor in the Ministry of Culture. The ambiguity surrounding al-Azhar's juridical power has not been resolved, as shall be demonstrated later.

The state, also, has made use of cultural production and the media in its battle with Islamist groups over the terms of religious orthodoxy and public morality. The policy of co-opting and neutralising the Islamists consists of producing an alternative understanding of

Islam. Thus, it sponsors religious newspapers such as *al-Liwa' al-Islami* and devotes more television and radio airtime to religious programmes. From the government's perspective, there is a need to discredit the radical Islamists and subvert their attempt to transform the status quo.

One example of the state's strategy was a televised series of public confessions by former members of Islamist groups. Known as 'the repentants' (*al-ta'ibun*), these former Islamists not only repented publicly for their actions but also condemned the militants. These confessions were broadcast in the spring of 1994. Their 'star,' 'Adil 'Abd al-Baqi, had been an emir of an Islamist cell within the al-Shawqiyun group, and he had close contacts with prominent Jihad figures. In a televised interview broadcast over three consecutive evenings, 'Abd al-Baqi aimed his attack at the deviant morality of his former colleagues. He spoke of how female members whose husbands had been branded apostates by the emirs were forced into divorce. The women were then made to remarry without observing the *'idda* (a Shari'a stipulation requiring a four month waiting period before a divorced woman can remarry). Given the central place of morality and sexuality in the Islamist discourse and the importance accorded to sexual propriety in the popular culture, the confessions programme proved to be an effective means of raising anti-militant sentiments.[19]

Similar themes were covered in the television drama series *The Family*, also broadcast in 1994. Over approximately thirty episodes, the series followed the lives of the inhabitants of a residential building in a middle class suburb of Cairo. One family was cast as a guardian of Egyptian values and customs, with the father portrayed as an upright character who sets out to reveal the falsehood of the Islamist discourse. This counter-attack assumes an orthodox position from which the views and practices of the Islamists may be classified as *bida'* (innovations). However, the overall strategy of falsifying Islamist propositions and arguments backfired when, in a dialogue with an emir and his followers in a mosque, the father objected to statements dealing with the afterlife and questioned the idea of punishment in the grave.[20] The objection to these views was articulated in terms of orthodoxy versus innovation. These utterances, which aimed at responding to the widely spread ideas about the afterlife, became the subject of public controversy and required an intervention from al-Azhar to clarify the matter.

The terrain of the confrontation spans the court system. Legal cases launched by Islamists turn state institutions into battlefields. This strategy has important implications. The overriding aim of legal cases undertaken by the Islamist lawyers is to bring the Law into conformity with the constitutional principle that the Shari'a is a main source of legislation. Furthermore, by bringing the state in as co-defendant in some cases, state failure in assuming responsibility for enforcing public morality is established, and, by extension, state guilt in promoting immorality is argued. Thus, cases against the billboards implied an indictment of state regulations and practices.

The lines of demarcation between the various Islamist forces are not clear nor are the boundaries between the Islamist opposition and the state. In looking at the instances of confrontation in the cultural sphere, what is revealed are the lines of convergence and divergence among the various protagonists. The events surrounding the case of Nasr Hamid Abu Zayd present us with a more pointed instance of a convergence of forces among conservative Islamists, militant Islamists and the state. The main actors in this case were Shaykh 'Abd al-Sabur Shahin[21] (an 'alim or religious scholar playing a mediating role), the courts, the Islamist lawyers for the prosecution and a secular writer as defendant. The case began when Abu Zayd's application for promotion to the level of Professor at Cairo University was rejected by the Promotions Committee. The decision was based on a report submitted by Shaykh Shahin, a committee member. It described Abu Zayd's thinking as atheistic and his work as blasphemous. Following the decision, a group of Islamist lawyers launched a *hisba* case aimed at forcing the separation of Abu Zayd from his wife on the grounds that he was an apostate. Initially, a lower court dismissed the case finding that the plaintiffs had no immediate or personal interest. This decision was later overturned by the Court of Appeal which confirmed *hisba* as a legitimate basis of litigation. In a more striking development, the Court of Cassation, the highest court of appeal, confirmed the Appeal Court ruling ordering the separation of Abu Zayd from his wife.

The text of the ruling employs discursive strategies similar to those of the militants. The Appeal Court verdict, which upheld the petition against Abu Zayd, was reached after establishing the validity of the apostasy charges. This was achieved through an investigation into Abu Zayd's religious convictions as reflected in his writings. The latter provided the proof of his *ridda* (apostasy), and Abu Zayd's propositions and arguments were construed as evidence of his *kufr* (infidelity). The implications of the case and the verdict are that, much like the radical Islamists, the state is now engaged in *takfir*. Indeed, the ruling proceeds by defining *kufr*, invoking the authority of medieval jurists like Ibn Hazm, and contrasting the literal 'truths' of the Qur'an with the falsehood of Abu Zayd's ideas and propositions regarding Qur'anic interpretation.[22] The court declared that the denial of these 'truths' constituted *kufr*. The possibility of invoking medieval juridical rulings is left open as a result of an ambiguity in the legal system that permits judges to draw on the works of the Sunni schools of Islamic jurisprudence in cases where there is no other relevant legislation or customary rule.

The arguments and the decision made in the ruling are based on the concept of truth grounded in the Text, and by implication, they advance a claim to monopoly over the Truth. The Truth of the Text is literal and supersedes reason and rationality; it is divorced from historical context and from time and space. The grounding of the truth in the Text understood in these terms is precisely what Abu Zayd's writings sought to challenge. It is important to note that the boundaries of 'the said' and 'the thought of,' as drawn out in the ruling, exclude meanings acquired in context and through usage. It thus seeks to fix the language in an ahistorical frame. Meanings acquired in translation or from interaction with other languages also are rejected. Thus, the idea of language as discourse, in which meanings emerge in an historically situated system of signs and symbols, is viewed as alien. The ruling affirms that, in searching for the meaning of the Text, the sole frame of reference is the Arabic language[23] and determining the meaning is referred back to the *'ulama* who are learned in the sciences of theology, interpretation, and jurisprudence.

In sum, the Abu Zayd ruling established the following: the court has a say in determining the faith of a citizen and by extension declaring her/him as *kafir* (an infidel); defence of the Muslim community or of the public interest can be declared by any member of that community; an individual may take action in defence of the community without having to establish a personal or immediate interest. This was confirmed in the Appeal Court judge's invocation of the concept of *maslaha* (utility or benefit) of the community to uphold the Islamist lawyers' grounds for legal action against Abu Zayd. The concept comes under the rubric of *al-amr bil-ma'ruf wal nahy 'an al-munkar* (enjoining good and forbidding evil).[24] This aspect of the decision, along with the repeated practice of using *hisba* against ordinary citizens – a practice which forces difficult choices on the state – has moved the government to try to restrict the use of *hisba*. Thus, following the Abu Zayd case, a bill codifying *hisba* was introduced and passed in the People's Assembly. The bill is designed to limit the right to initiate *hisba* cases with the public prosecutor.[25] This removes *hisba* charges from the arsenal of the Islamist lawyers and their clients. At the same time, the new law acceded to some of the Islamist claims. Thus, in the clarification brief which accompanied the project of the law, it was stated that 'it is known in the *shar'* (religious law based on divine revelations) that the good of the community cannot be established without applying the principle of enjoining good and forbidding evil.'[26]

The strategies and patterns of action described above reveal a process of redefining and re-appropriating orthodoxy. The invocation of *hisba* involves its reworking in practice. Indeed, in the current juncture, the commercial and market connotation of *hisba* is evacuated, while its application to areas of public morality and social regulation is reclaimed. Lacking the official character of the historical *muhtasib*, the contemporary *muhtasib* or 'inspectors' of public morality, are more akin to the *futuwwa* (tough guys/chivalrous gangs) who controlled, but also destabilised, their neighbourhoods in the past. This is particularly true of the militant Islamists who oversee social mores in the poor suburbs of Cairo. Similarly, the practice of *fatwa*-giving has escaped many of the restrictions applied to it in previous historical periods. Local preachers and emirs with no training in jurisprudence have taken on the position of mufti. Often, the issuing of a *fatwa* does not follow the rules set out in the traditional manuals.[27]

In this ongoing battle, state power, as represented by the police and the Censorship Board, is challenged. In response, these and other state institutions have assumed an active role in investigating violations and arresting violators. The state's desire to recapture positions of authority recreated and appropriated by the Islamists has necessitated that it moves into their territory. This move is bridged by al-Azhar, but not without creating tensions within the state itself.

Al-Azhar: The Guardian of Religious Orthodoxy

The Abu Zayd case confirmed that the state has adopted *takfir* as a weapon, which it wields through both al-Azhar and the court system. The involvement of al-Azhar in *takfir* is particularly significant. It should be recalled that in its ongoing struggle against the Islamists, the state has called on the Mufti of the Republic and on al-Azhar to respond to the claims made by militant Islamists. For example, the Mufti issued a report in 1981 refuting the ideas of militant Islamists particularly as expressed in the text *al-Farida al-Gha'iba* (The missing precept) by 'Abd al-Salam Faraj. In his report, the Mufti sought to define *kufr* and limit its use.[28] The definitions and arguments put forward aimed at removing the charge from the hands of the Islamists who made use of *takfir* as a weapon against the political authority, namely the government.[29] In numerous reports and statements, al-Azhar served a similar purpose. In the current juncture, however, the use of *takfir* against individuals is supported by the religious authority of certain sections within al-Azhar.

Al-Azhar's role is multi-layered and complex. As an institution, it comprises the Mashyakhat (the Grand Shaykh's office), the University, Majma' al-Buhuth al-Islamiya (The Islamic Research Academy), the High Council of Islamic Affairs and many standing committees. In light of recent developments relating to al-Azhar's role in the cultural, educational, and religious spheres, the politics of the institution must be nuanced. Clearly, the personal leaning of its head has an effect on its overall direction. Thus, a conservative outlook characterised the tenure of Shaykh Jad al-Haqq 'Ali Jad al-Haqq (d. 1996). On a number of occasions, Shaykh Jad al-Haqq publicly condemned writers for their critical reading of the early Islamic period and for their critique of the Islamisation of politics.[30] The institution has acquired a more liberal imprint under its current head, Shaykh Muhammad Sayyid Tantawi. However, it can be argued that there are bastions of conservatism within the institution. One such bastion, is Majma' al-Buhuth. The Committee for Research and Publication (CRP) within the Majma' has spearheaded the institution's claim to power over art, and is the only part of the official religious establishment in charge of overseeing and censoring books and artistic production. Its involvement in this domain is not clearly set out. In some instances, published material is referred to it by the Censorship Police (Shurtat al-Riqabat 'ala al-Musannafat al-Fanniya), or by the state security. Judges and public prosecutors have requested reports from the CRP when hearing court cases initiated by Islamist lawyers. In other instances, the CRP independently has submitted reports to these institutions on books it has qualified as 'contravening Islam.'

The CRP's yardstick for assessing this material is set in terms of orthodoxy in its simplest terms. Banning recommendations are issued against publications which contravene the Shari'a, or 'Islamic principles.' However, at a more basic level, they are aimed at whatever contradicts the principles of 'ma huwa ma'lum min al-din bi al-darura' (what is known, proven in religion by necessity), 'ma huwa thabit min al-din-bi al-darura' (that which is affirmed in religion by necessity).[31] In looking at the reports issued by the Majma', there is a noticeable absence of juristic exposés building on precedent and calling on classical jurists. The reports consist of summaries of the main ideas in the works examined, along with seemingly self-evident statements that a particular idea or a thought contravenes Islam, is insulting to the divine being or to the prophets. It should be noted that the CRP refuses to release the reports or the list of books that have been recommended for banning.[32] This appears as an issue of contention between the Mashaykhat (the Grand Shaykh's Office) and the Majma'. While the former has recommended the publication of the reports in Majalat al-Azhar, the latter prefers to preserve the secrecy of the decision.[33] The Majma' also holds that the topics reviewed are not subject to public debate.

The claim to power over art and literature is wielded by the Majma'. Throughout the 1980s, al-Azhar's Islamic Research Academy sought

and obtained the banning of numerous books. Further, it has bran-
dished *takfir* (apostasy charge) against various authors. Such was the
case with author Ala Hamid whose novel, *A Distance in a Man's
Mind*, was the target of a court challenge in 1991. The author was
sentenced to an eight-year prison term. The trial and the sentencing
drew on a report by the CRP. According to the report, the dialogue
between the characters in the novel reveals the author's apostasy.[34]
It is also reported that the Majma' puts pressure on state-owned publishing houses to withdraw certain books from print or from
distribution.[35]

In fact, looking at the instances of cultural confrontation, one can
argue that al-Azhar has been an important actor in the cultural struggle. This is illustrated by the activities of Jabhat 'Ulama al-Azhar, the
Front of al-Azhar 'Ulama, which originally was formed in 1946 and
reconstituted as a private voluntary organisation in 1967, then re-
vived its activities in 1993 under the directorship of Shaykh al-Tayyib
al-Najjar. The Front was supportive of the late Grand Shaykh Jad al-
Haqq in his differences with the then Mufti, Shaykh Tantawi,
regarding issues of bank interest, female circumcision, and the
International Conference on Population and Development.[36] The
Front publishes declarations in the form of *fatawa* (religious rulings). For example, it has issued a ruling of *takfir* against secular
writer and critic of the Islamists, Faraj Fuda. The Front judged that
'everything [Fuda] does is against Islam.'[37] This pronouncement laid
the ground for the *takfir* and hence provided justification for the
execution of the offender, an action which is stipulated as punishment for *kufr*. More recently, the Front issued a *fatwa* declaring
Egyptian thinker and philosophy professor, Hasan Hanafi, to be a
kafir (infidel).[38]

The Front and the Majma' are closely linked and have overlapping membership. Authors condemned by the Front often are made
subject to investigations by the Majma'. This is true of the latest case
of *takfir* and censorship brought against author and scholar Sayyid
Mahmud al-Qimani, whose book, *Rab al-Zaman* (God of the time),
was subject to a banning order based on a Majma' report submitted
to the state security prosecutor.[39] The latter sent the case to the North
Cairo Court, where it was dismissed on the grounds that the charges

made against Qimani expressed a difference of opinion and could not be resolved simply by negating one opinion with another.[40] The judge referred to article 47 of the Constitution, according to which freedom of expression is guaranteed to all citizens. The campaign against Qimani was led by Shaykh Yahya Isma'il, former secretary general of the Front. In an introduction to a book refuting Qimani's works, Shaykh Isma'il incited action against Qimani by classifying him as a *jahid* (an individual who denies God or any of his attributes).[41]

The divisions within al-Azhar have recently come to the fore in relation to the grand sheikh's decision to reform the religious educational system. A bill dealing with the reforms was presented to the People's Assembly. The bill pertains to reducing from four to three the years of schooling required at al-Azhar secondary schools. This would translate into a reduction of the overall volume of religious teaching at the secondary level. The Front and some members of the Majma' came out in opposition and attacked the grand sheikh personally.[42] The sheikh surmounted the opposition with the support of a leading conservative figure, Shaykh Mutawali al-Sha'rawi, who passed away soon after. In response to the Front's increasing power, the Shaykh has taken measures to rein in the outspoken critics. These measures may have been behind the resignation of the Front's leader, Shaykh al-Barri, and his replacement with the equally conservative, Shaykh al-'Ajami al-Damanhuri.

The tensions within al-Azhar are the outcome of different articulations of Islamist politics. On one hand, al-Azhar *'ulama*, including the Majma', see their role as supportive of the state and its leadership. The Majma', for instance, targets writings which may be considered as seditious and potential sources of *fitna* (chaos). On the other hand, the *'ulama* are divided on how to deal with issues of change and reform. For example, in addressing the questions that emerged in reference to the International Conference on Population and Development held in Cairo in 1994, some of the *'ulama* took positions closer to those of the Muslim Brotherhood. Sympathy with the Muslim Brotherhood or even affiliation with it is not new to al-Azhar. This association and convergence confirm the overlapping in positioning between state and non-state actors in some instances. The lines dividing state Islam and oppositional Islam are not clear-cut. In this regard, it is important to note the dynamics of interaction between the two and the impact this has on state structures.

Under the pressures for Islamisation, a religious institution, namely al-Azhar, has expanded its share of state power. In February 1994, the Department of Fatwa and Legislation in the Council of State issued Decree 58/63 in which it clarified al-Azhar's authority over artistic works and audio and audio-visual products that deal with religious issues or may conflict with Islam. This authority is understood as the power to prevent the publication, recording, printing or distribution of materials deemed to be contrary to or in violation of some religious principle. The Council redefined the purposes of censorship and enhanced al-Azhar's role in overseeing the audio-visual field.[43] According to the decree, al-Azhar's opinion is 'binding on the Ministry of Culture.' This generally applies to products dealing with Islamic subjects, although the precise limits or boundaries of al-Azhar's purview are to be defined by al-Azhar itself.

In practical terms, however, it is not clear to what extent al-Azhar's power is binding. On a number of occasions, al-Azhar's censorship powers were challenged in the courts. In one instance, the owner of a bookshop initiated a court case against the Islamic Research Academy which had issued a ban on the distribution of seven titles imported by the bookstore, including books by Abu Zayd, Muhammad Arkoun, and Fu'ad Zakariya. Al-Azhar was the defendant in the case. The court decision of January 1995 stated that the licensing of books and of audio and audio-visual material fell within the Ministry of Culture's jurisdiction, and not al-Azhar's.[44] According to the judgement, licenses are issued by the Ministry of Culture in accordance with Law 354 of 1954, revised by Law 38 of 1992.[45] It went so far as to state that al-Azhar's view, as advanced by Shaykh 'Abd al-Fatah Gazar, the then head of the CRP, is, in fact, not binding and is nothing more than an opinion.[46]

The censoring and licensing powers of al-Azhar vis-à-vis those of the Censorship Board also have been the subject of contestation. The State Council decree attempted to maintain an implicit division of labour: the Censorship Board being in charge of security issues and al-Azhar of religious issues. However, as these jurisdictions increasingly overlap, the Censorship Board has seized the opportunity to move into a terrain traditionally claimed by al-Azhar, specifically the licensing of religious works in the audio and audio-visual field. In a recent move, the Censorship Board sought to revoke licenses accorded by al-Azhar to audio-cassettes made by Islamist preachers. The Censorship Board considers that the cassettes are products that fall within its power purview. Al-Azhar's jurisdiction is limited to offering opinions on religious content, while political and security considerations regarding cultural products fall within the scope of the Censorship Board's power.[47] According to Mr Hamdi Surur, the former head of the Censorship Board, these considerations are given priority in licensing decisions on products that contain sermons or interpretations of a Qur'anic verse or a *hadith*.[48] In fact, the Censorship Board withdrew the licenses on the audio cassettes of some of the more fiery preachers, thus reversing an al-Azhar decision.[49]

Nonetheless, al-Azhar's powers have expanded and its role in the control of the cultural and intellectual sphere has been enlarged. This represents a significant change from the period of President Gamal Abd al-Nasser, when the al-Azhar came under government control with a reform law in 1961 and the powers of the rector were circumscribed. Al-Azhar performed a support role to the policies of the state: in the 1960s, it endorsed socialism; during the *infitah* period of the 1970s, it opposed communism.[50] Under President Sadat, its powers remained largely unchanged, although its symbolic importance was acknowledged by presidential decree 350 of 1975 stating that the rector of al-Azhar is the grand shaykh in charge of all religious matters.[51]

In the early 1990s, al-Azhar managed to regain some of its pre-revolution independence and power. With the 1993 ministerial decree, the Shaykh of al-Azhar acquired the status of prime minister in financial and protocol terms although not in relation to administrative affairs.[52] This elevated status coincides with a willingness to exercise more powers in censoring cultural and artistic products. As a mediator between the government and the militants, al-Azhar has gained a considerable degree of independence as demonstrated by the previous rector's *fatwa* against bank interests.[53] The greater role exercised by al-Azhar indicates the state's willingness to accept a religious authority as the ultimate referent in matters previously under the control of secular institutions.

Cultural and Moral Governance: Subversion of Power or Reversion to Social Control?

The instances of cultural confrontation discussed above indicate the centrality of the cultural domain for the Islamists' struggle for power. Their actions aim to reassert religious authority as the final referent in cultural issues. As noted by Aziz Al-Azmeh, the cultural and political project of the Islamists involves delimiting a number of areas as forbidden with respect to reason and aesthetic sensibility, widening the fields of the forbidden, and imposing the principles and conditions of the licit and illicit on reason, in the social space and in cultural life in general.[54] At work is the expansion of the mechanisms of orthodoxy into the cultural domain by assigning primacy to religious considerations in judging artistic products. Also at issue is the control of the public space. In subjecting the public social space to the grid of the licit and the illicit, the space is secularised and the profane banished. In the manner that women are produced as *horma* (inviolable), and thus segregated and hidden from public, the public space is to be covered (nudity, interaction between the sexes, immodest dress are core to *horma* regulations that are being reactivated and expanded to cover artistic representation). The defence of *horma* in the cultural sphere is undertaken with the zeal of defending one's honour. As such, Islamist activists have painted over billboards in which parts of the female body are exposed. Before initiating lawsuits, the Islamists issue warnings to the 'violators,' ordering them to cease and desist from the illicit act (showing a revealing image or exposing a thought or a representation which, according to the code, should be hidden and suppressed). The 'violators' thus are given a chance to repent.

Studies of contemporary Islamist movements have attempted to explain why moral constructs occupy a central place in Islamist discourses. According to Nazih Ayubi, Islam as a religion is not essentially or particularly political but is viewed as such because it is about the collective enforcement of public morals. Ethics and morality are not understood as primarily individualistic – expressed and shaped through individual action – but as social and collective.[55] From this perspective, it can be argued that the state's Islamic identity does not refer to a form of government but to a realm of government – the

governance of morality. Contemporary Islamists call upon and anchor their ideological productions in discursive traditions in which
sexual and moral constructs are intertwined closely. In matters concerning morality, a chain of discursive authority runs from the Text,
the Tradition through medieval jurists to contemporary preachers,
and commentators. For example, a discursive tradition, which assumes
the status of orthodoxy, is at work with respect to the question of
women's position in society. As noted by Valerie J. Hoffman-Ladd,

> From Shaykh M. Hassanayn al-Bulaqi's *al-Jalis al-anis fi'l-tahdir 'amma
> fi tahrir al-mar'a min al-tablis* ['The pleasant companion warning against
> the deception contained in the liberation of women'], written against
> Qasim Amin's *Tahrir al-mar'a* in 1899, to tracts distributed at mosques
> and universities in contemporary Cairo, the issue of female segregation
> has been intimately linked with public morality, true religion, the *sunna*
> and the early community.[56]

In taking account of a discursive tradition, its continuity and evolution, one should be careful not to postulate some unchanging Islamic
view or position on morality. A careful study of Islamic history demonstrates the existence of varying conceptions of morality and
sexuality and also of a tradition of religious scepticism.[57] A cursory
look at different periods of Islamic history indicates that along with
puritanical pursuits, there existed profane concerns. For example, at
the time of the Prophet erotic poetry was recited,[58] while in the medieval period, Muslim jurists developed liberal rulings on women's
sexuality and control of their bodies.[59] More recently, Shaykh Muhammad Galal Kishk revisited in an unconventional manner the
question of homosexuality in Islamic traditions.[60]

The cultural battle reactivates mechanisms of social control directed by religious authorities. The war is waged by the Muslims
against the unbelievers, or, in other terms, by upholders of the moral
code against the violators. This is not the battle of the poor against
the rich, of the oppressed against their oppressors, but of the right-
eous against the non-righteous. Anyone can join regardless of class
position or institutional affiliation. Thus, the *'ulama* and the preachers are joined by the mosque attendees, whether they are among the
upper middle class devotees at Dr Mustafa Mahmud's mosque in the
Cairo suburb of al-Muhandisin, or until very recently in attendance

at Shaykh Sha'rawi's Friday sermons; or whether they are members of the lower classes watching the same sermons on television, attending Shaykh Mahalawi's Friday prayers in Alexandria or attending prayer in the Islamist run-mosques in the poor Cairo suburbs of Ain Shams or Imbaba or in the disadvantaged governorates of Asyut and Minya.

The mechanisms and strategies employed in the cultural battle have significant effects. The application of the grid of the licit and illicit to cultural products goes hand in hand with the establishment of a juridical frame in which to judge the moral propriety of such products. In fact, the burden of making this judgement is lifted from the individual Muslim. A higher authority is claimed and a presumed act of delegation on the part of the believers takes place. The mufti, the sheikhs and the emirs are in charge. The powers appropriated by these authorities are those of naming and designating. Once the symbols of transgression are identified, it is the Muslim's duty to correct the situation. The act of naming an opponent joins the believers in the struggle. At the imagined level, the community is activated and, in mosques across the country, adult males are placed in a position to enjoin good and forbid evil. This call acquires force because the defence of Islamic beliefs and of the Muslim community parallels the defence of personal honour ('ird and sharaf).[61] 'Ayb (shame), a popular culture construct, and the religious principle of haram (forbidden/illicit) become intertwined. A morality police made up of Muslim soldiers is deployed – in such a manner, Faraj Fuda's killer and Naguib Mahfouz's attacker were enlisted. Whether avenging a major transgression such as blasphemy or restoring a social order threatened with fitna (chaos) due to women's presence or to their representations in public, the Muslim is engaged in defending his religion. This symbolic power endows the Muslim with the ability to fight evil around him. Al-amr bil ma'ruf wa al-nahy 'an al-munkar is a claim to power which requires no sanctioning from the state.

The investment of moral constructs in the public space extends the field of control over which the Muslim can act. The believer's power as waliy amr (guardian) is not only exercised in the family through control over female members; it extends to the control of women in society. This power also effects a spatial control. The Muslim re-claims the public space which is represented and perceived as undermining his power in the private space. The billboards, for instance, are seen to injure the *haya'* (shyness) of women and induce sexual desires in men, bringing chaos into society.

The activities of the militant Islamists in Cairo and in the governorates of Upper Egypt involve, at once, the control of public space and the imposition of the moral code. Thus, in Ain Shams and other Cairo suburbs, the Islamists enforce public morality, enjoining women to wear the veil, ensuring the segregation of the sexes in public, forbidding music and dance, and applying the *hudud* (religious ordinances) as pertaining to sexual transgressions.[62] Islamist practices aimed at the control of the neighbourhood reinscribe the activities of the *futuwwa* in the *hara* (quarter, neighbourhood or alley) and reproduce the effects of what Janet Abu Lughod termed 'defensible space.'[63] Popular traditions provide the symbols of collective action. *'Ayb* is merged with *haram*. Rather than achieving emancipation, the strategies and goals pursued by the Islamists involve practices which aim at control (containing sexuality for instance) through the imposition of a narrowly defined morality and the re-establishment of the guardianship of Islamic authorities.

Conclusion

The crystallisation of Islamist political activism in the cultural arena brings disparate elements of the movement together and signals the development of an area of convergence between the state and the various Islamist forces. This form of Islamist politics revolves around questions of morality and is focused on the cultural domain. It deploys the discursive strategies of religious orthodoxy as well as the mechanisms and practices of societal regulation with the aim of controlling the public space. Informal groups such as the Islamist lawyers act as a new force through their court challenges of violations of the moral code. In this atmosphere, the degree of intimidation is greater and violence against intellectuals and artists finds justification in declarations of *takfir*. This area of activism is one where state policies of co-optation of the Islamists are at work. Various state institutions have been involved in the production of a public morality which is compatible with the Islamist vision. State-sponsored religious television programmes and publications, new state regulations investing censorship power in al-Azhar and, finally, the courts' engagement in the cultural battle in relation to morality are all factors that point to the increasing Islamisation of state institutions. Islamisation, here, is understood as the enforcement of public morality in the name of religious orthodoxy. At the same time, the restructuring of relations between and within state institutions has resulted in tensions and strains as shown in the case of the rifts between the Mashyakhat al-Azhar and the Front of 'Ulama.

The dynamics of cultural politics in Egypt operate in a manner that engages the Muslim in a position of defender of the faith. Membership in the community of Muslims invests the individual with the responsibility of safeguarding morality in public. The terms of this activism reinscribe the mechanisms of orthodoxy in structures of social action that are rooted in popular traditions. However, the scope of the Muslim's activity is limited and is carried out under the tutelage of some Islamic authority.

4

Contemporary Islamism as a Popular Movement
Socio-Spatial Determinants in the Cairo Urban Setting

This chapter is a revisiting of the question of militant Islamism in Egypt. Its purpose is to rethink the main arguments and explanatory frameworks relating to Islamist activism in general and the militant and violent type in particular. It presents some new propositions about the phenomenon and provides elements for a deeper understanding. This revisiting is undertaken in light of certain developments over the last decade or so, which may be summarised as follows: 1) the heightening of Islamist violence, marked by confrontations with the government in and around Cairo and in the provinces of Upper Egypt,[1] 2) the emergence of clear socio-spatial dimensions to Islamist activism. For the purposes of this chapter, my analysis pertains to these developments in the Greater Cairo area.[2]

The chapter is guided by several interrelated aims, some of which are given only preliminary attention here. First, it points to the links between Islamist action, on one hand, and a particular social geography of the city and the historical modes of urban organisation, on the other. Here, I draw attention to the history of urban activism in the popular quarters of the city, underlining the role of popular classes in politics, the grounding of their activism in the social structures of

82

the neighbourhoods and their patterns of organisation. Second, it outlines certain characteristics of the present urban context; specifically the informal housing communities and the social landscape characterising them. The argument here is that Islamism has found a home in these communities because their spatial, social, cultural and economic characteristics have contributed to their emergence as 'spheres of dissidence.'[3] Third, it examines the Islamist modes of implantation and action and the ways in which these are interwoven with the space, as exemplified by the informal housing communities of Ain Shams and Imbaba in Greater Cairo. Fourth, it highlights the importance of certain contemporary Islamist practices, which recall earlier forms of social organisation and regulation. Fifth, it situates Islamist activism within an overall framework, which takes into account the variables outlined above in addition to the role of ideological practices in mobilising support. In this regard, I will underline the limits to mobilisation which arise out of the Islamists' articulation of the principle of 'enjoining good and forbidding evil.'

The central argument is that militant Islamism has developed as an appropriation of spaces that have emerged with the ongoing processes of urban growth and expansion. There are indications that the new landscape does not represent rupture with social traditions and popular modes of life, but is, rather, a variation on the historically evolving urban tapestry. In socio-spatial terms, the Islamists are 'of' the popular classes, diverging from them only in some of their radical ideological practices.

The chapter is divided into five sections. Section one highlights certain elements in the explanatory frameworks used in relation to militant Islamism. Section two provides a brief historical overview of Cairo's urban social organisation. Section three sketches the new popular neighbourhoods, drawing a composite image of their social space. Section four outlines the Islamist mode of implantation in the new quarters. Section five highlights the popular movement dimensions of Islamist activism and the limitations of their ideological practices in the new quarters. The conclusion attempts to draw out the case for and against the development of militant Islamism as a full-fledged movement of the popular classes.

Islamism as a Contestation Movement

Militant Islamism is conventionally associated, at the ideological level, with Egyptian radical thinker Sayyid Qutb and, at the level of practice, with the 1970s groups influenced by his ideas. Among the earliest of these groups were al-Fanniya al-'Askariya (the Technical Military Academy) and al-Takfir wa al-Hijra (Excommunication and Flight), while the later ones, which continue to be active to this date, are al-Jihad Organisation and al-Jama'a al–Islamiya (the Islamic Group).[4] These groups share what is commonly referred to as a 'Jihadist' ideology. The main tenets of this ideology revolve around the idea of restoring *hakimiya* (God's governance) and the evaluative assessment of present-day society as *jahiliya* (state of ignorance before the advent of Islam). The concept of *jihad* (struggle) is central to their militant ideology, serving to justify the use of violence as a mode of action against state and society. The purpose of *jihad* is to establish the Islamic state and apply the Shari'a.[5] These two objectives are shared with moderate Islamist groups such as the Muslim Brotherhood Organisation.

Studies of these militant groups and their ideologies have generated typologies of organisations and individuals in their attempts to explain the nature of the movement and provide a framework for understanding. It is not my intention here to review the now immense volume of literature on the topic.[6] Rather, I will briefly recall the main contours of two key approaches in the literature on the subject. The first takes Islam as a starting point, and bases itself on the history of Islamic ideas. Through this prism, the movements appear as an expression of unchanging principles which guide the believers; hence their fundamentalism.[7] This corresponds to the revival thesis advanced by Sivan and others. Within this same approach, a more nuanced view is given in the reform thesis, which sees in Islamism the articulation of the religion's inherent, transformative potential.[8] The approach as a whole tends to attribute continuity to Islamic ideas and thought, and posits them as the embodiment of some religious essence.

The second approach is best described as the psychosocial model. Its earliest expression is found in studies of the socio-economic background of the first generation of militant Islamists, who emerged on the scene in the 1970s.[9] The model has yielded a socio-psychological profile of the ideal type militant: a recent migrant to the city, highly educated, a disenchanted product of modernisation. This perspective described the relationship between the movement and its context as being based on factors such as social dislocation and alienation. Within this conceptual framework the Islamists represent a rejection of their social environment. They occupy a vanguard role by virtue of their distinction from the rest of society. This approach's emphasis on Islamists' elitist ideology and high level of educational achievement leads to a downplaying of the movement's popular dimensions. In this vein, Hamied Ansari affirmed:

> the militant view is confined to a segment of the population on the margin of society. It has no impact on the urban masses or traditional rural society. Islamic militancy is especially appealing to the young men or to the rural migrants who became caught in the web of an urban society whose most manifest feature is the unbridled consumerism resulting from the liberalization policy initiated by Sadat. To this segment of the population which is experiencing an acute sense of deprivation, the resort to Islam was more a sign of social protest than a way of life.[10]

In a more recent study, Saad Eddin Ibrahim has noted changes in the social profile of the membership of Islamist groups: a decline in the percentage of university students active in militant Islamist groups, and an increase in the share of what he terms the lower middle class.[11] Further, Ibrahim has included the 'alienated masses' among those who suffer from relative deprivation. Although Ibrahim has adjusted the profile, the explanatory framework of the psychosocial approach remains intact. There are problems with this conceptual apparatus. First, it views the people as divorced from their social setting or, at least, psychologically removed from it. Thus, it leaves out both the efforts of the disaffected to create an alternative set of living conditions, and their engagement in the production of that environment. Second, the greater emphasis on psychological factors attracts attention away from the structures of social action which emerge in everyday life, and from those structures which can be recalled as acts of historical retrieval and remembering. As a result of these conceptual restrictions, we lose sight of the spaces of protest and the structures of oppositional action in which the people operate; by extension, we do not see in what ways and in what terms the Islamist insertion into the popular spaces has occurred.

A number of studies have, however, paid attention to the issue of popular activism. Situating the Islamist challenge within a wider historical context, Afaf Lutfi al-Sayyid-Marsot analyses contemporary Islamism as an urban protest movement.[12] Al-Sayyid-Marsot shows how Islamic groups represent a type of collective action which involves popular mobilisation, and describes how this type of action is rooted in the changing dynamics of state-society relations in Egypt. These changes took place in the structures of mediation, whereby the role of the 'ulama (learned men of religion) as intermediaries and popular leaders was 'devolved on new socially mobilised groups.'[13] Similarly, Guilain Denoeux recognised the importance of Islamic urban networks in the mobilisation of opposition against the state.[14] However, in conceptual terms, Denoeux alternates between the two approaches outlined above. In line with Saad Eddin Ibrahim, he emphasises that the ideological principles of the Islamist groups responded to the needs of the uprooted, alienated, educated youths.[15] At the same time, drawing on Emmanuel Sivan, he argues that the groups are a contemporary manifestation of the original founding experience of Islam, i.e. the hijra model (the flight of the prophet and the believers from Mecca to Medina).[16]

The approach developed in this essay stresses the importance of socio-spatial factors in analysing contemporary Islamism and in exploring the popular movement dimension of Islamist militant action. In other words, the study seeks to explore how the Islamists anchor themselves in certain spaces. An important aspect of my analysis is the study of the historical dimension of urban activism, in which activists draw on earlier experience and show where continuities and breaks occur. The attention given to space nuances the similarities and differences encountered in the urban landscape, both historically and in the contemporary period. This points to the need for comparative studies of old quarters in their evolution and in their relation to the new popular quarters, including the informal housing communities. As will be apparent from the analysis below, some characteristics of the old quarters and their social modes of organisation have persisted to the present. In addition, these have been transported to the new quarters and, in the process, have been reinvented and transformed. The comparative historical view helps locate contemporary Islamism within the developing socio-spatial configuration of the city. The approach I am proposing proceeds in a similar vein to the study of 'comparative history of urban collective action' outlined by Edmund Burke III.[17] Such a study is focused on the evolving patterns and forms of urban contestation, and on tracing the links between the changes in these forms, on the one hand, and the processes of social transformation, on the other.[18]

Popular Forces and Power Relations in the Cairo Urban Setting

A central aim of this essay is to bring into focus the analysis of societal forms of organisation in explaining modes of contestation, including militant Islamism. The anchoring of Islamist forces in particular urban spaces with distinct characteristics can help account for the nature of their organisation and their patterns of action. Greater insights can be gained by situating this process of anchorage in an historical context, in which specific groups acted as forces of contestation and urban unrest in various Middle Eastern countries and historical periods.[19] This is not to argue that the contemporary Islamists are an extension of these earlier forces, but to draw out the importance of certain forms of social organisation which are reproduced or transformed over time, highlighting continuities as well as ruptures. This constitutes an element of a wider framework which can illuminate our understanding of one of the most important forces of contestation today: militant Islamism.

A starting point for reviewing city organisation in the Ottoman period (sixteenth to nineteenth century) is its subdivision into quarters, with territorial, social and political boundaries.[20] The basis of this division was residential, professional and religious. In the popular quarters of Cairo, professional communities organised along craft lines, known as guilds, were juxtaposed to residential neighbourhoods. Superimposed on this framework was a religious type of organisation (primarily the Sufi orders). The whole formed a complex urban network characterised by the overlapping of residence, professional, and communal affiliations, parts of an overall system of power and control with many layers. This same feature facilitated mobilisation of popular groups in times of crises.[21] As André Raymond notes, '... the inscription of the political and social forces in the geography of the city ... was a fundamental phenomenon.'[22]

The guilds were more than mere economic units; they had rules and structures of a social and political nature, with their heads (*shaykhs*) being chosen by the membership and confirmed by the *wali* (governor). The *shaykh* was in charge of collecting taxes, overseeing rules of apprenticeship, and maintaining order.[23] In addition, some *shaykhs* were heads of Sufi orders based in the quarters. An added dimension was the presence of organised youths or gangs with links to these orders. Their names varied from the pejorative *"ayyarun'* and *'zu'r,'* to the more positive, such as *'futuwwa.'*[24]

How did all of this fit into the system of social and political control? In principle, the quarters were headed by *shaykh al-hara*, who was the representative of the city governor and acted as an informant to authority. Other state agents included the *muhtasib*, who oversaw pricing in the market and the preservation of public morality. Another layer of state-society mediation and control was occupied by the official *'ulama*.[25]

The positioning of the *futuwwa, shaykh al-hara, muhtasib, 'alim*, and Sufi leader was not static. The local groups extended their powers over their quarters when the central administration was weak.[26] Popular forces, particularly the *zu'r*, rose in contestation at different periods and for various reasons. They also constituted a force to be mobilised by different contenders for power, including the state itself. During the Ottoman period, Raymond notes, government sometimes sought their help, but more often looked upon them with suspicion.[27] The *futuwwa* gangs played an important role in mobilising the population of the quarters in the seventeenth and eighteenth centuries. It is these groups which responded to the *wali*'s oppression, and which were mobilised under the leadership of the craft-Sufi heads and other religious figures.[28] Raymond affirms the gangs' role in making history as seen in their collective power against the ruler. The threat to unleash gangs to loot and plunder forced rulers to retract from imposing higher taxes or raising prices. In a sense, the gangs preserved the moral economy of the city.[29] In time, these popular groups became preliminary forces for contestation of and opposition to the French occupation (1798–1801), and were instrumental in the investiture of the country's leadership in the person of Muhammad Ali.[30]

After a strong central administration was put in place under Muhammad Ali in the nineteenth century, the political power of these forces waned, only to be reasserted at critical junctures.[31] In any case, the terms of social control and local practices of power persisted. For example, the *futuwwa-'alim* coalition of the past was no longer operative, but, the *futuwwa* continued to influence the life of the quarter.[32] Thus, while overt popular contestation was contained by an emerging strong state, socio-spatial factors allowed for continued autonomy and other forms of activism.

Here, we should turn to the social organisation of the quarters.[33] Janet Abu Lughod stresses that within the terms of social and political organisation sketched above, the quarter acted as protector and constituted 'defensible space.'[34] This aspect of the quarter's character developed as a consequence of spatial and social organisation: spatial markers indicated where the public space ended and semiprivate and private spaces began. At the *hara* (alley/neighbourhood) level, this spatial differentiation was expressed in a street system which included a central branch or street (*darb*), from which small alleys or passages called *'atfa* branched into a *zuqaq* (dead end alley).[35] The hierarchical street system allowed for the maintenance of social autonomy, and enforcement of social rules regarding gender relations.

As a social unit the *hara* has persisted in the popular traditional quarters of the city, along with many of the rules and regulations which made the local neighbourhood operate as an extension of the family. In the twentieth century context of rapid social transformation, which brought about new economic, social and cultural developments for the popular classes to contend with, the old social practices grounded in the space were reworked. Regulation of malefemale relations, and efforts to cope with new financial burdens of education and marriage were issues to be dealt with within the historically developed modes of socio-spatial interaction. Recent studies have shown us how this is accomplished[36] and how the quarters, centred on alleys, continue to represent the everyday communities of the people, although the *hara* was officially abolished as an administrative unit and the office of *shaykh* discarded in 1962.[37] The *hara* continues to exist as a social and territorial unit in the old quarters and, to a lesser extent, in other parts of the city. At the same time, the *hara* has undergone many changes. For example, Stauth notes that the integrative functions of *hara* social relations and institutions began to weaken with the introduction of factory relations into the workshop production of the quarters.[38] As a result, the normatively grounded attitudes of reciprocity, arbitration and sexual segregation, which represent important rules in the construction of social and public life, required renegotiation.[39] The modes of survival and transformation of the old popular quarters are instructive for our understanding of the new popular neighbourhoods.

In the post-1952 period, new residential and housing areas for the popular classes have sprung up through state planning and community efforts. These differ from the old popular quarters in terms of street layout and residential organisation. Those areas which emerged as a result of state planning were mainly large industrial zones with popular housing units (*masakin sha'biya*) in the form of low-income apartment blocks for workers in the Cairo suburbs of Helwan and Shubra. State-planned residential areas were laid out along class lines, with middle class suburbs designed for the professional elites forming the social base of the new regime.[40] In the new working class areas, traditional layers of control and mediation disappeared and in their place there emerged a system of surveillance centred around police stations – control of workers was a preoccupation of the regime.[41] These areas have been the sites of workers' protest, erupting from factories and perhaps drawing on the surrounding housing areas where family and kin reside. The industrial zones, though originally planned by the state, have also become sites for informal housing communities. Since the 1960s, this type of community began to spread to the outskirts of the city, and, today, such areas house one third of Cairo's population and have emerged as the new popular quarters. It is to these communities that I now turn.

The New Popular Quarters and Islamist Oppositional Movements

Before proceeding to an examination of the key features of contemporary urban social organisation, I would like to note the particularities of the Islamist presence in the urban setting. An investigation into the areas where Islamist activism and confrontation with the government has occurred reveals a concentration in popular neighbourhoods and quarters – namely those which have emerged 'spontaneously' and have come to be known as informal housing communities. These have mainly developed on the periphery of Greater Cairo (Cairo, Giza and Qalyubiya) as well as in nine other Egyptian governorates. Islamist implantation in these areas is discussed in greater detail below. At this point, however, we should map the evolution of this presence over the last two decades.

The importance of spatial determinants is indicated by the al-Takfir wa al-Hijra group's strategy of separation by segregation in the peripheral areas of southern Cairo. The group's flight from the inner city was ideologically justified in terms of *hijra*, modelled after the migration of the Prophet from Mecca to Medina. This tenet was not espoused by the Jihad group, but many of its members lived and operated in peripheral areas such as Boulaq al-Dakrur, Matariya and Sahil, forming cells headed by emirs as in the Nahya district of Imbaba.[42] In fact, the places of residence in the early 1990s of members of the new military section of the reconstituted Jihad (known as Talai' al-Fatih or Vanguard of Conquest) confirm a particular pattern of spatial distribution. This pattern also crystallised in other groups from the mid-1980s on. First, we find new groups emerging in these spaces, notably al-Najun min al-Nar ('Escapees from Hell'), and al-Samawiya (named after its leader Taha al-Samawi), whose members resided in Boulaq, Matariya and Imbaba. Then, a clear case of territorialisation develops, with full-fledged efforts at appropriating the peripheral spaces. The informal housing communities, therefore, served not only as places of residence and hiding, but also as areas of militant concentration and activity.[43]

We should now turn to the new urban popular quarters and examine their spatial features and socio-economic configuration. This is necessary in order to shed light on contemporary Islamism as a form of contestation shaped by the setting in which it operates.

The establishment of informal housing settlements and the practice of squatting on public land in Cairo are not, in themselves, new phenomena.[44] However, the large-scale development of informal housing communities is a more recent occurrence, dating from the mid-1960s. In simple terms, these communities arose in response to the increased popular need for urban housing and the state's failure to meet that need.[45] Population growth, dislocation and resettlement and rural-urban migration were all factors contributing to urban expansion. State urban housing and planning did not keep up with this expansion. The state began providing fewer subsidised rental units in the mid 1960s, and by the early 1970s had moved into the production of medium-cost and luxury flats for private ownership. As a result, responsibility for much urban management and housing provision was assumed by the people themselves. In Cairo, this translated into the appropriation of public land and illegal construction on agricultural land. The process of informal housing development has, thus far, resulted in the emergence of seventy-four informal settlements in twelve areas of the city.[46] The housing in these areas ranges from temporary shelter made of tin huts and shacks to permanent structures several stories high.[47]

Informal housing communities have developed as spaces of urban contestation and have come to represent an important arena of Islamist activism. The anchoring of Islamist groups in these communities must be understood in terms of the physical characteristics of the spaces and the forms of social organisation which are inscribed in them. In spatial terms, these communities exist on the periphery of the city and are not easily accessible – given that their rise was not part of state planning, they cannot be accessed via paved roads and have no means of public transportation. Some are rather forbidding to outsiders due to a rocky landscape or otherwise inhospitable environment. As the maximisation of housing space is a valued objective in the development of these communities, streets tend to be narrow with little public space and with buildings running back to back and side by side for kilometres, as is the case of Munira in Imbaba.[48] The high population density makes control and surveillance difficult. The narrow streets, unpaved roads and labyrinthian layout render the areas uncharted territory for outsiders, including the state authority. In fact, until recently, the agents of state control – particularly the police – were absent from most of these spaces.

As communal efforts undertaken to resolve the housing problem, the informal communities have arisen in violation of government rules and regulations concerning construction. This process of development has given the communities a certain degree of autonomy from the government – the latter having been completely absent during the communities' founding stages of planning and construction. Unable and unwilling to meet popular housing needs, the state turned a blind eye to the informal housing communities.

Community solidarity and forms of collective action have developed through the process of implantation. Forms of social organisation and community control differ according to the history of development – whether communal or managed by contractors. Where squatting on public land was collective and in defiance of the state, the communities have organised along lines such as kinship, place of origin, and date or period of arrival. As a consequence, in places such as Izbat al-Haganna in Madinat Nasr, Manshiyat Nasir in the Muqattam and Istabl Antar in Fustat Hill, a power hierarchy has emerged with modes of control based on these various lines of social differentiation. This pattern is less likely to develop where contractors controlled the process of implantation, dividing the plots and putting up illegal private construction. This latter type of division is found in Munira al-Gharabiya in Imbaba. However, even in Imbaba, a communal type of implantation has taken place in some sections such as Izbat al-Sa'yada, whose inhabitants migrated from Upper Egypt following the initial settlement of a single individual and his family.

Studies of the informal housing communities reveal a mode of action and relationship to government which reflect activism and initiative.[49] The residents pursue strategies of engagement and disengagement with the government depending on their needs, employing tactics which bring about either visibility or invisibility, to suit their situation. Residents of the communities organise and engage in collective action to pressure the government to provide services, confer legal status on them, and acknowledge their legitimate right to continue to live in the spaces they have appropriated.

In other instances, the residents choose to meet their needs through private means, by collectively investing in the provision of the services: purchasing cables and transformers for the connection of water and electricity, paying for sewage tanks and the removal of solid waste.

The social groups residing in the informal housing communities make up the expanded popular classes. These are the social forces that developed with the growth of the commercial and service sectors of the economy under the policies of *infitah* (open door) and privatisation, and with the accompanying restructuring of the labour force.[50] 'Popular' is defined in opposition to the dominant forces – the political and economic elites. It also refers to the economic and social position of a number of classes or fractions of classes which, because of the blurring of boundaries, are not easily distinguishable. The fluidity and blurring of lines has to do with occupational mobility and the fact that members of these classes hold more than one job simultaneously. A common feature between them, however, is the predominance of informal economic activities. This applies to the artisans, petty traders, low-level service sector workers, construction workers and craftsmen. Many of these workers are grouped under the category of *hirafiyyin* (craftsmen or tradesmen). Levels of skill vary and so do positions within the craft, from the self-employed and workshop owners, to contractual workers, to daily workers. Informal economic activity signals a change both in the structure of work and the social organisation which accompanied the move to the new quarters.

Before proceeding to discuss other characteristics of the popular classes, it is important to reflect on the working classes' position as one of their constitutive components. In looking at the Egyptian setting we find that there is a need to nuance the terms of this inclusion. First, the construction of *masakin sha'biya* (popular housing) in housing areas designated for state workers allowed for working class concentration in distinct districts and neighbourhoods of the city. Second, the patterns of working class activism are inscribed within state corporatist structures which were put in place by the Nasser regime after the 1952 revolution. Thus, working class forms of contestation are framed by terms of negotiation and exchange that have been worked out with state-controlled unions. These factors have

served to distinguish the working class in terms of residential distribution, relations with the government, and everyday forms of social
organisation. I will come back to the question of the apparent absence of Islamist mobilisation among the working class.

There is a residential aspect to the identification of the popular
classes. Until recently, the category referred to the residents of the
old quarters. It would seem appropriate now to include the new neighbourhoods. The latter are distinguished in a number of ways. They
are mainly inhabited by young 'nuclear families' that have come from
the villages or that have moved from the old quarters, leaving their
extended families behind. The physical characteristics of the new
neighbourhoods are different from the old, but, as Singerman points
out, the popular classes 'take the *hara* culture with them.'[51] Thus,
the popular classes are also distinguishable from other social strata
in cultural terms. This has to do with the people's claim to authenticity. Values, norms and practices associated with the popular classes
are seen as true and authentic and opposed to the 'fake' values and
lifestyles of the upper classes. The socio-spatial factors outlined so
far are important to the constitution of the popular classes as a political force.

A study of Manshiyat Nasir shows the predominance of trades
work among the residents. Most of these tradespeople work in the
informal sector.[52] This type of work composition is also reported in a
study of Izbat al-Hagana.[53] A report commissioned by the governo-
rate of Giza has 50 per cent of the residents of informal communities
listed as peddlers, daily workers and craftsmen.[54] In the current socio-economic juncture of economic liberalisation and privatisation,
the employment ranks of the informal sector are expanding, due to
the convergence of different types of entrants. On one hand, we find
individuals with lower levels of education and limited skills and, on
the other, university graduates. In fact, Hoodfar's study of households in one of the new neighbourhoods shows that, increasingly,
young males are leaving school at an early age to learn a craft. This
represents a family-based response to the changes in the job market,
whereby a higher education neither improves job opportunities nor
brings higher income.[55] A similar pattern is revealed in a 1989 study
of Munira al-Gharbiya in Imbaba, showing a high rate of illiteracy

among children over ten years old (49 per cent). The study reports that 20 per cent of children under the age of fifteen have entered the labour force and that 35 per cent of the total number of children in the households surveyed engaged in craft-type employment.[56] The entry into the artisan/tradesworker class by the educated segments of society is another development. Many of today's construction sector workers, such as house painters, plasterers and tile layers, are university graduates with engineering and law degrees. Indeed, these degree-holders find themselves among the group of *arzuqi* workers (daily job-seekers) who bide their time in coffee shop cum labour markets, waiting for employment.[57]

Networks based on kinship and regional origin are avenues of entry into the job market for the residents of the informal housing areas. In Manshiya Nasir, different kin groups enjoy links to particular trades. Thus, those originating from the Araba, in the Upper Egypt province of Sohag, have better access to the building trades and to such jobs as house painting and plastering.[58] In Manshiya, the residents supply 20 per cent of the labour force employed in the workshops and stores of the area.[59] The social networks of the Manshiyat residents extend beyond the place of origin and the borders of the community to include other quarters of the city. In fact, Tekçe, Oldham and Shorter contend that 'the patterns of interaction are becoming similar to those of the older urban neighbourhoods.'[60] In her study of Izbat al-Hagana in Madinat Nasr, al-Maghazi confirms the importance of familial and neighbourhood networks to the social interaction and economic activity of the residents, many of whom establish workshops or small stores in the community. The informal labour market is, in many ways, self-regulating. Its structures and regulatory institutions operate in a manner similar to the guild system with, rules of entry, apprenticeship and forms of solidarity and sociality which are now centred on coffee shops rather than workshops.[61]

The commercial life of the neighbourhoods revolves around the market which runs through the main thoroughfare, where shops and kiosks are located. There is little space for cars to pass through. Informality is once again the predominant character of these markets. However, they have their '*shaykhs*' who act as mediators with government, or who organise the trade of particular goods.[62] The informal markets are also sites of confrontation with the police, whenever this latter tries, from time to time, to impose 'law and order.'

The above composite portrait of informal housing communities highlights the characteristics of the new popular neighbourhoods. This is a first step towards integrating them into the analysis of contemporary social and political activism in Egypt (the informal communities have been the subject of anthropological and sociological studies, but there has been little attempt to incorporate them into political studies). On one hand, the informal housing communities appear to represent marginality and invisibility, and have thus been officially discounted. The common term used to designate them is *'ashwa'iyat'* (haphazard), which stresses the absence of planning and organisation, and their lack of integration into the wider community. However, this characterisation is belied by the few available studies. In terms of organisation and spatial arrangements, the communities actually tend to show a degree of planning, and a utilitarian approach to the space.

As for their relationship to the state, we can find dynamics of both engagement and disengagement. It is their positioning in relation to the wider society which is more complex. As noted, the communities tend to exist in relative separation, as a result of the physical characteristics of the space and their lack of integration into the main municipal road system. However, in their pursuit of a living, the residents have established familial and market-linked networks which extend beyond their communities. In this, they are not very different from the old popular quarters. In fact, many of the residents of the old quarters have moved to informal housing areas. Some were even at the forefront of the original establishment of informal communities, after their former homes collapsed or had to be evacuated.[63] According to Eric Denis, these neighbourhoods are 'veritable cities, popular districts with commerce, markets, multitude of private services that make up for the absence of the state and its schools, clinics and bus lines. It is here that one now finds the people of Cairo.'[64]

The conventional view is that the popular classes are apathetic, and that if they engage in action, it is only as a result of their social frustration or the manipulation of their religiosity. Yet, a closer look at the strategies of community development and consolidation pursued by these classes tells a different story. In strategies of engagement and disengagement, they developed practices which challenge state authority. Through community organisation and the establishment of informal networks, the groundwork for autonomy was laid. Part of my contention is that Islamist activism should be placed within a broader social context, which takes account of the different forms of social and spatial organisation that have come about with the socio-economic changes of the current juncture. Islamism is not a marginal religious or political movement or merely a militant ideology with few adherents. Rather, it is a form of contestation that finds ground in spaces where oppositional positioning develops. André Raymond has observed that while popular quarters and classes seem to erupt on to the scene in historical periods of crises, the conditions for such eruption are rooted in modes of social and territorial organisation. This observation has relevance to the contemporary context. Indeed, militant Islamism should not be viewed as the activism of a marginal and alienated group, but rather through the prism of the social geography and the urban landscape in which it has taken root. The Islamists anchor themselves in oppositional spaces already formed or in the process of formation. The terms of this opposition are spatial, social, cultural, economic and political. As noted by Denis, these neighbourhoods 'propose a reformulation of the popular city, recovering the social role of the street.'[65] The dynamics of Islamist insertion into this setting and the logic of their action are factors which influence their ability to direct popular activism and its eruption onto the urban scene.

Islamist Implantation in the New Popular Quarters

As noted above, the presence of militant Islamist groups in peripheral areas of the city dates to the early period of activism in the 1970s. However, a crystallisation took place in the 1980s. An important factor in the consolidation of Islamists in the informal housing communities was al-Jama'a al-Islamiya's decision to migrate to Cairo from Upper Egypt, in response to increased pressures from the state security services and following confrontations with the police. Their destination, in most cases, was the informal housing areas. Ain Shams and Imbaba were favoured because of their characteristics, as noted above: peripheral location and a degree of invisibility. Ain Shams is located on the north-eastern edge of Cairo. Imbaba is situated in north Giza, falling within the boundaries of Greater Cairo. These two areas are not necessarily peripheral in terms of their geographical distance from the centre, but in terms of their lack of integration into the main road and transport systems and the social services network. For example, as late as 1993, Munira in Imbaba was accessed by an informal network of unlicensed vans. Its main thoroughfare was unpaved and visitors had to negotiate their way over old railroad tracks and barbed wire in order to enter the area. In the late 1980s, Ain Shams had only two paved roads.

Imbaba was originally an agricultural urban fringe which, under the industrialisation policies of President Nasser, saw the establishment of factories accompanied by some popular housing construction. Migrants to the city flocked to the area, where contractors put up cheap housing units. This early association with an industrial base accounted for the spread of socialist ideas and activism in the 1960s and 70s. The area's potential as a locus of protest is borne out by the fact that it was one of the first places where the bread riots broke out in 1977.[66]

The Jama'a found in these spaces an appropriate territory for mobilisation and action. Their organised implantation in Imbaba was in the mid-1980s, when a small cell under the direction of Rifa'i Ahmad Taha, a leading member now residing outside Egypt, met with a number of residents and formed the group's nucleus. This nucleus was composed of young migrants of Upper Egypt origin.[67] Through religious education, they managed to recruit more youths. An aspect of the Jama'a's attraction was its confrontational stand vis-à-vis the government, a stand which distinguishes it from the Muslim Brotherhood (MB). According to a leading member, the youths rejected the MB's soft position. Here we have a clue to the youths' preference.[68] Occupying a position of conflict and confrontation with the state was more appealing. It was not the religious ideas per se that were at issue but the practical conclusions drawn from them, more specifically the positions of resistance they made available.

As part of this organisation, the Jama'a sent a speaker and representative to Imbaba, and divided the area into ten main sections, positioning emirs in the main streets and alleys and in the mosques.[69] Following conventional Jama'a strategy, new recruits were given religious education in mosques or zawiya (small mosque or prayer room); the lessons were given by the local emir and outsiders were easily identified.[70] The Jama'a controlled five mosques in the main streets of Munira, giving them access to many of the worshippers. The mosques were sites from which they could control the main streets, as well. As part of ideological and political consolidation, the Jama'a used videocassettes, journals, and weekly popular meetings to disseminate their views. For instance, it has been reported that at least one of these meetings attracted 600 attendees.[71] Gatherings spilled over into the street, and thus were visible to other non-participating residents. The weekly speeches were broadcast over microphones and heard beyond the vicinity of the mosque and the main street. The Jama'a succeeded in attaining a visible presence where the state and its agents were absent.

Moreover, the group provided social services through a 'social work committee.' The committee helped poor residents with health care and education, setting up projects that included support for orphaned students, and the distribution of books and food.[72] Money was raised from merchants in the market, a practice which was classified as zakat (alms collection) by the group, but as itawat (protection money) by its opponents. In addition, the Jama'a was active in the area of social relations, enforcing social mores and regulating gender relations. In resolving disputes among the residents, the emir bypassed the traditional tribal council, whose powers were waning in the face of spreading anomie and drug abuse.[73]

A similar mode of implantation took place in Ain Shams, where Jama'a members exercised wide-ranging powers over some of the districts and neighbourhoods (e.g. Alf Maskan, al-Zahra and Masakin Ain Shams). There are some indications that this implantation involved modes of planning parallel to those undertaken in Imbaba. For example, directives were given to place Safwat 'Abd al-Ghani, a Jama'a military strategist and a prominent figure of the Jihadist current, in the Adam mosque.[74] Another important figure, Hasan al-Gharabawi, was relocated there by the Shura Council in Asyut. Al-Jama'a controlled a number of mosques, namely Adam, Fatima al-Zahra and al-Anwar al-Muhammadiya. Weekly seminars were held in the Adam mosque. Jama'a members exacted donations from the merchants in the Ibrahim 'Abd al-Raziq market, where they were actively propagating their ideas. The funds were used to finance the social work committee which operated from the mosque. In addition to preaching and providing social services, the Jama'a attended to matters of social mores – forbidding mixing between the sexes, banning music, and monitoring entry into the area. It enforced the rules and applied the *hudud* (religious ordinances).

In each of the above cases, the group came into conflict with the state. The immediate causes for this confrontation differ, and reports tend to conflict. However, it was official cognisance of the growing Islamist challenge which brought the state to act. The police took action in Ain Shams in 1988. It penetrated the area by force, cleared the market and set up roadblocks in the streets and alleys, as well as checkpoints at the main entrances of some of the neighbourhoods. Demonstrations ensued and people marched on two police stations and set them on fire. They also burned police security cars. Islamists and their supporters blockaded themselves in the mosque and were besieged by the police. The clashes lasted four days, ending with hundreds of arrests. The government was again moved to act in 1992, in the face of local and international media reports claiming that Imbaba had fallen under Islamist control. Thousands of police personnel were brought in to 'recapture' the territory. The clashes lasted for three weeks. Following this, the government intensified the politics of security, opening access roads to the area and lighting the streets. It also embarked on a project of upgrading for some areas and planned removal for others. The implementation of the new policies has been gradual, and it is too early to determine the outcome.

The Popular Movement Dimensions of Militant Islamism

Earlier studies of the first militant groups elaborated an ideal type of the Islamist militant: a university student or young graduate, usually in the engineering or medical faculties, and of rural origin.

According to Saad Eddin Ibrahim's work on the 1970s generation of Islamists, the ideal type militant was a high achiever. More recently, Ibrahim has found that the 'ailment' of the high achiever has spread to the 'younger and less educated Egyptians.'[75] Alienation, deprivation and discontent are components of what he terms the 'inner sociological logic' of Islamist activism. As noted above, however, it is more helpful to approach militant Islamism in terms of its social rootedness, rather than in terms of uprootedness. This requires a more differentiated account of the ties that bind the militants to their social context. I will turn to this account below.

Increasingly, the militants include artisans or *hiraffiyin* (tradespeople). This is confirmed by data drawn from police case files pertaining to a 1986 investigation of some members of al-Najun min al-Nar and al-Samawiya, to the arrests made in the Ain Shams events in 1988, and to those members of the new Jihad-Talai' al-Fatih group who were brought up on charges in 1993. The occupational profile of the Samawiya group, based on the list of seventy-six accused and brought to trial, is as follows: twenty-nine technical workers in the service industry (including three owners of workshops); eleven students in vocational training schools and high schools; three cab drivers; two traders; two mosque keepers; one farmer; a popular singer; twelve university graduates (of whom three were teachers, two engineers, one doctor, and the remaining six in accountancy and clerical jobs); six university students; three enlisted in the army, for whom no educational background was specified. The occupations of six others were not indicated.[76] For al-Najun min al-Nar, the list of thirty-three accused are grouped into the following occupational categories: sixteen professionals; ten craftsmen; two traders; two unemployed; one student; two unknown.[77] The list of the accused in the Ain Shams events shows a very similar breakdown.[78] Among the first group of Talai' al-Fatih members to be arrested, totalling fifty-two individuals, a similar pattern emerged, with many having vocational training and working in trades, particularly house painting and petty trading. There were also some students among their number.[79]

In terms of age composition, this new generation of Islamists maintains the youthfulness of its predecessor. Looking at the age breakdown of the members in the cases examined above, it is found that 75 per cent of activists were below the age of thirty and that only 25 per cent are thirty or above.[80] Data regarding the marital status of activists is sketchy. The question raised here is whether militancy is more prevalent among a particular group, namely single young men with little familial responsibilities and more mobility. The predominance of younger members would confirm the association of activism and youth.[81] However, it should be noted that a number of the emirs were married and had children, and that the wives were engaged in support activities, such as hiding weapons. There is a degree of intermarriage among group members. Activists arrange for their sisters to marry fellow members, thus forging a bond as brothers-in-law. Sisters also introduce female friends to their brothers as suitable marriage partners.[82] Membership of the Jama'a is viewed as a means of securing a partner and gaining financial support for the marriage. At the same time, established marriage links aim to solidify the relationships among group members.

As noted earlier, the apparent absence of Islamist mobilisation among the working class (al-'umal) can be explained in terms of the form of incorporation which has characterised the latter's relation to the state in the post-revolution period. Within the state corporatist arrangements framing the workers' activism, protest became focused on sit-ins and strikes, which usually ended in negotiated settlements.[83] Workers' demonstrations have taken place around the areas of work and, again, the unions have acted as intermediaries to avoid long drawn out standoffs. The established working class's oppositional tactics have intensified in the 1990s in response to the liberalisation and privatisation policies.[84] The militant Islamist ideological discourse does not seem to address itself to this situation. However, we cannot generalise that there are no workers among the Islamists, nor that there is an inherent animosity between the working class and Islamist activists. It should be recalled that the Muslim Brotherhood was active in working class areas in the late 1930s, and by the mid-1940s, it carried out an organisational campaign among the workers of Shubra al-Khayma.[85] The ideological principles of the Brotherhood, which were framed in moral and cultural terms, had their appeal under conditions of colonialism and the foreign ownership of industries. However, these principles became less salient with the Egyptianisation of industry and the subsequent move to 'corporatist nationalism' in the 1950s.[86] At the ideological level, the discourse of today's militants suffers similar limitations on its ability to appeal to the workers. Nonetheless, there are cases of militant Islamist activism among the workers in some of the industrial areas of Upper Egypt, namely Naj' Hamadi and Dishna.[87]

Militant Islamist operations carried out in Cairo in the 1990s were directed internally by *hirafiyyin*: emirs in many of the areas were also tradesmen. Among the emirs of the Jama'a, we find an electrician (Shaykh Jabir of the Imbaba group), and a law student/poultry merchant (Gharabawi of Ain Shams). In addition, tradesmen were the targets of the religious lessons held in militant-mosques run in the popular neighbourhoods of Alexandria.[88] In sum, those making up this social force, tend to have a high school level technical education, be engaged in petty trade, and employed in a wide range of jobs in the service and construction industries: as mechanics, house painters, plumbers, carpenters.[89] Members of some of the Islamist groups tend to reject government employment on a matter of principle, in favour of self-employment. They set up businesses and establish job networks as part of their strategies.[90] Hence, their responses are not different from others in the popular classes, who recognise that there are no jobs to be had in the government.

Most of these newly-created jobs are held in the informal economy. In urban areas, informal jobs and informal housing go together. More than half of the workers in the informal sector live in the informal housing communities, especially Ain Shams, Imbaba, Boulaq, Matarya, and Haram.[91] Within this sector, are found un-registered, small businesses which employ less than ten persons. Many of the jobs involve menial labour. In 1985, it was estimated that there were 2,887,000 jobs in the informal sectors of production, commerce and services.[92] In her study of a popular quarter in old Cairo, Singerman confirms the pervasiveness of informal economic activity, which constituted a primary source of income for 38 per cent of the economically active members of her sample, and a supplementary source of income for 60 per cent.[93] Further, production workers were heavily represented in this type of activity, most being *hirafiyyin* working in small manufacturing workshops.[94] These informal economic activities depend on occupational and familial networks. Islamists are part of this socio-economic configuration. The importance of informal networks as 'avenues of participation' and quiet resistance has been demonstrated in recent studies, which note the activism in survival strategies and networks of reciprocity among the popular classes.[95] To this picture should be added the open resistance and militant oppositional potential which contemporary Islamism can and does capture.

In occupational and residential terms, the Islamists are located among the popular classes in the new popular quarters. The views of the Jama'a members in these areas are shaped by lessons in the *zawiya* and by popular religious education through cassettes and the sermons of popular preachers. They attend weekly seminars that include religious speeches and updates on Jama'a activities and news of Muslims in other countries. Thus, we witness a shift in terms of membership and location of recruitment and means of organisation. Islamist activism has moved from the university to the neighbourhood. However, the mosque and religious education remain central.[96]

In attempts to avoid police surveillance, residential flats have come to serve as new gathering-places.[97] Direct access to the followers is possible through the use of video-senders, whereby the Jama'a is able to programme and broadcast certain videotapes directly into the homes of members and sympathisers.[98] To tune in, viewers are notified in advance of the transmission times of this alternative programming. In addition to juristic pamphlets, political newsletters and bulletins are now used.[99] These analyse sociopolitical and economic conditions and deal directly with the people's difficulties, tackling issues such as increases in bread prices, government investment policies, and so on. Thus, 'educational' activities pay greater attention to issues of daily concern, and address questions of exploitation and oppression. There has also been a marked shift in focus away from the problem of the infidel ruler to that of official corruption.[100]

My emphasis on the occupational and residential factors aims to highlight the location of Islamism within a particular urban context, which shows the movement's popular dimensions. Thus, the analysis nuances earlier views which pointed to its elitist-vanguardist nature, evidenced in social background variables and the groups' approach to state and society. In both Ain Shams and Imbaba, the Islamists have engaged with the people. As noted above, they resolved disputes among neighbours, provided social services and religious teaching. Many of the members come from families that know each other and are tied by kin relations. This provides the groups with familial, popular protection, which is vital to their capacity to confront and resist the authorities. Reports indicate that while committed members in Ain Shams numbered in the hundreds, the number of sympathisers who could be mobilised reached into the thousands.[101]

My exposé indicates that there have been significant transformations in the social makeup of the militants and in their engagement with society. However, elements of elitism or distance from society continue to exist in their ideology and practice. This may be attributed in part to the fact that the intellectual leadership seems to remain with the first generation or historic leadership and its disciples,[102] many of whom are either in prison or residing abroad. A more important factor, which I have noted in my earlier work and which is consistent with the late Hisham Mubarak's assessment, is the ideological limitation of the Islamists' capacity to engage in popular action. Such constraints derive from the group's emphasis on the principle of *al-amr bil ma'ruf wa al-nahy 'an al-munkar* (enjoining good and forbidding evil). In some respects, the application of this principle recalls popular practices of social control and is thus acceptable. However, it also expresses an attitude of intolerance which contradicts with popular norms of toleration and moderation. I will discuss this briefly.

Certain acts of violence carried out by the Islamists are directed against what they see as violations of rules of public morality. Under the rubric of *al-amr bil ma'ruf wa al-nahy 'an al-munkar*, they commit acts of social violence directed against fellow citizens, including organised attacks on video clubs, cinemas and liquor stores. Other acts aim at enforcing an adherence to moral strictures usually relating to interaction between the sexes, the dress code, and popular entertainment activities at weddings and during festive occasions. It is in these areas that the ambiguity lies. In challenging the state and society, the Islamists often invoke popular traditions of male-dominated interaction between the sexes and family relations. Popular traditions thus serve as a frame of reference for contestation. As an oppositional strategy, this involves the merging of popular values with Islamic traditions. An example of such merging is the overlap of *'ayb* (shame) and *haram* (illicit) in the popular imagination. *'Ayb* is a principle of social control that is applied to many spheres and relationships, particularly the family and gender relations, while *haram* is a principle stipulating religious restrictions. In practice, these principles fade into one another. The Islamists' concern with social mores in terms of *halal* and *haram* (licit and illicit) intertwines with the *'ayb* tradition.[103] Their ideas of gender segregation draw on *horma* (sanctity) regulations concerning the inviolability of women and the spaces with which women are conventionally associated. Historically, these regulations were enforced in the *hara*, which Islamist action, in the present, seeks to reinscribe in the new neighbourhoods. It should be noted that the housing conditions in some dwellings have served to undermine these regulations. The crowding of male and female family members in a single-room dwelling, and of whole families in shared accommodation transgresses the norms. Popular concerns with such issues have been expressed in questions directed to Lajnat al-Fatwa (Religious Ruling Committee) of al-Azhar.[104]

Tahakum (arbitration to God) is a central idea in the Jihadist ideology and constitutes another area where the normatively grounded attitudes and practices of the quarter can be merged with Islamic principles. Past and present popular quarters have a tradition of arbitration, in which disputants turn to respected members of the neighbourhood as referees. The Jama'a has stepped forward to occupy this role. Islamists have inscribed themselves in the space as mediators or agents of *tahakum*, to whom conflicting groups refer to sort out disagreements.[105] The offices of the Jama'a have reconciled disputing spouses, reinstated a son's financial obligations toward his mother, settled outstanding debts, and so on.[106] The intensity of the Jama'a's involvement in social relations cannot be fully established from available data. However, what needs to be stressed is the symmetry between their modes of operation and popular avenues of social regulation in particular spheres. Here, the Jama'a and the people converge in eschewing the involvement of public authority.

In a sense, the Jama'a members occupy a multitude of roles, ranging from the *futuwwa* to the *shaykh al-hara*. Like the *shaykh al-hara*
they control the boundaries of the community, monitoring entrances
and identifying insiders from outsiders. Many of the practices recall
the traditional *futuwwa* acts.[107] In dealing with violations of the moral
code, the Jama'a issued warnings. For instance, in the late 1980s and
early 1990s, the Jama'a dealt with violations of the moral code by
issuing warnings to 'violators' and calling them to the mosque for
disciplinary meetings. The emir or the group instructed transgressors on correct practice and advised reform. Failure to comply was
met with punishment which included beating and flogging. Jama'a
members appropriate the role of protecting women and safeguarding their *sharaf* (chastity). In imposing control in the home, the Jama'a
seemed to operate a system of surveillance which allowed it to detect
illicit relations between men and women in the neighbourhood.[108]
In Ain Shams, alleged illicit conduct was punished by public flogging. In Imbaba, the Jama'a attacked flats where 'immoral' acts were
reputed to be taking place and charges were made against the inhabitants. Furthermore, there are reports of neighbourhood fights
between Islamist activists and coffee shop and video-club proprie-
tors.[109] These events indicate not only that a different life-style was
pursued by some of the residents, but also that those who differed
were not easily deterred by the Jama'a's practices.

The Jama'a members' interventions extend to economic activities
and other types of social relations: they oversee market activities,
and engage in neighbourhood brawls in their role as mediators and
arbiters. It should be recalled that the various *futuwwa* practices lie
on a continuum from protective, integrative functions, at one extreme, to the destabilising, disintegrative activities associated with
the gang leader – the *baltagi* (thug) type – at the other.[110] According
to some commentators, Shaykh Jabir, the Imbaba emir, was a *baltagi*
and not a religious leader.[111] There is an ambiguity in the role of the
defender-protector who uses bullying and intimidation – popular
acceptance of this behaviour takes into account the level of violence
used and the goals being pursued. In these roles, we see the practices
of the old quarters reappearing. However, there are limits to the Islamists' success in redefining popular practices. The extremism in

tone and action which tends to accompany the Islamists' assumption of these roles contradicts the no-fuss spirit of *awlad al-balad* (sons of the country), resulting in a loss of popular support for the Jama'a.[112] Thus, the dynamics of their popular insertion are more complex than they appear at first sight.

Islamists anchor themselves in spaces which, because of their characteristics of autonomy, informality and self-regulation, are open to oppositional activities. Islamists are thus enmeshed in the web of social relations found in these areas. They may have a programme of change, but they are likely to lose ground if they push too far on certain issues. There are rules governing their reciprocal relations with the communities. As participants in familial, economic, and religious networks they gain community support for their activities in facing the government. Yet their use of force to apply a strict or puritanical code contradicts popular norms of tolerance and moderation. In support of the first proposition, I draw on the facts surrounding cases of confrontation with the state. In Ain Shams, the Jama'a relied on familial networks to supply the numbers needed for the demonstrations that followed the August and December 1988 standoffs with the police. It has been reported that the December conflict started as a dispute between several vendors and a single police officer which escalated when the police used this as a pretext to regain control of the area, thereby drawing in the Jama'a. Thus, the Islamists' involvement overlaps with popular antagonism towards authority. In Imbaba, neighbourhood youths of the *futuwwa* type joined the Jama'a and provided the needed muscle in clashing with the police in 1992.

This pattern of clashes is also found in other instances of social violence which do not involve the Jama'a. A recent study of violence in Egypt between 1967 and 1992 shows that popular riots and demonstrations often begin as conflicts with the police. In these cases, police mistreatment of citizens tends to spark off urban riots, in which the residents of the victim's neighbourhood are mobilised. They usually march on the police station involved and clash with the officers. Such incidents have occurred in popular quarters such as Sayyida Zaynab, Ataba and al-Madabigh. The crowd is often composed mainly of *hirafiyyin* (plumbers, bakers, and construction workers, for example).[113] Popular resentment towards the police is undoubtedly intensifying, as police brutality has become the norm. A standard repertoire of urban unrest appears to be developing: street clashes with the police in response to excessive police force and arbitrary arrest, followed by marches on the police station and ending in additional arrests. No doubt, this patterning of relations has resulted in the transformation of some of Cairo's police stations into veritable fortresses.[114]

Strong popular engagement in the Islamist clashes with the police are evidenced in the fact that in both the Imbaba and Ain Shams cases the confrontation extended over periods of several days to several weeks, and required the deployment of large numbers of police personnel. The Ain Shams operations were executed in two stages – in August and December of 1988. After gaining control of the Imbaba territory, a police unit was stationed in the area for some time. 'Combing out' operations continue to be staged in these areas despite the large numbers of militants arrested. State action against the militants has comprised the repossession of the mosques, and the closure of the zawiya, in addition to campaigns aimed at discrediting the militants and undermining their popular appeal. Here we have clues as to the Islamists' ability to capture oppositional potential and channel it into organised social activism which goes beyond what Asef Bayat terms 'quiet encroachment.'[115] According to Bayat, the absence of structures of popular collective action accounts for the lack of a sustained challenge similar to that seen in Iran's shantytown dweller movements. The latter involved intense and prolonged mobilisation and protests. However, if we take into account the standoffs in Imbaba and Ain Shams we find that the structures discussed above provided the bases for widening the Islamists' conflict with the government to include greater segments of the population.

There are macro-structural elements which favour popular engagement in support of the Islamists. These do not arise out of alienation and uprootedness, but out of the new dynamics of state-society relations. It should be recalled that formal political organisations are ineffective in representing or mobilising the people. The social/moral contract between the people and the state of the Nasserist period has weakened, if not dissolved. The deal organised around the suspension of citizens' political rights in exchange for social rights is no longer operative. Today, there is little in the way of social benefit coming from the state. Increasingly, the people have to depend on their own resources, and a gradual process of disengagement is taking place. The corporatist structures are being dismantled, and with them the people's side of the bargain.

Before further examining the limitations on the Jama'a's ability to transform itself into a full-fledged popular movement, I would like to underline the elements of organisation which can help it do so. The Jama'a operates as a trans-neighbourhood group through a network of mosques and flats, particularly in the new quarters and some of the old quarters. In the records from the Jihad trial, we find that potential recruits were taken from their neighbourhood mosques to attend mosques in other neighbourhoods, in order to hear the emir/preacher. There are also indications that a level of co-ordination exists among the different neighbourhood cells of the Jama'a. The active members enjoy a degree of mobility, and are able to relocate from one neighbourhood to another with the help of other Jama'a members. These elements of their organisational structure are important for any attempt to establish a citywide popular movement.[116] However, the group experiences both internal, ideological and, by extension, operational, constraints, and external constraints that come with the government's policy of encirclement.

If the advocacy of violence vis-à-vis the government is a source of attraction for the youths, the policy of social violence detracts from their ability to reach wider segments of the population. The popular cultural practice of providing *satr* (protection or cover) to an errant member of the community is a factor in approaching social and religious transgressions in a discrete manner. Peaceful avenues of conflict resolution emerge out of a desire to avoid division and the entrenchment of animosities. Thus, the Jama'a's public flogging of violators denies them *satr* and brings shame on individuals and their families.[117] Restrictions on listening to music and celebrating weddings are likely to be viewed as intolerant. The resilience of peaceful modes of regulating moral violations appears at this stage as a factor in making militant Islamism less appealing. Finally, the extreme violence which characterises the attacks on tourists and Copts in the last few years, and particularly the Luxor massacre, have brought shock and condemnation from all sectors of society.[118]

The question of the violence implied in the *jihad* principle may, in the end, represent what Gehad Auda sees as a paradox for the militants.[119] Their advocacy of exercising *jihad* to change un-Islamic practices has involved dispersed violent action, which lacks direction and brings chaos. In principle, anyone can engage in *jihad*, and this wrests control away from the hands of the leadership. The lawlessness of this type of situation, as noted above, is not always constrained by popular norms because some Islamist principles clash with these norms. Finally, we should note the state's involvement in discrediting these acts as un-Islamic. State *'ulama* have mobilised on a number of occasions to show the deviation of the militants from the 'true' understanding of religion. Further, the government is pursuing a policy of cultural Islamisation through religious television programmes and newspapers. This constitutes an attempt at constructing an alternative Islamic view – one focused on rituals and appearances.[120] The question of whether this type of Islamisation would marginalise the militants or serve to reinforce their ranks is contingent on how the various forces involved position themselves in response.

Towards a Conclusion: Is Militant Islamism a Protest Movement of the Popular Classes?

This chapter has attempted to show the popular movement dimensions of contemporary Islamism by underlining the socio-spatial determinants at work. It highlights the spatial grounding of Islamism in the urban setting and points to a transformation in the social composition of the membership. The occupational profile of the members testifies to the particular socio-economic setting from which they are drawn, and the particular social relations and networks within which they operate. These factors support the argument for the popular dimensions of the movement. In fact, the Islamist mode of action has responded to these determinants; moving into neighbourhoods, basing themselves in mosques, *zawiyas*, and flats, and engaging in social work and awareness-raising activities. These popular dimensions are undermined by an element of ideological practice, that of *al-amr bil ma'ruf wa al-nahy 'an al-munkar*, which, in certain respects, merges with popular traditions, while contradicting them in others. The emerging picture is that the Jama'a members are neither uprooted nor alienated. They are part of the social fabric. They may pull it in extreme directions, but they are woven within it. The use of violence to oppose the government or undermine its respectability gives vent to popular grievances, but extreme violence is likely to appear senseless.

The mobilisational potential of militant Islamism seems to lie in its ability to ground its ideological principles in the social antagonisms and the oppositional positions that are part of the urban landscape. The Islamists' activism and appropriation of space recall popular traditional practices and reinscribe historical modes of social organisation. To this extent, they conform to the people's perceptions of authenticity. In order to expand their popular support, they must operate within the socio-spatial framework of the communities. The Islamists' insertion into this setting has so far been beset by limitations because of constant government crackdowns and their own limited scope of ideological manoeuverings.

5

Islamist Politics in Algeria and Tunisia:
A State-Society Perspective

In the 1980s and 1990s both Algeria and Tunisia witnessed the rise of Islamist movements. The trajectories of these movements have differed. By all indications, Tunisia has overcome its Islamist 'problem,' while Algeria, since 1991, has been experiencing a protracted war between the state and armed Islamist groups. There are immediate and simple explanations that may account for this difference. The Tunisian Islamists never won a national election only to be later denied a popular victory. In addition, the Tunisian state early on followed a policy of repression and eradication and thus managed to contain and eventually eliminate the Islamists. From an economic point of view, Tunisia's restructuring policy has proved successful and the people have been spared the economic woes of the transition period. On the other hand, the Algerian government had flirted with the Islamists and turned to repression late in the game. Government mismanagement of the economy and the corruption of the political leadership inhibited any effort at lessening the economic difficulties of the population. While these features of the Algerian crisis and the Tunisian 'success' are important, they need to be placed in a wider framework that takes into account the different settings that provided the infrastructure for the emergence, expansion or containment of Islamism. That is, we need to look at the social, economic, political and cultural variables that are at play in each case. Of importance,

also, is the trajectory of the movement itself and its terms of insertion into particular settings. The following questions are a starting
point of our analysis: how are patterns of interaction between state
and society structured? What are the social, economic, political and
cultural factors shaping state-society relations? What are the terms
through which Islamist movements come to articulate a change or a
transformation in state-society relations? In integrating these questions into the study of the Islamist movements in Algeria and Tunisia,
the analysis is guided by the aim of bridging macro and micro levels
of explanation and bringing into focus state-society patterns of
interaction.

1. ISLAMIST POLITICS IN ALGERIA

The Algerian Polity: A Brief Overview

Since its inception, the Algerian state has been run by two seemingly contradictory, yet complementary, impulses: one tending
towards division and fragmentation, the other towards concentration and unification. They are complementary because both express
the will to power and the power plays of those who took over the
state in 1962, at the end of the war of independence waged against
the French colonial power. The existence of different ideological currents within the nationalist leadership was not necessarily a cause of
fragmentation nor a pretext for homogenisation. However, both processes did occur, unfolding as the expression of the contending groups/
clans' struggle for a monopoly of power.[1] The *modus operandi* aimed
at eliminating adversaries and developing a core or minimum set of
principles around which all clans could claim legitimacy. These core
principles developed around the revolutionary credentials of the leaders and the state developmentalist project. This became the subject of
what Lahouari Addi calls 'l'unanisme obssessional' (an obsession with
unanimity).[2] As a result, conflicts over language and the relationship between religion and politics remained unresolved. A partnership
of sorts was at the base of elite consensus, allowing the various clans
to identify with the state project and, eventually, to go about priva-
tising its assets for their own benefit.[3] In this context, power was

personalised by the holders of office and by those occupying higher positions in the state structure.

State apparatuses served to consecrate unanimity at all costs. This effort engaged the FLN (Front de Libération Nationale) – the single party – and, behind it, the army – the two institutions claiming a monopoly over the revolutionary and nationalist legacy. Though a façade for the army, the FLN was an important part of the edifice of surveillance and control under President Boumediene (1965–1978) and more so under President Chadli (1978–1991). With mass organisations such as the UGTA (the workers' union), the UNJA (the youth union), and the UNFA (women's federation), all appended to the single party, the structures and the processes of an exclusionary corporatist state were set in place. Further, the FLN local party cells carried out spying activities and acted as auxiliaries of the police and the army, inhibiting the emergence of autonomous social forces.[4] It is significant that this people's party was actually seen as a web of informers whose leaders became important in the party without having developed a social base. The overall effect of this was the development of a disjunction and eventually a rupture between state and society.[5] At the ideological level, the leadership articulated a populist discourse affirming unity between the revolutionary state and the people. However, it is in the name of this unity that all structures of intermediation were abandoned, most spaces of societal autonomy were invaded, representation from the bottom up was denied, and the local level was neglected on the assumption that it should be merged with the nation. On these premises, basic liberties were sacrificed.[6]

Like other populist authoritarian forms of government, the Algerian state was built on a denial of the political.[7] The various Algerian constitutions and charters negated the possibility of class antagonisms and struggles and rejected the idea of pluralism. Nationalism, revolution and the Islamic tradition were put forward as the elements of a formula that would shape the people into a unitary entity whose defining features were the Arabic language and Islam. Further, this populist formula conceived of the people as the beneficiaries of their nationalist, socialist state.[8] In the 1960s and 70s, at the level of policymaking, this translated into welfare provisions such as free education, public health care, housing and employment. As the embodiment of the nationalist developmentalist project, the state became the main proprietor and employer. However, the state managed to escape any responsibility for insuring the equality and equity of its citizens.

The political and military leadership, acting as a founding group with special privileges, converted its revolutionary capital into physical capital through its appropriation of land in the villages and towns, and real estate in the city. Further, the developmentalist policies favoured the creation of administrative and technocratic positions to be filled by the middle strata employed in the state sector. Thus, the new state engendered its bourgeoisie. The latter merged with the commercial elites of the previous era and, together, they monopolised the political and economic apparatuses of the state, controlling public enterprises, goods and resources.[9] For the rest of the population, the industrial sector's rate of job creation was limited. By 1970, this sector had created only 150,000 jobs[10] and by 1987 it provided 350,000 jobs.[11] As a result, employment opportunities were rapidly diminishing for the younger generations.

By the 1980s, clientelism and clannism, being at the heart of political power, soon spread to other levels of the administration so that services and goods could only be obtained by those with personal connections (*piston* in the local idiom).[12] With the liberalisation of the economy and the reform of the welfare structures, the distributive policies were more circumscribed, reaching only to the networks and circles of power holders. People with no connections had to depend on themselves, which often meant acting independently of the state or against it. As will be shown, it is precisely in the developing oppositional spaces that the Islamist movement was able to amass its support. It was able to do so among segments of the population that had embarked on a strategy of disengagement from the state.

The disengagement of societal forces took place in various spheres. As noted, a disjunction developed in the political sphere as the populist rhetoric, evoking the identification of the state with the people, came to be seen as nothing more than rhetoric. In the economic sphere, disengagement was achieved through the development of the informal economy. This economy did not necessarily escape state control, but it operated beyond state regulations.[13] The unregulated economy, comprising small and big merchants, contractors and *trabendistes* (traffickers/smugglers), represented an area of relative autonomy. Finally, the informal housing areas and the popular quarters of the city emerged as spaces of dissidence. The Islamist movement with its various wings – the Front Islamique de Salut (FIS), first and foremost, and then the armed groups – was able to invest itself in these spaces. The pertinent question is how and why did it achieve this investment.

Societal Disengagement: The Informal Sector and the Reactivation of the *Houma*

Societal disengagement from the state is a multifaceted process which has been unfolding gradually at the local level, in popular quarters and communities. Its nodal points are in the urban neighbourhoods: in the mosques, economic enterprises, cultural and sporting associations, and in the overall web of social relations that traverse these instances of societal interaction. Despite state efforts to effect an *encadrement* of the population, political disjunction has been reinforced through these nodal points, as evidenced in the role of popular and peripheral urban quarters, local notables, informal economic activities, independent mosques, sports clubs and teams.

Islamist activism in Algeria is concentrated in urban areas. A brief look at the election results of 1990 and 1991 confirms the massive following that the FIS enjoyed in the cities. In elections to the Popular Municipal Assemblies (Assemblés Populaires) in 1990, the FIS won a majority of the popular vote (55 per cent). Its proportion of the vote was much higher in urban areas, where it won 90 per cent of all votes cast in urban agglomerations of over 20,000 inhabitants. This corresponds to support from 75 per cent of all urban dwellers.[14] Further, 90 per cent of the 188 seats won in the first round of legislative elections were located in urban constituencies. Finally, it was in the peripheral suburban areas that the FIS delegates amassed a virtual totality of votes (93 per cent). In Algiers, the FIS's performance varied depending on the type of quarter(s) making up the constituency. Old popular quarters close to the city centre, and peripheral suburban quarters in the informal housing sector, were the main sources of support.[15]

The sites of Islamist activism are the old quarters and peripheral suburbs in cities such as Algiers, Constantine and Tlemcen. The physical location of both the old quarters and the peripheral communities within the country's urban areas attests to the social and spatial hierarchy and segregation that has characterised Algeria historically. These spaces articulate the progression of the political and social life of the city from the pre-colonial, to the colonial and to post-colonial times. This progression took the form of a layering of divisions and conflicts. In contradistinction to the old city, with its historical architectural structures and forms of urban sociability, the French colonial administrators built 'la ville nouvelle' for the colonists. Spatial segregation underscored the relation between the indigenous population and the colonisers. An additional layer took the form of the bidonvilles (urban squatter areas) that housed the rural migrants who had come to the city in search of employment and to escape the impoverished conditions of the countryside. In the post-independence period, the construction of peri-urban and spontaneous housing developments represents a later phase of the historical development of the city and a further layer of social differentiation. It should be noted that with the departure of the French, the appropriation of the vacant homes and apartments in the colonial quarters allowed for the consolidation of the social and political elites associated with the nationalist struggle. At the same time, the spatial movement of the population was linked to a wider process of social mobility.

As such, a multitude of settings and urban forms has come to characterise many Algerian cities. The division of urban space into the old city and the colonial and post-colonial quarters is an important dimension of the socio-historical development of the country and is clearly linked to social, economic, cultural and political processes of differentiation. For instance, in Algiers, the social and economic differentiation of the city's residents is inscribed in spatial divisions: the lower strata, engaged in trades, tends to be concentrated in the old city; the new political elite, in the colonial city; the rising middle strata occupy the new development areas; while workers, craftsmen and merchants, settled in the informal housing sector, are located mainly on the periphery of the city. In the new state-sponsored development areas, there has been no clear-cut territorialisation of the various social strata. However, other markers reinforce social divisions. For example, within the new development areas, the villa sections stand in clear contrast to the apartment blocks and low-income housing units established by the state.[16] These different forms of urban organisation shape social relations, patterns of interaction and positioning vis-à-vis the state.

The investigation of the informal urban sector in Algiers presents us with indicators of changing state-society relations and societal transformations. Informal housing developments date to the colonial period and particularly to the 1930s. Originally, they took the form of *gourbivilles* and were concentrated around the old city. The expansion of the informal housing sector, however, took place in the 1960s, and accelerated in the 1970s and 80s with the decline in state provision of social housing. During this latter period, most public housing was geared to accommodate the higher state cadres and the middle strata.[17] Similarly, private construction companies targeted the more affluent segment of the population. As such, low-income housing was limited. In 1994, the housing deficit amounted to 1.2 million homes.

In Algiers, the informal sector developed mainly in the city's eastern and southeastern peripheries, in the two neighbouring *Daira* of Dey Hussein and El-Harrach. In addition to the community of El-Harrach, the *Daira* of El-Harrach includes the communities of Eucalyptus and Baraki, which, together, account for 80 per cent of all illicit housing in the city.[18] The process of autonomous construction shaped the constitution of the communities and their relations of force. The majority of the communities of the informal quarters were established through the installation of communal blocs of families originating from the same region of the country.[19] Homes were built in closely-knit blocs for persons sharing a common family lineage. Promoters undertook the division and the sale of lands. Some of these promoters acquired the land as grants from the state in recompense for their nationalist support. Others were state officials holding doctored ownership papers. In many instances they represented figures of local power in these communities. Positioned at the interface of the entrepreneurial stratum and the notability, they owned shops, artisanal businesses and *hamams* (public baths), and provided employment for many.

The socio-economic profile of the population in the informal housing sectors of Algeria resembles that of Egypt. Most of the active population is engaged in the tertiary sector of the economy and in sub-proletarian activities.[20] A key area of employment is small enterprises engaged in artisanal production and commercial services. The level of tertiary economic activity in the communes of El-Harrach and in Eucalyptus is higher than in the rest of Algeria. The establishment of these enterprises in the informal sector was aided by the urban form itself, which facilitated a blending of ateliers and residences. Shops and workshops were located in the basements or on the upper level of houses.[21] The economic activities of the small merchants and artisans were to a great extent disengaged from the state. For many, the capital for establishing their enterprises came from private banks, and the input needed for production was procured from the illegal trade maintained by the *trabendistes*. It should be pointed out that not all residents of the informal housing sector engage in informal economic activities. In fact, some studies on that sector in Constantine show that the state has remained the main employer for the majority of the active population.[22] However, in the 1980s, the informal economy became a primary source of income for a growing proportion of the workforce throughout the country.

The strength and expansion of the informal economy gave weight to different social actors and gave rise to a network of hierarchical relations in the quarters. In this network, three groups can be identified: the local notables-entrepreneurs, the small merchants and the *trabendistes*. These social actors are enmeshed in the web of economic and social relations at the local level. At the same time, they are part of a national economy that has become more distributive than productive by virtue of its dependence on commerce and the circulation of mostly imported goods. In this setting, the trabendiste emerged as the central figure of the Algerian economy.[23] The notables-entrepreneurs are well placed in the informal sector. Using their connections with the public sector, they are able to procure goods and materials that can be resold at a high rate of profit.[24] This activity is one kind of trabendo to be distinguished from the traffic in goods smuggled across the border from Spain, Morocco and other countries.[25] The notables-entrepreneurs supply cash, permits and protection to the those engaged in the latter type of trabendo.[26] A certain hierarchy of relations may be discerned in these operations: patrons supply capital, while intermediaries act as go-betweens for the patrons and the sellers. Small merchants and artisans are also linked to the trabendo, as buyers or by virtue of having a family member engaged in trafficking. As noted above, their own economic production owes much to clandestine construction, having built their workshops as part of the unauthorised houses they live in. The trabendo trade furnishes them with inputs unavailable from the public sector.

Integral to the informal economy has been the co-optation of a segment of the young adult population into the clandestine trade. As public educational and employment avenues became closed to the majority of urban youth, opportunities opened for earning a living through informal economic activities. It is worth noting that 80 per cent of high school students fail their baccalaureate exams and find themselves out of school each year. In addition, a large number of students end up leaving school prior to final exams.[27] Thus, the trabendo offers them employment and places them in patronage networks with connections to the Islamists.

Two spaces of urban sociability have served to organise these youths: the mosque and the sports team. The mosque was central to the constitution of the new urban quarters. The process of mosque construction, and the space it occupied, underline the centrality of the mosque in the reorganisation of urban space.[28] In building these mosques, the residents of the new quarters created spaces of autonomy. Many of the mosques were established without permits, on land without clear property titles. Promoters and local notables, merchants and other quarter residents were all engaged in their establishment. Both promoters and residents sought legitimacy for their homes through the mosque. Acknowledged as an instance of *horm* (sanctity) by all, the mosque's protection extends to the homes surrounding it.[29] Thus, to prevent the local authority from removing their illegal homes, promoters and residents championed the construction of mosques. For local notables, the sponsoring of mosques is viewed as a necessary affirmation of their social position. Similarly, for small merchants, contributing to the building of a mosque brings social recognition and some upward mobility.

The services provided by the mosque extend beyond the religious needs of the community. It provides water, a place of rest and shelter. It also permits the development of solidarity relations and social relations based on allegiance and clientelism without a necessary religious colouring.[30] In Boudghène, an informal settlement in Tlemcen, the mosque is reported to have served as a kind of community headquarters.[31] It was active in a social sense, affording the residents a place for meeting to resolve neighbourhood conflicts and to establish mutual aid societies.[32] In the Benchergui settlement in Constantine, the community used the mosque as a meeting place to discuss collective projects and to appoint a representative committee in charge of articulating common needs.[33] As such, the mosque generated a space of communication and territorialisation for the residents. This function harks back to the idea of the *houma* (quarter) with its collective identity, interests and symbolic values.[34] But this reactivation of the *houma* involves a reworking of familial relations and bases of solidarity.

The *oulad al-houma* (children of the quarter) functions as an alternative type of fraternity and solidarity to the family. Overcrowded homes and disputes over the use of household space put strains on family relations.[35] The average number of members per household was between seven and eight, while the average dwelling size was two rooms. For the young of the household, limited living space, and a lower standing in the household rank, were reasons to seek alternative forms of fraternity. The spatial segregation between the rich and poor quarters of the city meant that they had nowhere to go outside the quarters. Coffee shops in the city-centre were beyond their means.[36] The mosque was one place for the development of this alternative fraternity. It served as a meeting place for the youths and as a shelter away from their crowded residences. Vergès notes that, progressively, the mosque became the principal space for maintaining sociability.[37] Beyond the discussion of religious matters, the youths found a forum to discuss everyday problems, family troubles and the like.[38]

Along with the mosque, sports teams contributed to the reactivation of the spirit of *oulad al-houma* among the youth. Sports associations are attached to local territories and each quarter has its own team. At the national level, teams are identified with their cities. The state attempted to frame the youths' sports activities by organising competitions under party auspices (e.g. *cross du parti*).[39] In 1975, it attempted to attach associations to national societies with the declared aim of undermining the influence of local notables. This move was a legalisation, or a recuperation of an existing collective practice of *houmistes* (youths of the quarter).[40] However, this aspect of the reform did not overcome the territorial reference of the quarter.[41]

The sports activities at the quarter level have reinforced the *oulad el-houma* collective with its male character, fraternal values and valorisation of the male community. Women are excluded from this kind of societal embedding. Inter-quarter tournaments and sporting events are occasions for the expression of solidarity. Youths are organised to travel collectively to the football stadium. The groups of supporters develop out of the activation of a community maintained by the quarter's football team committee which takes charge of transportation to important matches. In Bab el-Oued, an old popular quarter of Algiers, the committee meets in a coffee shop where players and supporters gather.[42] National matches represent opportunities for the articulation of collective grievances. During the 1980s, the youths' chants at these events changed as their opposition to the state grew. Thus, from exhorting the president to remove the minister of sport ('Chadli change nous houhou'), they move on to demand housing and foreign currency ('nous voulons des logements, des devises'), and then to a call for the removal of Chadli himself ('houzou Chadli').[43]

The FIS Insertion into the Urban Quarters

As an expression of a desire for the re-Islamisation of society, Islamist politics in Algeria predates the rise of the FIS and may be seen to have had its early stirrings in the state itself. The presence of a strand of religio-cultural nationalism in the nationalist movement and the struggle for independence marked the ideological orientation of the post-colonial state. This current is identified with the Islamic thinker Ben Badis and the Association of Ulama which merged with the FLN in 1956. It emphasised the religious identity of the national community and stressed the need to preserve its authenticity understood as the Islamic religious values regarding the family, gender relations and so on. The incorporation of this current into the state was assured through the Ministry of Religious Affairs and the Ministry of Education.[44] Through control over religious and educational institutions, the state sought to affirm its Islamic and Arab identity.[45] The policies followed in this regard were at times in contradiction with the socialist revolutionary ideals advocated by a segment of the leadership and political elites. All the same, the notion of Islamic socialism was propagated. The Islamising tendency in the FLN left an imprint on a number of policy areas. This is particularly true of the family code approved by the National Assembly in 1984. The code instituted men's guardianship over women. An official Islam sponsored by the state found expression in the public media and educational institutions.[46]

In association with the Islamising current of the FLN, organisations such as al-Qiyam al-Islamiya (the Islamic Values), established in 1964, aimed at rectifying the moral order, from which the people were seen to be deviating under the influence of internal communist and westernising forces identified with the Francophones and leftist-educated groups.[47] The association was dissolved in 1966, but its members continued to preach its brand of morality. Along with the state affiliated 'ulama, a number of independent religious figures – notably Shaykhs Soltani, Sahraoui and Sahnoun – propagated a critique of the leftist direction of the Boumediene regime, signalling the deterioration of social mores associated with the secular educational system and the entry of women into public employment.

The concern with morality and authenticity found appeal in the university where the Islamist movement as an organised form of protest took form. Two religio-ideological currents were identified within the movement: the *salafi* and the reformers. The reformers were mainly French-speaking or bilingual with scientific and technical training. They were influenced by the thought of Malik Bennabi, and tended to emphasise the Algerian dimension of Islamic identity. They became known as the Algerianist (Djaz'ara) wing.[48] The *salafi* were Arabic-speaking with training in languages and religion. They were attracted to conservative religious figures and ideologues of Egypt's Muslim Brotherhood as well as to the Saudi Wahhabi tradition.[49] The two currents came together in the formation of the FIS in 1989.[50]

The Islamist presence in the university could be explained in reference both to conjunctural conditions and to longer-term developments. The university was embroiled in nationalist politics that, at times, amounted to nothing more than personal squabbles and rivalries. Students were mobilised by the Boumediene regime to support the agricultural co-operative enterprise. The main organ for this was the communist-affiliated student union (Parti de l'avant-garde socialiste) which stood in conflict with the Arabising Baathists.[51] The conflict was drawn along linguistic and ideological lines to which an Islamist colouring was added. With the move away from socialist policies, the Islamists gained a freer hand in the university.

How did the Islamists develop from a university-based movement to what, by 1990, appeared to be a popular movement with national support in municipal and *wilayat* elections, winning the first round of legislative elections in 1991? Why did it fragment and experience attrition in active membership in favour of the armed groups?

The Islamist movement was transformed into a popular movement through a process of investment in the spaces of autonomy that emerged with societal disengagement from the state. With informal housing, the informal economy, and the social and cultural structures of the quarters, the infrastructure for dissidence was laid down. In a sense, these quarters existed in opposition to the state. As Safar-Zitoun notes, in Algeria 'l'urbanisation s'est dévelopée contre l'État.'[52] The quarter, through its mosque, sports association and football team, produced a reterritorialisation of identity that was oppositional to the state.

The FIS implanted itself through the mosques and sports clubs. The implantation into the quarters was part of a deliberate strategy that included merging with locally developing relations of power. The FIS organisation had at its base the quarter committees (*al-ahya'*) which met in the local mosques and designated Imams among the militants.[53] Following the events of October 1988, the FIS leadership undertook to place imams in the popular quarters of the cities. In quarters like Belcourt, Kouba, Bab el-Oued, the Qasbah, Eucalyptus and Baraki, FIS imams became stars attracting a wide following. The mosques where these imams preached reinforced the territorial identity of the quarter. Thus, quarters like Belcourt or Kouba recovered the historical centrality of the mosque and its Friday *khotba* (sermon) as territorial and symbolic markers. At the same time, these mosques served as meeting places for residents from different quarters who wanted to hear the sermons of the famous preachers: Ali Benhadj in al-Sunna mosque of the Bab el-Oued quarter, Al-Aid in the Fath al-Islam mosque of Triolet quarter, Abdel Malek mosque of Colonne quarter, Kamel Nour in Kaboul mosque in Belcourt.[54]

The FIS was also founded by local imams who were emerging as figures of authority in their quarters.[55] Their engagement in the FIS may well be explained by their desire to extend their influence beyond their local setting. This was the case, for example, with Ahmad Merrani the imam of a mosque in the old quarter of Algiers. Merrani began his religio-political career in the Oued Koreish mosque in the Qasbah.[56] Merrani's social profile and practices betray aspirations that parallel those of the merchant notability of yesteryear. He is a merchant who uses his wealth to fund a charitable association that gains him notoriety among his fellow merchants and artisans and earns him their financial support.[57] In addition, Merrani claims supernatural powers that he uses to heal members of the community. The administering of healing powers to help people who believed themselves to be possessed by evil spirits responds to the need to regulate social claims and contestations developed in relation to the present context. The blending of religious teaching with *karamat* (supernatural gifts) appeals to the popular imaginary and is akin to the way in which merchant/Sufi leaders had acquired followings during previous historical epochs.[58]

The FIS was able to find a constituency in the small merchants who were looking for alternative circuits of power that can be based locally and that can be mobilised in face of the government. The notables-entrepreneurs had earlier on grasped the utility of the Islamist connection. They cultivated an image of being God-fearing since it was good for business. Contributing to the mosque, undertaking the pilgrimage and donating to charity were practices that helped develop this image. They also fostered links with the national leadership of Islamist organisations both to ensure relations with all power contenders, and out of ideological affinity with the FIS's economic liberalism and its support for commercial activities.[59] Emblematic of the notables-entrepreneurs who pursued these strategies are Mohamad Abed in Constantine and Hadj Saddok in Algiers.[60]

The FIS and Oulad al-Houma

For the youths, the FIS succeeded in bringing about a meeting of the mosque and the stadium.[61] As noted above, the youths' structures of action were framed by the sporting associations and by the production of the *houma* as a form of territorial identification. FIS militants organised classes in Karate and other martial arts that attracted the youths. In addition, leisure activities such as camping trips, excursions and football matches were sponsored by the FIS committee in the mosques.[62] Thus, the youths frequented the mosques for sociability as well as for religiosity. The mosque, like the café, was a place where *oulad el-houma* could meet. Further, the imam acted as their confidante, listening to their troubles concerning school failures or employment.[63] The youths' involvement in collective action until 1988 was framed by their quarter-based affiliation, and by their sports activities. Looking at earlier events of urban protest in Algeria, certain patterns of action can be discerned. It is within these patterns that the FIS was able to insert itself. The FIS succeeded in constituting the mosque as a space for the mobilisation of the youths.

In 1986, a youth-based contestation movement made its mark on the political scene. It began in October of that year with strikes in the high schools of Algiers then took shape with the November demonstrations of students in Constantine and other cities to the East, namely Skida, Batna and Tebissa. However, it was in Constantine that serious confrontation with the state representatives of law enforcement and civil order took place.[64] The Constantine demonstrations soon extended from high schools to universities. The student marches were directed at the seat of the party. The agitations then spread to the peripheral quarters. Among the youth who participated in these clashes were workers, the unemployed and those excluded from school and facing the draft into the army.[65] The youths took control of the city for three days. They set up barricades in the streets and intensified and multiplied points of confrontation with the police in the peripheral quarters. They then moved to the city centre.[66] The most important challenges by non-students took place in the centre where the youths converged. The conjunction of the Medina and the colonial city in the centre shaped the unfolding of action. The colonial city is where the public buildings are located. It has an open layout with wide streets and boulevards, while the Medina has the traditional spatial configuration of narrow winding streets, culs de sac and so on. The contiguity of the two settings allowed for passage from open to closed space. That is, the youths met in the open space of the Place des Martyres in the centre, then attacked public buildings and retreated to the old city. This mode of attack and retreat continued for several days until, eventually, the security police regained control without encircling the Medina.

In Constantine in 1986 (and later in Algiers in 1988), the Islamists joined the youth movement as it unfolded. They were not the instigators. The events articulated the anti-state sentiments of the younger generation. They also mobilised other social groups with defined demands and occupying clear antagonistic positions. Thus, in Constantine, big commercial shops were attacked. In the city of Attabia, inhabitants of the popular neighbourhoods gathered to reclaim housing. In response, the residents of the villas in the upper class quarter of Bentchikou, situated next to a *bidonville*, barricaded themselves.[67] It would appear that the transition from an anti-state to a social movement was smooth.[68]

Significantly, the first incident of the October 1988 revolt took place in a high school in the El-Harrach, the disadvantaged eastern suburb of Algiers.[69] Youth gangs demonstrated and were pursued by the police. The next day, there occurred a repeat of the previous day's events, but this time in the west near the general police quarters. On October 5, the youth gangs descended on the centre, vandalising public and private property along the way, from boutiques to state offices.

Among the targets of their wrath was the Riadh el-Fateh, a commercial centre built as a monument to the Chadli regime, identified with the state bourgeoisie, and frequented by the *tchi-tchi* (westernised young men from elite families) and the nouveaux riches. Violent exchanges with the police broke out in the popular quarter of Bachdjarah where a police station was set on fire. By Friday 7 October, the demonstrations spread to other cities, both large and small.[70] The main actors in the crowd were the youths, predominantly male high school students and unemployed. In Algiers, they came from the popular quarters and the peripheral areas to the centre. Earlier, these youths had made of the stadium an arena of contestation.[71] During the October events, they called on their stock of stadium chants. The merger with the Islamists occurred on 10 October when Ali Benhadj called for a march to proceed from the Belcourt mosque to the National Security headquarters where state forces opened fire. This was an important moment when the Islamists linked up with a growing contestation force.

The FIS mobilisation activities in the period of the general strike of June 1991 (called to protest the new electoral divisions) should be placed in relation to the modes of appropriation of public space and the transformation in spaces of opposition and conflict that had occurred in the 1980s. The FIS call to occupy the two main public spaces in the centre of Algiers followed the logic of earlier youth demonstrations. The Place des Martyrs and the Place du 1er Mai, 2.7 kilometres apart, are situated in the lower part of the city. Islamist militants and sympathisers occupied the space for a week. By virtue of the duration of this occupation, the event may be seen as unique.[72] Yet, it embodied the desire to take over the city, a desire expressed in earlier movements and action. The two places are located on the borders of the popular quarters: Bab el-Oued and the Qasbah, Oued Koreish, Climat de France, Diar Kef for the Place des Martyrs; El Madania, Sidi M'hamed, Belcourt, Diar al-Mahçoul for the Place du 1er Mai.[73] The prolonged occupation of the two central open spaces of the city extended the oppositional effect invested in this type of action. In other words, in earlier events in Constantine and Algiers, the invasion of the centre posed a challenge to state authority, but was limited in its extent. The long duration, the intensity and the orchestration of action – with meetings in all quarters of the city – had as an objective to bring about a fundamental change in the political scene, if not to bring down the president and the government.[74]

Mass participation in the June 1991 event was encouraged and harnessed by the integration of practices of urban sociability, including collective outdoor prayers, communal food preparation and eating, and hashish smoking. Marches proceeded from mosques, and supporters converged from the peripheral quarters onto the centre. At the symbolic level, the event achieved a conquest of the city and of power. For an entire week, the strikers remained in the open space, moving from one quarter to another, and did not need to resort to the attack-retreat tactics of the earlier demonstrations. Eventually, they were confronted by the police and, in response, blocked access to El-Biar, El-Harrach, Kouba and Bab-el-Oued. To regain control, the army was ordered into the city and further clashes ensued. Following this, a state of siege was declared.[75]

FIS Practices of Governance and Social Control

The FIS strategies and activities were interwoven with modes of action anchored in the quarter. Furthermore, they developed around particular spaces such as the mosque, the café, the stadium and the street. Linked to this was the FIS's moral and social agenda which responded to the desire to reinstitute societal control over sexuality and gender relations which were perceived as two key areas of social life that were in need of regulation given the changing social environment and the contradictions these changes brought about. Most notably, there was more interaction between men and women in public at the university and in the workplace. In some of the popular quarters, up to 40 per cent of women were in paid employment.[76] The segregation of the sexes, historically achieved in spatial arrangements in the Medina, was undermined in the colonial city and again in the contemporary city with its various urban forms.

Collective housing, the co-habitation of more than one family in a single dwelling and shared accommodation in many of the new and old quarters, forced a rearrangement of space which undermined rules of *horma*.[77] Male spaces were no longer separated from female spaces, and no delineation between collective and personal space or common and private space was established or respected. Further, because of the limited economic means of many families, men and women were marrying at a later age. The postponement of marriage left young people in a state of extended adolescence, living with their parents and unable to establish independent households.[78] More importantly, the rules governing sexuality dictate pre-marital celibacy for young men and women.[79] The mosque and the preachers help reintroduce the terms by which sexual propriety is maintained and transgressions punished.

For young men, the mosque and its fraternity supported celibacy as a morally justifiable norm. In addition, a process of 'apprenticeship' operated through the religious *halaqat* (circles) and *durus* (lessons). Through the *halaqat*, the youths gained religious knowledge and thereby attained qualifications that they could use to reverse the hierarchy in family relations. Young men armed with Qur'anic citations, *hadith* and the discursive frames set out by the imams, claimed new positions of authority, instructing their parents on correct practice and permissible conduct (*yadzuj*). For instance, sons reproached their parents for watching television.[80] Most importantly, they asserted their *nif* (honour) and *redjla* (virility) through the surveillance of their sisters and the enforcement of *hijab* (veil).[81]

Imposing order in public took the form of cleaning the streets, but also of monitoring male gangs that did not respect the modesty of women in public.[82] Bekkar notes that women's support for the Islamists was motivated in part by their desire to counteract 'the obscenity of the street.'[83] Women's modesty is sought out through the adoption or enforcement of *hijab*.[84] At the same time, practices of surveillance by the family and by the neighbours ensure the *encadrement* of women's movements. The mosque and the coffee shops, located at the entrances of the quarters, are places where men monitor women and their observance of social mores.

The FIS discourse and actions deal with issues of morality and norms governing public space.[85] The leaders' speeches and tracts and the mosque sermons reaffirm the rules of morality and castigate the transgressors. Militant actions are also undertaken to preserve sexual and moral norms. As such, the banning of satellite dishes, the banning of the distribution and consumption of alcohol, and forbidding male-female mixing in public are all rigorously pursued by the militants.[86] Many of the FIS policies during their short tenure in the communal and *wilayat* government were focused on these issues.[87] In response to the residents' complaints about drug-trafficking in their area, the FIS mayor of Eucalyptus created a volunteer group in charge of over-seeing order and dealing with the drug problem.[88] In a number of other communes, the mayors decreed a ban on co-education.

In designating the mosque as a site for holding municipal office, the FIS attempted to effect a shift in the ordinary person's perception of government.[89] The idea that the community's ruling body was meeting to discuss local affairs in the mosque conferred on it a sense of honesty and integrity derived from the sacred symbolism associ-ated with the space. At the same time, it appropriated the egalitarian symbolism of the prayer meeting by announcing that all discussion will be made public following the Friday prayer.

In sum, the FIS gained support from a population that occupied an oppositional position vis-à-vis government. A large number of resi-dents in the popular quarters that voted for the FIS lived in homes that were neither regularised nor officially recognised. They ran the risk of eviction or having their homes demolished. Between 1983 and 1985, the government, in accordance with a presidential decree, removed over 170,000 inhabitants of these quarters from their homes. Forty-seven per cent were sent to their *wilaya* of origin, 29 per cent were moved to the eastern peripheral suburb of Algiers, and the rest were either awaiting decisions on their cases or were considered to have departed of their own free will.[90] Others were removed by the government from the Qasbah and Bab el Oued to collective housing on the periphery. There, the inhabitants felt isolated and cut off from their old quarters where they were better integrated into the city.[91]

The Turn to Armed Struggle

The FIS invested the structures and spaces of collective action that developed or were reactivated during the 1980s. The takeover of mosques, the holding of national congresses uniting adherents, and practices of intermediation were all part of this investment. The popular and peripheral quarters expressed allegiance to the regime proposed by the Islamists in the form of a massive vote in their favour in the 1990 municipal and *wilayat* elections and in the first round of legislative elections. The shift to violent action took a more defined shape sometime after the army's interruption of the electoral process. Martinez suggests that the lull in the supporters' action indicated the limits to which the FIS adherents were willing to go. The armed action ensued in full in 1993 and can be seen as a reaction to state repressive policies and, in particular, against the repossession of the mosques and the policy of encircling the popular quarters by the security forces. Added to this was the sustained harassment and imprisonment of youths suspected of being FIS sympathisers.

Once unleashed, violence acquires a dynamic of its own. Here, violence, as a mode of action, has no singular objective and its ethos and terms of justification merge the religious with the profane. Thus, the targets of violence, the methods used and the discursive tenets supporting it multiply and diversify. In this seemingly chaotic situation, the settling of accounts becomes possible through the adoption of a war strategy aimed at eliminating one's opponents. In a sense, what transpired with the commencement of violent action was that it created an opportunity to get rid of one's real and symbolic foes.

Different logics of violence are at work in the Islamists' turn to armed action. They correspond to two distinctive Islamist armed formations. On one hand, are the armed bands based in the quarters, on the other the armed groups whose violence is directed at the state. The latter differ from the former in terms of the kind and level of violence used.[92] Despite these distinctions, there are links, mergers and overlapping positions. The youths of the quarters who form the armed bands seek to preserve their local autonomy. According to Martinez, the local emirs stepped in to fill the vacuum created by the departure of the notables-entrepreneurs following the irruption of violence, and to re-establish the economic and social exchanges that the latter sustained.[93] This would represent a process of social mobility and ascension parallel to the one that unfolded following the war of independence. The factor of mobility supports Martinez's contention that an imaginary of war has served to catapult various groups into positions of power at different junctures of Algerian history.

The territorialisation of identity that the quarter and its sons represent is reinforced through the armed band. Armed bands were formed to defend the quarters against state military and security intervention, but they soon became enmeshed with the economic networks of trabendo and, in due course, turned to banditry. On the one hand, the emir/armed leader is a son of the quarter, acting as an avenger of the people against the injustice of the state. On the other, the financial demands that he places on the people weaken their sympathies toward him. The workings of the bands hark back to the zu'r gangs of the urban quarters in Cairo and Damascus. Like the zu'r of fourteenth-century Damascus, the bands dismantled in 1992–93 were disciplined and well structured.[94] They were composed of students, technicians and workers. According to Martinez, from 1994, adolescents became preponderant,[95] as gangs of delinquents were incorporated into the bands. In joining the armed Islamist bands, 'bad boys' and delinquent youths passed into more esteemed positions, such as 'bandit of honour,' redrawn under the Islamist sign.[96] At the same time, there are parallels between their mode of operation and that of the zu'r gangs. The band provides protection services, exacts donations and runs extortion operations. It also controls the quarter territory, monitoring the space, positioning informers on street corners and watching out for police patrols. For the big traders and merchants who have delicate relations with the official administration and the police, the trabendiste crossover to armed Islamist bandit introduces a new and favourable variable.[97] These traders and merchants have benefited from the destruction of their public-enterprise competitors and from their enhanced economic autonomy that has resulted from the bands' territorial control.

Quarter-based action is transcended by the armed guerrilla formations such as the Groupes Islamiques Armés (GIA) and the Armé Islamique du Salut (AIS) that pursue a war against the state.[98] The strategies of these two formations derive from competing visions of the purpose and use of violence: the former adopting a strategy of all out-war, the latter engaging in a strategic war in support of a political solution involving the FIS.[99] Unlike the armed bands, these groups are implanted in the central zone encompassing Algiers, the Kabilye and the Mitidja (the GIA) and the interior (the AIS).[100] The Mitidja small towns of Sidi Moussa, Boufarik, Borj al-Kifan, Khemis el-Khechna and Larabaa represent the domain of the GIA. The guerrilla groups are none the less linked to the armed bands of the quarters. The latter provide logistic support to the guerrillas and execute some of the operations ordered by the *moujahidin* leaders.[101] A number of leaders of the armed groups continue to operate in some fashion from their quarters. Some were gunned down there by the police and security forces.

The recourse to violence finds justification in the militant Islamist ideology and its concept of *jihad* and in the practice of *takfir* (declaring someone an infidel). The symbols and agents of infidelity are everywhere such that an entire society may be condemned as 'infidel.' In such an instance, change must be brought about by installing an Islamic government that would enforce the rules. In other words, an all-out war against society does not seem to follow from the canonical articulation of *jihad* by its militant ideologues (Qutb and later Egyptian Jihadists). It may be argued that the strategy of terror is a *jihad* of sorts on the part of the militant Islamists. This is true to some extent. The assassination of journalists, writers, artists and intellectuals enters into the Islamist armed groups' strategy of terror.[102] However, many other acts of violence appear either to be committed at random or to fall outside the framework of terror against the presumed signs and agents of infidelity. The purpose of many of the massacres remains a mystery given that an Islamist motivation or involvement is difficult to establish on any grounds.[103]

The extent of the violence witnessed in Algeria cannot be accounted for simply in terms of a strategy of action pursued by some factions of the Islamist movement. The generalised terror involves other actors besides the Islamists. Agents of the state and of law and order, in particular the security services and the military, have adopted a policy of terror against the Islamists and anyone suspected of being a sympathiser. Thus, entire neighbourhoods are encircled and their residents made subject to arrests and interrogations. Mass detentions and torture follow. Random killing may also be used to sew seeds of fear and suspicion and, thus, inhibit any independent or oppositional activities.[104]

The violence involving the government and the Islamists has

served as a smokescreen for the settling of criminal accounts, clan wars and other types of illegal activities such as theft, arson and so on. An amorphous actor under the name of the *mafia-politico-financière* emerges as the culprit. This nebulous formation is made up of the barons of the state sector, the military entrepreneurs, the contractors and the *tchi-tchi*. The facts surrounding the assassination of Boudiaf in 1992 and other political figures point to the involvement of military warlords.[105] Finally, the violence seems to have allowed for the smooth transfer of public assets into private hands.[106]

Conclusion

The trajectory of the Islamist movement in Algeria is tied to the setting in which it emerged. The local actors, including the small *trabendistes*, the military entrepreneurs, the small merchants, the university students and the unemployed, shaped the movement and its direction. The merchants and the entrepreneurs, along with quarter inhabitants, spearheaded mosque construction. The mosque was conceived as the main social and cultural infrastructure of the community and not just as a place of worship. As the informal economy became more preponderant, trabendo activities developed around a hierarchy of relations involving the entrepreneurs, the merchants and the youths. The urban setting, where historical traditions and new forms of sociability interacted, structured the patterns of relations among the various forces.

The FIS developed as a major oppositional force anchored in emerging spaces of autonomy and dissidence. The youths constituted an important social force that was positioned against the state. They established new fraternities through the mosque and then the armed groups. In trying to understand the violence witnessed in Algeria following the interruption of the elections in 1992, many factors appear to have been at work. On one hand, the intervention of the army and the intransigence of its Generals vis-à-vis the FIS and its sympathisers added to the anti-state feelings. At the local level, the youths were engaged in securing their territories at the level of the quarter. The dynamics of the informal economy characterised by clandestinity facilitated the passage from protection of the *houma* to banditry. However, as the stakes increased with the ongoing process of privatisation, violence became a convenient strategy for capital accumulation. The armed groups were drawn into the web of the *mafia-politico-financière*. Thus, the extent and level of violence need to be situated in relation to the condition of generalised corruption that has existed in Algeria for over two decades.

2. ISLAMIST POLITICS IN TUNISIA

In contrast to the Algerian case, the story of Islamism in Tunisia appears complete. The movement is thought to be at an end. Studies dealing with the case have shifted focus from an account of conditions of the movement's emergence to the causes of its decline or fall. This is captured best in the idea of 'montée et declin' (rise and fall) expressed in the title of Elbaki Hermassi's 1994 article on Tunisian Islamism.[107] In a retrospective, reflective and auto-critical study, noted sociologist Abdelkader Zghal reviewed the predominant modes of questioning and inquiry into the Tunisian Islamist movement.[108] In his view, the questions developed within a common sociological paradigm and were shaped by the developments at moments of inquiry, whether the rise, affirmation or eradication of the movement as a political force. The questions pertained to the reasons for the Islamist appeal among university and high school students[109], and the socio-economic background of Islamist adherents and sympathisers.[110] The findings of this existing research represent Islamism in Tunisia as an expression of protest among educated youth against their condition of blocked mobility resulting from a shrinking job market during the 1970s and 80s and the expansion of the gaps between the social classes.[111] In reviewing the Tunisian case, I expand the analysis of Islamist activism as a social movement to take into account the dynamics of state-society interaction both at the local and global levels. I also examine the insertion of Islamism into the Tunisian socio-political setting, looking at sites of activism and patterns of action. Of particular importance to this undertaking is the issue of the Islamist's mode of implantation into the urban setting in Tunis. The analysis highlights how certain spaces of oppositional action emerged and how opposition was contained by the dominant modes of interaction at the local level and by state-society relations of incorporation at the macro level.

Dynamics of State-Society Interaction in Tunisia: An Overview

Post-independence Tunisian politics has been marked by a highly centralised bureaucratic state and by the development of structures of societal incorporation and control. The Tunisian state is generally viewed as omnipotent and, in one formulation, as a 'tutelage state;' a state at once exterior to society and imbricated in it through the institution of the party-state and its corollary, the politico-adminis-trative apparatus.[112] The party-state is exterior to society, yet it penetrates into all its aspects and spreads its tentacles into all social crevices. In the workings of this system of domination, clientelism serves as a fuel. This captures the structural basis of political control, but leaves out the role played by social forces in shaping patterns of interaction with the state. As such, it becomes important to inquire into how societal forces position themselves in relation to this sys-tem of domination and how they relate to the structures of control.

In structural terms, the party (the Neo-Destour 1934–63, which was renamed the Parti Socialist Democratique [PSD] in 1963, and the Rassemblement Constitutionnel Démocratique [RCD] from 1988) developed as the framework of incorporation and territorial enframing of the population. This has been achieved by means of country-wide hierarchical organisation intertwined with the state administration, itself hierarchically structured into national, regional, local and sub-local levels of government corresponding to a territorial division of nation, region, *délégation* and *secteur*.[113] The party structure paral-lels this administrative hierarchy and territorial division, having at its apex a political bureau and a national congress to which regional federations are subordinated. The federations subsume the local and sub-local levels of party cells or chapters.

This centralised structure does not exhaust the political field and is not the only locus of political power. Rather, complex processes involving state and non-state actors, different contexts and multiple forms of interaction and relations of force are also productive of the political field. Decisions at the centre and interventions from above are subject to manipulation and instrumentalisation from below. Technocratic, administrative and partisan authorities at the national level represent a multiplicity of competencies and interests which interact with the web of local actors and social forms of organisation. In other words, structures of control from above do not neutralise or negate social relations of power. In some instances, they represent the framework and the arena in which conflicts and antagonisms are played out. They are also the locus of manoeuvres to acquire or enhance individual or group power. This is confirmed by the fact that at the local level, social relations of power have often been acted out within the party cell. Societal structures of authority, whether based on kin or market relations, or a combination of the two, have found in the party cell an additional, and, perhaps, an unavoidable arena of power play. Physical and symbolic capital, constituting the basis of power and prestige, could be validated in the party cell, the federation committee and so on. From this perspective, the framework of local partisan politics enhanced the position of figures of notability, and brought about the rise of some and the demise of others. The relay functions of the politico-administrative structures and the resources they possess have made them both channels of power and offices of mediation that can be fashioned by societal modes of organisation.

The following analysis examines Islamist activism within the framework of state-society interaction, with a view to bringing the multitude of spaces structuring action (oppositional and consensual) to bear on our understanding of the trajectory of Tunisian Islamism. In looking at local relations of power, and at the links and exchanges between the local setting and other instances of state power, we are able to focus on the positioning of actors, on the spaces of action governed by local relations of power and on the dynamics of interaction with these instances. By situating the Islamist movement in the socio-political setting in which it operates, it is possible to assess the opportunities and constraints that have shaped it.

Islamism in the Tunisian Socio-political Setting

Before situating Islamism within the wider setting of state-society relations, we should look at the immediate conjuncture of its early stirrings. The movement's beginnings, and its early form, owe much to the socio-political juncture of the late 1960s and early 1970s. This is the period when the experiment with socialism under Prime Minister Ben Salch was on the wane and the move towards a free market economy was underway. Socialist activism, which had been the dominant form of political expression, was out of step with the turn taken in the economic sphere. In other words, the socialist discourse was no longer sponsored or tolerated by the state. At the same time, the liberal wing of the PSD was marginalised and finally pushed out.

In this context of weakened ideological force and diminished political coherence at the centre, Islamism was articulated as the expression of social contestation against the loss of societal control – a loss exemplified by the 'free' dress habits of women, the mixing of the sexes and the waywardness of youth symbolised by the presence of too many coffee shops.[114] The early expression of Islamism in Tunisia, then, bears similarities to the Egyptian and Algerian cases. The noteworthy difference lies in the fact that the nucleus of the new movement formed around theology graduates of Zaytouna seminary and was thus tied closely to establishment Islam. Elbaki Hermassi has interpreted these origins as a sign of protest against the dismantlement of the social and cultural order of Zaytouna. Abdelkader Zghal, on the other hand, views them as the desire of Zaytouna notables to regain political sovereignty.[115] However, while the Zaytouna origin is clearly an attempt at the reassertion of religious knowledge as a source of symbolic capital and power, it should be noted that the decline of Zaytouna preceded its downsizing by President Bourguiba to a faculty of theology at the University of Tunis.[116] Rather than reacting to Bourguiba policies affecting the religious establishment, the Zaytouna nucleus drew on a frame of reference within which it was possible to recuperate certain mechanisms of control in the family and in the public space.

The nucleus of the movement which, in 1981, became known as the Movement of the Islamic Tendency (MIT), found in the mosque an appropriate space for voicing its social contestation.[117] The group targeted high school and university students for support. The first recruits, thus, were young and at an early stage of intellectual formation. Founding teachers organised learning and discussion circles (*halaqat*) between sunset (*maghrib*) and evening (*'isha*) prayers in mosques of the old city of Tunis: in Sahib al-Tabi' in Halfawin quarter, in Sidi Mehrez in al-Saha in Bab-Souiqa, and Sidi Youssef in the Qasbah. Their teaching concentrated on ethical and religious matters. This strategy allowed the group to compete with the state apparatus of indoctrination and to present itself as an alternative to the contending socialist forces on university campuses.

In 1974, the Islamist activities in the university began to take shape and claimed space in the form of mosques and prayer rooms. Meanwhile, the shift to a market economy during the early 1970s allowed for a convergence between certain state interests and Islamist interests around a common opposition to leftist sympathisers on university campuses. Certain forces within the state facilitated the Islamist presence by granting permits for the establishment of prayer rooms and for the publication of two journals, *al-Ma'rifa* and *al-Mujtama'*. These focused on questions of women's dress and loose morals. Their major themes echoed those found in the writings of the Muslim Brothers of Egypt concerning the decadence of the West, the failure of its model, the moral corruption of its leaders and the estrangement of the people from Islamic values.[118]

In this early phase of the 1970s, the loci of the movement's activities remained the universities and high schools. Hermassi's profile of adherents and sympathisers during this period indicates that 80 per cent were students and teachers and the rest low-level employees and technicians.[119] Among the university students, he noted a concentration in science faculties. In terms of socio-economic background, the students came from families in which the fathers had low levels of education and held low-level jobs.[120]

Both Hermassi and Zghal explain the appeal of the Islamist discourse among the students in terms of frustrated aspirations or what is viewed as blocked mobility.[121] There are a number of observations that should make us question this explanation. First, the discourse in its earlier articulation was not concerned with issues of social justice and equality. By contrast, the socialist discourse

articulated by the leftists on university campuses appeared to address the students' immediate concerns. In fact, the left continued to
attract student sympathisers. Second, the Islamist students did not
develop a position critical of government until they broadened their
agenda in the 1980s. As such, the Islamists' concern with religious
practice and morality was dissociated from political opposition and
action. The focus in their discourses on social mores and sexuality
underlines the desire to reinscribe mechanisms of social control in
public and private. Hermassi, indeed, points out that the questions
pertaining to the family and the position of women in society were
the primary preoccupations of the movement in the 1970s.[122] The
predominant concern, in Ghanoushi's words, was with 'the manifestations of moral delinquency.'[123] These were most evident in the
university where mixing between the sexes took place, women
adopted a Western style dress, and the non-observance of religious
practices was not necessarily hidden. In this context, religious conservatism was a reaffirmation of patriarchal values in the household
and in the public sphere especially in the university, the school and
the workplace.

Souhayr Belhassen's study of Islamist women in Tunisia gives us
insights into power contestation in the family setting.[124] She notes
that young women from popular class backgrounds adopted the veil,
not necessarily in submission to pressures coming from Islamist
brothers, but in a reassertion of their economic independence and
revalorisation of their position in the family. Further, the veil was
perceived as a tool in the fight against sexism.[125] In this sense, the
Islamist discourse is open to subversion, although within certain
boundaries. It is interesting to note that some of the women expressed
critical views of their families' mode of adherence to the religion.[126]
They also adopted a critical stance towards government discourse
and the process of secularisation.[127] Belhassen notes that the women
sought to build up networks of support in the school, university and
workplace.[128] They also constituted themselves as a community in
the mosque.[129]

The Islamist movement's non-involvement in the socio-economic
issues of the time and its distance from the popular sector was the
subject of an auto-critique by the leadership in the second phase of

development. Further, social, economic and political transformations brought about a change in the Islamists' ideological discourse and activities. The 1978 riots mark a turning point in this respect. The Islamists condemned the social action organised by Tunisia's labour federation, the UGTT, but they learnt important lessons from it about syndicate activism. Later, with the 1984 riots, they would come to understand the social and political role of the street. In light of this, the Islamists moved to enlarge their social base through activism in the UGTT and other organisations. Thus, in addition to the control of the educational syndicate, the Islamists made some gains in the UGTT, electing seventy members out of 220 delegates to the Union's general congress in 1984.[130] The MIT showed a strong presence in certain regions, gaining a majority of votes in regional elections to the UGTT executive in Baja and Bizerte.[131] During that same period, it moved into the arena of public agitation and escalated its confrontation with the regime. The removal of President Bourguiba in 1987 by his prime minister, Zayn al-Abidin Ben Ali, put an end to this confrontation. This was followed by two important turns – first on to the political road then, in 1990–91, on to the road of violence. This chronology follows a simple narrative of rise and fall. However, the question posed here is not simply why this sequence of events occurred, but how we account for Islamist activism, its failures and successes, its opportunities and constraints. Looking retrospectively at events, concerned actors and observers point to certain determinant factors to explain the 'demise' of Islamism in Tunisia. These have to do with fatal errors committed by the leadership. First, the leaders of the Nahda (the new name adopted by the movement in 1987) refused to enter into a dialogue with the left and opted to 'go it alone.'[132] Second, the leadership overestimated the level of street involvement on which the movement could count.[133]

Tunisian Islamism, as a student movement, was necessarily limited by the absence of an alliance with other social forces, in particular workers and the sub-proletariat. As such, in its first phase, it was unlikely to take power or become a partner in a political transition. Unfortunately, there is no data on the occupations or socio-economic backgrounds of activists in the later phase. However, available data on Islamists facing court trial in the mid 1980s give us some indication of the basis of activism. In terms of strategy, the leadership seemed to have bet on institutional penetration, particularly into the apparatuses of physical oppression – the army and the police. To this end, they recruited members from the ranks of the army and police corps. This is confirmed by the fact that sixty military men were among the accused in the 1987 trial of activists charged with plotting against the regime. Furthermore, in the 1991 trials military men made up a full one-third of those accused of devising another plot which included the assassination of President Ben Ali. Of the 300 men brought to trial, 100 were from the military, holding the rank of major or below. Several were in the air force with access to sensitive security information.[134]

In addition to this institutional strategy, there is evidence that the Islamists took steps to appropriate spaces where state presence and relations of power were undergoing change and where state-societal processes of intermediation were being transformed. In the 1980s, Islamist activism took on a social garb moving into spontaneous housing quarters and rehabilitated shanty-towns of Tunis. The salience of the Islamist implantation into the popular urban sector has to do with two significant determinants: the structures of oppositonal action and the social relations of power at the local level. In the following discussion, I review the patterns of urban social collective action as manifested in the key events of societal organisation in the urban popular quarters. This sheds light on state-society dynamics of interaction and on the positioning of Islamists in this setting.

Islamism and Urban Oppositional Action

The Islamists' inroads into the urban areas gave them a degree of popular support that manifested itself in their final confrontation with the Ben Ali regime in 1990–91. With the escalation of violence in early 1991, Islamist action represented an attempt to draw out the link between its university base and the popular classes. In this respect, university protest activities were intensified and supplemented by agitation in the urban sectors. On one hand, students rioted on university campuses bringing classes to a standstill. They also attacked faculty deans and campus security personnel. On the other hand,

militants moved into high schools, targeted RCD offices, police stations and government offices in such popular quarters as al-Ouardia
(a planned popular 'city'), and Ben Arous (an industrial sector in south
Tunis). These actions were often accompanied by demonstrations and
ended in clashes with the police. The strategy, as noted earlier, was to
activate the power of the street.[135] However, popular support was
not forthcoming, in contrast to other events (to be discussed below)
that brought out large segments of the population in sustained opposition in 1978 and 1984. In order to understand the limited popular
sector involvement in 1991, we need to look at the structural conditions of the earlier period and the structures of oppositional action
that prevailed. We also need to take into account the social changes
and transformations that were underway.

We turn briefly to the 1978 riots, with a view to identifying opportunities for and constraints on contestation. The 1978 events began
with the UGTT call for a general strike. Labour activism and opposition aimed at a restitution of rights that were withdrawn as a result
of the reconfiguration of the national economy. By the end of the
1970s, while absolute salaries rose, the workers' share of the GDP
fell from 41 to 33.5 per cent.[136] The decline of the workers' share of
the national wealth had to do with changes in the state's policies
concerning capital accumulation. In the 1960s, under the import-sub-
stitution industrialisation regime, the state blocked the rise of workers'
salaries, but also controlled the prices of consumption goods, particularly basic food items. In the 1970s, the state shifted to export-led
growth, moved to encourage private capital investment, liberated
prices and continued to block salaries. Under these conditions, the
divergent interests of labour and capital crystallised. State policies
lined up on the side of capital and were reoriented with the aim of
relying on an entrepreneurial class to invest in the export industry
drive.[137] From 1970 to 1974, there was an unprecedented level of
strikes. During this period the UGTT, with its strong popular base,
emerged as the main force of opposition to the Bourguiba regime.
The Union organised workers' protests and strikes at periods of sal-
ary negotiations. It also sharpened its view on class issues and class
interests.[138] The state responded to this increased combativeness by
trying to diminish trade union autonomy and by trying to pose a

counter-force of controlled workers' representation.[139] Such interventionist manoeuvres, however, sparked the call for a general strike.

Of particular interest here is that the strike and demonstrations mobilised a social force with grievances and demands within a particular frame of organised action. At the same time, as an event of contestation, the action encompassed wider social forces such as youths, professionals and the unemployed. Moreover, it unfolded in a number of cities. The account from Tunis is highly instructive of the conjunction of labour and urban politics. In Tunis, hundreds of residents gathered at the offices of the UGTT in the city centre (Place Mohammed Ali). The gathering grew strong due to the presence of youths between the ages of twenty and twenty-five years. The records of arrests indicate that most of the protesters were residents of the old city and the informal quarters and included workers, students and the unemployed.[140] In the confrontation with the police, some protesters dispersed to the new city, passing through the centre. Police use of firearms and tear gas forced the rioters to retreat into the old city, seeking refuge. The police, however, encircled and then entered the Medina in pursuit of the fleeing groups. Once inside, they opened fire on inhabitants who interceded in an attempt to end the confrontation.[141] As Lowy notes, the incident broke the rules of urban protest according to which the Medina was a safe retreat. Merchants and traders in the Medina tried to help, but in the face of police force they were not willing to risk their homes and lives.

The 1984 week-long riots provide us with further insight into oppositional action during the 1980s. The riots erupted in response to the removal of subsidies on bread and other basic consumer goods. The first action took place in the interior of the country in Bouzi, Kebili, Thala and el-Hama, all in the disadvantaged south and centre regions which were favourable to revolt and *jacquarie*.[142] The crowd took over the street and attacked public buildings and magazine shops. Other riots broke out in Kasserine in the centre of the country. There, the army was called in and bloody clashes ensued. Violent demonstrations in Gafsa and Gabes followed. In Tunis, the action started three days later, and spread throughout the capital, with young people and women making up the crowds. The agitation began in the high schools of the popular quarters, but drew participants from the rich quarters as well. In the Medina and in the city centre, clashes exploded and could not be controlled by a contingent of some 4,000 police officers.[143] Protesters set up fiery barricades using overturned cars, buses and old tires. Food shops in the city centre were emptied and set on fire. Violent exchanges occurred in the squares around the Medina and in the neighbourhood of Bab Souiqa. Much of the action was sustained in Melassine, Jbel Lahmar, Ettadhanum and al Ouardia, all popular quarters of the city. Sub-proletarians from these areas made up a good portion of the troops.[144] As in 1978, the army and the police fired on protesters, then moved into the Medina to dislodge them.[145] In containing the challenge, the state deployed a high level of violence. It then restored the food subsidies.

In these two key events of oppositional action in the post-independence period, the main social forces of contestation were workers acting within the framework of the UGTT, the popular classes and youths. An important regional dimension underpinned contestation, with the towns of the south representing zones of dissidence.[146] It was in these spaces that Islamism had to activate if it was to develop a wider social base and represent a significant protest movement. Following the 1984 events, the Islamists attempted to link up with the popular sector. In the context of political struggles over Bourguiba's succession, elite rivalries and intrigues contributed to the weakening of the party framework of *quadrillage*. The mobilisation of popular opposition was possible under these circumstances. However, the Islamists seem to have managed only a limited extension of their spaces of activism. In 1986, Islamist action in the university followed the established pattern of confrontation with leftist students: strikes and the disruption of classes. On a number of occasions, the security forces intervened and university faculties were closed down. In one instance, 1,000 students were interrogated.[147] In 1987, agitation in the university was followed by a call for civil disobedience in the form of mass demonstrations in all large cities and towns.[148] This plan failed as a result of popular distance and continued police repression.[149] In that year, the Islamist militants attempted to widen their base of support, taking to the street on many occasions. For instance, in April, following the imprisonment of Rachid Ghanoushi, they descended on the capital demanding his liberation. Public demonstrations were repeated in May and, in July, the Islamists called for a march of re-sistance.[150]

The failure to involve the popular sector and popular forces in confrontational activities was repeated in 1989 and again in 1990–91. Following the legislative elections of April 1989, an atmosphere of confrontation between President Ben Ali and the Islamists developed. Both sides were drawn into an open dual that each seemed to have perceived as the logical climax to their power struggle. The strategic considerations at play centred on the Islamists' showing in the elections. While they fell short of securing a popular victory, the Islamists nevertheless confirmed their position as the main power contenders and opponents of the regime. This may have prompted the regime to find a way of containing the movement's further expansion. For the Islamists, pursuing the legal strategy of elections when they had been denied formal presence and recognition may appear to have been a miscalculation. In any event, it would seem that the 'inconclusive' results of the elections contributed to mounting tensions. Dispersed incidents in December 1989 included a hunger strike by Zaytouna theology students, a UGTE call for a general strike and confrontation with police in Manouba mosque in Tunis.[151] Reports of urban action are given for September 1990 and refer to Nahda/Islamist members testing the degree of popular support. This began with organised demonstrations in popular quarters every Friday following the prayer.[152] The 1991 attack by fringe Islamists on an RCD office in Bab Souiqa in the old city, resulting in the death of one of the guards, served as the catalyst for a state policy of liquidation. The focal point of the policy's implementation was the university – the Islamists' stronghold.

The events of 1991 underline the fact that after two decades of opposition and activism, Islamism as an oppositional movement remained largely confined to the university. Following police raids on university campuses and dormitories, students called for strikes, held vigils and engaged in clashes with the police. The student action brought the university to a standstill. Between 5 and 8 May, two students were killed in clashes and ten were injured. Outside the university, mobilisation took place in high schools where the administration was attacked and classes disrupted. There were incidents in Tunis where a group of fifty persons engaged police on the borders of the Medina, a favoured strategic space of action.[153] This did not spread to other quarters. On 7 May 1991, the UGTE called for a general strike, but activities remained within the university boundaries.[154] On 21 May, the minister of the interior announced the discovery of a five-phase plot against the regime which occasioned a clampdown on opposition and the spiral of repression that neutralised the Islamists.

Efforts were made to connect the university with the popular quarters. The proximity of some of the university residences where action was taking place may have encouraged the participation of high school students in some quarters; however, residents' involvement appeared limited. Events were confined to the Faculty of the Manouba, the ENSET, and the Lycée Technique du Tunis. In other regions, a number of schools were involved in the agitation although, according to press reports, they added up to no more than twenty-seven schools out of a total of 600.[155] At the centre, the press reported incidents in high schools in Dowar Hicher (an informal quarter in the west of Tunis) and in Melassine (a rehabilitated squatter quarter in Tunis).[156] In general, the protest was contained and confined to the university. The deployment of the state's repressive armada was no doubt effective in containing what appears to have been the Tunisian Islamists' last stand. Yet it should be noted that in addition to force, other measures of containment and neutralisation were used. These measures were focused on reaffirming the state's control over urban space and at strengthening the mechanisms and channels of incorporation. Before considering these measures, we should turn to the local urban setting and dynamics of power traversing it.

The urban setting in Tunis: Local-level politics

Writing in the 1980s, a Tunisian urbanist noted that the social divisions of the Tunis urban space were demarcated by separation between the various geographical sectors making up the agglomeration. Residing in the north, which includes the two coastal beach suburbs, are the privileged population and a fraction of the middle classes. Concentrated in the south-west and north-west of the city, are

medium quality and popular housing quarters (79 per cent of workers' housing, and 90 per cent of spontaneous housing). The city centre
is dualist: the centre-east is the colonial city with a population close
in its socio-economic characteristics to that of the north, while the
centre-west, the Medina and its *faubourghs*, has a similar profile to
the west and the south.[157] The socio-economic divisions have been
inscribed in the historical progression and changes of the urban form,
each of the sectors having emerged in particular historical periods.[158]

In treating Islamist activism as a protest movement, the approach
developed here is concerned with the oppositional spaces where Islamism either emerges or is implanted. 'Spontaneous' quarters tend
to represent such spaces because of the dynamics involved in their
construction and development. As we have seen, the key events of
oppositional action in post-independence Tunisia originated in the
disinherited regions of the south and in the disfavoured urban quarters of large cities, with Tunis representing the locus of action.

Recognising the potential challenge represented by these spaces,
the Tunisian post-independence state pursued policies aimed at the
control of space. From early on, it was alert to any spaces that may
not be within its structures of enframing. In this respect, it continued the colonial policy of eradicating the unplanned settlements in
the urban sector. Within this framework, the state removed the squatter settlement of Borgel and attempted the removal of Jbel Lahmar.[159]
Bourguiba himself was conscious of the contestatory potential of these
areas since they had served as hiding places during the nationalist
struggle against French colonial authorities. In his discourse, he enun-
ciated his view that these spaces were a threat to state power that
would not be tolerated and asserted that if, in their eradication, lives
were lost, it would be a necessary cost.[160] Bourguiba expressed these
views on the occasion of the 1964 confrontation which took place
between the inhabitants of Borj Ali Raïs and the National Guard.[161]

Following the 1978 events, the state intensified its efforts to regain control of spontaneous and irregular quarters. In this respect, it
adopted a policy of rehabilitation of the *gourbivilles* (shanty-towns).
The policy was supported by the World Bank. Funds were allocated
to upgrade Melassine (in the centre-west) and to remove certain sections of Jbel Lahmar. Planned quarters for rehousing, such as

al-Khadra and Ibn Khaldun, were designed to receive these residents.[162] In the early 1980s, the new informal quarters such as Ettadhamun, Douar Hicher and M'Thalith were integrated into the rehabilitation programmes. During this period, state intervention policies in the urban sector aimed at the reduction of social tensions through the provision of collective social infrastructure and services.[163] Infrastructural development and social service provision were intended to supplant political control achieved through party cells, administration, the *omda* and *délégué* (governor's representative). The emergent dynamics of this multi-layered intervention are the key to understanding state-popular quarter relations and the local setting in which Islamism operated.

This setting is characterised by a dense web of actors and interactions. In the case of informal quarters, it includes the *délégué*, the party cells, the residents, the clandestine real estate promoters, and the representatives of urban authorities. The web is spun around relations of exchange and patronage, regulatory norms and so on. Islamist activism in the popular quarters is positioned in relation to this setting. Looking at quarters with a documented Islamist presence, it emerges that this was felt most when traditional local actors were weak or absent and when relay structures with the state had little physical or social capital. The case of Islamist implantation in Ettadahmun, Melassine and M'Thalith highlight the processes of engagement in the local setting in terms of opportunities and constraints. We should also keep in mind the dynamics of local politics underpinned by political actors representing the state, the social notability and popular forces.

Ettadhamun presents us with an important case of changing power dynamics.[164] The quarter was formed in the 1970s as a result of clandestine construction. Unauthorised developers sold parcels of land to poor families who were former occupants of dilapidated homes in the Medina and were migrants from rural areas. In this space the developers emerged as the local notability. In the early phase of construction, they offered instalment payments, as an alternative line of credit to state financial institutions. The developers established *hamams* (bath houses), grocery stores and other local businesses including textile workshops. These enterprises operated on credit systems and thus facilitated the purchase of goods and services. They also were a place of employment for some of the residents. In time, the notability sought to formalise its status by spearheading an initiative, supported by the residents, for the authorisation of a party cell. Once this was granted, a party bureau run by the developers was set up. This was a strategy of legitimating the settlement, securing delivery of public services and rising up in the authority structure of the party.

Prior to the adoption of the rehabilitation policies, demands in the informal quarters were made through the party cells and there were dispersed instances of state intervention. M'Thalith, renamed Ennour in 1981, in south Tunis is a noted exception. There, the inhabitants were better organised due to tribal linkages among them. Furthermore, the Islamists were active in the area. This explains why the authorities were more responsive to the demands of the residents than to those of the other quarters. Prior to the urban public authorities' engagement in quarter management, the development of the politico-administrative frame in M'Thalith was limited. In Ettadhamun before 1979, local actors included the *délégué* of the Manouba delegation under whose jurisdiction the quarter came. Other important actors included members of the party cell bureau. With the implementation of the rehabilitation programmes, and in response to the regulation imperative, the government created a new *délégation*, that of Ettadhamun, composed of three *secteurs* (Ettadhamun, Douar Hicher and M'Nihla). Further, the area was constituted as a commune and was organised into five circumscriptions for PSD cells.[165] The politico-administrative personnel and the partisan activists in the PSD acted as intermediaries between the residents and the urban authorities. They lobbied on the residents' behalf for services and performed regulatory functions. For example, the *délégué* raised funds, calling on the promoters for contributions to social solidarity projects and to aid poor families.[166]

In the mid 1980s, the notables/promoters moved to the rich quarters, creating a vacuum in governance structures in the quarters that was filled partially by the Islamists. The latter's ability to work within the area may have been facilitated by the social character that the mosque had come to acquire. Local notables in the 'informal' quarters established mosques to legitimate their status. In Ettadhamun, the mosque was used by the inhabitants to organise the delivery of needed services. Most important was the regulation of the ad hoc sewage system.[167] The mosque organised teams in charge of the maintenance of improvised drainage arrangements.[168] In addition, it sponsored mutual aid activities. With the departure of the notables, the Islamists began to engage in the familiar social welfare activities: raising funds for charity, helping out needy families, attending to the resolution of social conflicts in the neighbourhood. They also offered karate classes and organised football matches and tournaments.

In Melassine, a similar process of transfer of authority from party notables to Islamist sympathisers took place. Vasile notes that a competition for control over the local space ensued following the relocation of the party cell in the 1970s. The outcome of this struggle was decided when the party cell office was transformed into a mosque.[169] This takeover represented a collective response to the problem of maintaining order and containing behaviour that transgressed social norms. The transformation of space into a site for religious practice was aimed at a reversal of its appropriation by some of the youths as a place to drink and socialise.[170] The construction of the mosque was sponsored and paid for by the inhabitants.

The Islamists' ability to take root in the popular quarters in Tunis was limited by the historically constituted structures of *encadrement* and by the state's ability to reactivate these structures. Societal instrumentalisation of mediating agents and spaces represented additional impediments to Islamist insertion. This said, it should be noted that the Islamists managed to activate in mediating spaces. In Ettadhamun, for example, the offices of the party cell were used as spaces for performing the prayer. Following the 1978 events, the state adopted a rehabilitation policy guided by the imperatives of regulation and social integration. There were moments when control through local structures was loose. In addition, the Islamists were able to activate in the established spaces of mediation. At the same time, the *délégué* tried to neutralise them, although some state agents may have bet on an Islamist success in the 1980s and, accordingly, formed alliances with local activists.

The history of urban management in Tunis underlines consistent and continued policies of social and political control. Structures of enframing waned at times, and regulations were loosened. However, from early on, state penetration into the new popular quarters was assured. In this vein, the 1990–91 escalation of conflict with the Islamists was accompanied by a strengthening of state regulatory and control policies under which some integrative functions were subsumed. The plan of urban integration for quarters like Ettadhamun, Douar Hicher, M'Nihla had been under way and yielded some results. Security and integrative aims were part of the basic rehabilitation policies of the 1980s. Strategies for attaining these aims took the form assigning numbers to houses and streets, paving roads, and undertaking the cartography of these areas. Urban authorities saw to the provision of water and electricity, while sewage connections were installed for primary and secondary users.

In 1991, the state reinforced the regulatory policies of the 1980s. It is interesting to note that at precisely the time the Islamist urban protests were taking place, President Ben Ali paid unannounced visits to Melassine, Ettadhamun, Hraira and other popular quarters of Tunis. During these visits, he reassured the residents that sewage services would be provided and that living conditions would be ameliorated. Immediately following this, a new rehabilitation programme was announced for 220 popular quarters. Funds were allocated for the provision of water and electricity services. Follow-up mechanisms were set in place under the jurisdiction of the minister of the interior. Concurrently, the state expanded its structures of enframing the population within new organs of control, such as the *lijan al-yaqadha* (awakening committees in charge of monitoring Islamist activities) and *lijan al-ahya'* (quarters' committees). The decision to create *lijan al-ahya'* was announced on 10 May 1991 as an initiative recommended by the president.[171]

A temporal and spatial enframing of the population has been accomplished with programmes of leisure for youths and a plan of municipal action in the domain of culture.[172] Under the Eighth National Plan, disfavoured quarters throughout the territory were assured access to education and improved recreation facilities for the young. Further, the age of attending basic education was raised from sixteen to eighteen years, while obligatory schooling extended to the first cycle of high school. State action designed to control space took full force. The new spaces of quarter committees represent further instances of state *quadrillage* and of recomposition from below.[173] The quarter committee president must have support from RCD cell cadres. Authorisation for constituting the committee is obtained from the Ministry of the Interior.[174] The members and heads of the new committees often are RCD bureau members. They are in charge of promoting civism, and directing citizens' initiatives in neighbourhoods towards apolitical activities. The regime's policy of promoting civism rests partly on a temporal marking of activities exemplified by the declaration of numerous national days to celebrate or reinforce state-guided civic participation. Hence, there are national days and week-long festivities producing the effect of *marquage du temps* (temporalisation). Among these are national days of hygiene and environmental protection, a day of knowledge, a national day of the tree and the 7 November week.

The reinforcement of a state presence at the local level constitutes an important component of a global policy of control and incorporation. This policy should be examined from the perspective of the changes and transformations taking place at the macro-level in Tunisia.

Islamism and the Macro-Setting

The structural factors inhibiting Islamists' implantation in the popular urban quarters, in combination with developments at the macro-level, created a context that is less than favourable to Islamist activism and opposition. Here, we should note the economic transformation of the late 1980s and the 1990s, the reconfiguration of the political scene and the ongoing process of social restructuring. In the decade following the economic crisis of the early 1980s, a transformation from a rentier to a productive economy was achieved through the expansion of the industrial sector and its further integration into the global economy.[175] The Tunisian structural adjustment programme (SAP) has been evaluated as a success.[176] State compensatory policies attenuated the impact of the SAP measures on the salaried component of the middle strata and on the popular sector. The former continues to benefit from credit lines designed to assist with home purchasing and the acquisition of consumer goods.[177] Social programmes such as the Fonds de Solidarité Nationale (known as Fonds 26/26) are directed to the less well-off segments of the popular strata. Further, with the introduction of programmes supporting micro-enterprises, the ranks of the self-employed and the small business sector have expanded. The overall effects of these policies and programmes has been a reconfiguration of the social structure, marked by an expansion of the middle strata, including professionals, entrepreneurs and artisans, all with interests tied to the state.

With the country's further integration into the global economy, the Ben Ali regime's suppression of the Islamists has been presented as a security imperative designed to safeguard the economic gains that accrued from tourism, foreign investment and international aid. In the 1994 presidential and legislative elections, President Ben Ali's main campaign slogan was *al-balad al-amin* (the safe country). The theme of security figured prominently in his discourse and in political slogans. For instance, ads were run in which electors professed their choice of Ben Ali to secure their future (*lidamani mustaqbali*).[178] The security motif was played up by drawing comparisons between a stable Tunisia and an insecure and unstable Algeria in 1991. Comparisons were also drawn with Egypt, although the contrast was less stark. Official newspapers juxtaposed stories of the Tunisian state's control of the Islamists with reports of Islamist violence in both Algeria and Egypt.[179]

In addition to the acquiescence of the country's large middle class, the regime benefits from a cowed political opposition and a corporatised women's movement. Following the 1991 confrontation with the Islamists, opposition political parties closed ranks behind the regime. Leaders of these parties condemned the Islamist action and pledged their support to the president.[180] To this crescendo of support was added the voice of the neutralised UGTT.[181] The left, as politically and intellectually constituted, opted for a secular authoritarian regime as a lesser evil to Islamist government. In the meantime, the ruling party (RCD) was revitalised, recruiting a younger leadership and renewing its mobilisational drive.[182] RCD members infiltrated societal associations with the aim of bringing them under control.

Finally, the women's movement has proven beneficial to the regime in its counter-offensive against the Islamists. The UNFT (the women's union) was engaged in the neutralisation campaigns. Its president called for 'a dialogue within the family to undermine the enemy of the nation' and appealed to the president to safeguard the achievements of Tunisia. To ensure women's support, measures promoting their labour rights and improving their status within the family were adopted.[183] As part of the strategy of incorporation, a number of women were admitted into the party central committee and one woman into the political bureau.[184] A whole range of reforms affecting the status of women was introduced.[185] The independent women's association was legalised and a fund to support divorced women was established.

The championing of women's interests is exhibited by the Ben Ali regime as evidence of its progressive character. The regime proclaims itself to be the woman's defender against the Islamists. This strategy is pursued within an overall policy of repressing all opponents, critics and potential challengers. Repressive measures have been applied against the press, the intellectuals and the political opposition, including both men and women.[186] An elaborate system of surveillance and control under the direction of the security apparatus is at work.[187] The prevailing situation in 1999 may be summed up in the words of Zakiya Daoud's description of conditions in Tunisia in 1991: 'en privé, tout le monde denonce cette dérive dangeureuse et totalitaire et souligne que la police est omnipresente, la presse verouillé, le processus de démocratisation bloqué. À l'étranger, toutes les associations de droits de l'homme multiplient les avertissements à l'endroit du pouvoir Tunisien.'[188]

Conclusion

In its early phase of development, Tunisian Islamism emerged as a student movement. Its outlook was conservative with a strong focus on morality, male-female relations and sexuality. These concerns articulated a desire for the preservation of societal mechanisms of control within the family and in the public sphere. The movement's ideological discourse and strategies of activism underwent changes in the 1980s. These changes were shaped by the context of labour activism and modes of urban oppositional action. In recognising the importance of widening their basis of support, the Islamists became active in popular quarters. Their ability to engage the popular sector was constrained by the historical structures of state-society incorporation at the local level and by societal forces' instrumentalisation of mediating spaces and agents.

Macro-changes in the economy and the social structure appear to favour the regime's pursuit of the security option. The expansion and multiplication of mechanisms of control and incorporation has served to neutralise Islamist opposition and to suppress other forms of independent activism.

6

The Paradox of Islamist Politics

In light of the multiplicity of expressions of Islamism and Islamist politics, many scholars have embarked on reassessments of the significance and potential of Islamist movements. The variety of Islamist currents, strategies and modes of action are viewed as evidence both of the movements' weakness and strength. On the one hand, the proliferation of groups and organisations claiming Islamist credentials and agitating on the ground of some Islamic principle is read as a sign that the movements are flourishing. On the other, it is construed as a sign of disintegration and dilution. In this chapter, I assess the potential and limitations of Islamist movements and Islamism. I do so by engaging with the thesis that political Islam has failed and with the argument that the age of post-Islamism has arrived.

In an interesting study of contemporary Islamism entitled *The Failure of Political Islam*, Olivier Roy contends that Islamist movements have lost their revolutionary character, ceased to be radical and have become nothing more than groupings of run-of-the-mill neo-fundamentalists.[1] Roy finds evidence for this transformation in what he calls the lumpen-proletarianisation of the movements and in their social democratisation. By this he means that neo-fundamentalism, defined as morality-focused activism, has become prevalent within the movements. This is signalled in the Islamists' increased focus on the Shari'a rather than on new political forms, models for society or an agenda for a brighter future. Islamists have neither established a new society nor altered the political landscape in the Middle East. For Roy, the Islamists' failure is rooted in their tendency to equate virtue with the establishment of the good society. The failure thesis has gained popularity and has been taken up by analysts in the media writing on the current state of Islamist politics.[2]

In a more recent work, Roy extends his thesis to argue that we are witnessing the advent of post-Islamism.[3] He finds confirmation for this contention in the movements' shift towards Islamo-nationalist type ideology where the slogan of the *umma* (the community of Muslim believers) is internalised and where activities are confined within the bounds of the nation-state.[4] Further, post-Islamism is evidenced in the emergence of a social dynamic – re-Islamisation – that is expressed in Islamic terms but is autonomous from the state and no longer involves the takeover of state power. Roy argues that re-Islamisation operates only at the level of the social and does not entail the unification of religion and politics. As a result, a new secular space has emerged in Muslim countries. This conclusion, however, rests on a problematic conception of politics; one that limits 'the political' solely to activities that concern the state and government.

Roy stresses that there has not been a decline in religious observance and belief in Muslim societies. Hence, post-Islamism refers to the dissociation of the religious field from the political. This dissociation is marked by the individualisation of religious practices and their segregation in closed communitarian spaces. The end result is a differentiation between citizen and believer. Post-Islamism is also characterised by the development of practices that, while inscribed in the religious sphere, do not constitute either a critique or an alternative to the ideologies and strategies of the Islamists. These practices simply subvert, ignore or reappropriate the strategies of active Islamists. At the same time, while the road to the Islamic state is blocked, there is an ongoing redeployment of religious significations to other fields. Linked to this is a continual dilution of Islamism. Roy asserts that the deployment of Islamist idiom and grammar has come to articulate strategies such as notabilisation and corporatism that are not necessarily Islamic. In the political realm, the nation-state is reinforced through the incorporation of the Islamists into the political game.

I will assess these arguments on two different levels of analysis. The first addresses the geopolitical and strategic successes and failures of Islamists. The second probes the social and normative changes that Islamist movements have helped to bring about.

The Failure Thesis and the Geopolitics of Contemporary Islamism

I begin this review with an evaluation of the Islamists' success in achieving their declared goals and objectives. First, it is important to note that Islamists, like other political activists, change their strategic aims and may alter their overall direction in the course of their activism. As such, it is necessary to distinguish between the militants' declared goals and objectives of the 1970s and 1980s and those of the 1990s. In its earlier phase, Islamist politics took the form of militant action for the takeover of state power, the establishment of the Islamic state and the reconstitution of the *umma* – the transnational community of Muslims unbounded by the nation-state. On the whole, Islamist movements have not been able to deliver on these objectives.

Islamists have expended considerable effort to achieve the important goal of reconstituting the *umma*. Roy contends that this goal has been abandoned in favour of a nation-state-based *umma*. In the 1970s and 1980s, Islamists championed causes and undertook actions that transcended their own nation-states: taking up arms in support of the Afghan resistance, the Islamic Republic of Iran's policy of exporting the revolution and its policy of the *mu'allafa qulubuhum* (literally those whose hearts are won over).[5] However, by the 1990s, the export of the revolution was no longer a priority for the Iranian government. Whether from a standpoint of strategy or feasibility, the 'Islamist International' is not in the offing. The call in 1997 by two top militant leaders, Ayman al-Zawahri and Usama bin Laden, for the creation of an international Islamist front against the 'Crusaders' and Jews was rejected by other Islamist groups, in particular, al-Jama'a al-Islamiya in Egypt and its affiliate members abroad.[6] Divisions among the various factions of the Egyptian Jihad and Jama'a al-Islamiya on this and other issues have intensified. In fact, the emphasis on activism abroad favoured by Egyptian militant groups with bases in Afghanistan and Albania has proven ineffective especially in the face of continued containment by national and international policing and security authorities.

The call for an international Islamist front is tied up with some militant groups' confrontational stand vis-à-vis the West. The front is conceived as an agent of war against the USA. One of its strategies is to organise attacks against Western countries. This strategy does not seem to have found appeal among militants. This should be understood in relation to the shift in direction taken by some of the participants in Islamist movements at the national level in key countries such as Egypt. Indeed, the call to establish the front coincided with a peace initiative, directing all militants to cease violent activities, launched by Egyptian militants and supported by Shaykh 'Omar 'Abd-al-Rahman in his declarations from his prison cell in the USA. At the national level, the militancy that marked the movement's early phase was subject to review, and new terms of engagement were recommended. In Egypt, the peace initiative signalled a redirection. At the same time, more moderate groups such as the Muslim Brotherhood in Egypt, and Hamas in Algeria, have continued to pursue accommodationist policies.

A doctrinal review is clearly on the agenda of some activists who pursue engagement through legal channels. In Egypt a group of dissidents from the Muslim Brotherhood has renounced the idea that Islamists hold the absolute truth. From its perspective, the Islamists' interpretations of traditions are efforts of human understanding. Thus, questioning or opposing an Islamist claim does not constitute rejection of Islam, but simply a disagreement over interpretation. Further, this auto-critique rejects rulings that the existing government is un-Islamic and the present-day ruler a *kafir* (infidel). Accordingly, the practice of *takfir* (declaring someone a *kafir*) is rejected, and the invocation of the principle of *al-amr bil ma'ruf wa al-nahy 'an al-munkar* (enjoining good and forbidding evil) is abandoned.[7] In terms of strategy, this trend favours participation within the system and within the constitutional and legal framework of political action. Consequently, the Muslim Brotherhood dissidents who advocate it have set out to establish al-Wasat, a centrist party that does not insist on qualifying the existing state as un-Islamic.[8]

An important dimension of the redirection of Egyptian militant activism is the practice of doctrinal review and self-critique. It should be noted that the peace initiative was launched by imprisoned leaders of al-Jama'a who had authored and subscribed to the policy of *hatmiyat al-muwajaha* (the inevitability of confrontation). This same leadership later embarked on doctrinal rethinking, producing new documents that have been discussed in prison.[9] It is reported that the idea of rebelling against the ruler (*al-khuruj an al-hakim*) has been reinterpreted to mean opposing government through no-confidence votes and other tactics in parliament. The adoption of violence as a strategy has thus been subject to reassessment. A spokesperson of the Jama'a explained that violence did not achieve positive results and had proved ineffective as a strategy of action. He reasoned that because violence was not an end in itself, it had to be abandoned. Meanwhile, working with the people in the university and the neighbourhoods had proved to be an effective tool of Islamisation and mobilisation. As an extension of this repositioning on the part of al-Jama'a, militant members have, like the dissident Muslim Brothers, explored the idea of establishing a political party and, following the peace initiative, have discussed openly the possibility of seeking recognition for such a party. Gamal Sultan, a spokesperson for al-Jama'a, stated that the project of forming a party represented an alternative mode of activism, particularly since the Jama'a militants had chosen to respect their leadership's call to end violent operations.[10]

Other groups with histories of violent activism have also articulated an absolute rejection of violence. In Morocco, the group known as al-Islah wa al-Tajdid (Reform and Renewal) has renounced violence as a strategy. Al-Islah originated in the 1970s as a small nucleus of militants. Known then as Jama'a al-Islamiya , the group claimed to represent the only true Muslim society – a claim which justified the use of violence against non-members and, in particular, against its opponents. In later transmutations, the group repositioned itself on the political scene, entering into an alliance with a legal party (the MPDC or Mouvement Popularie Démocratique et Constitutionnel) and pursuing integration into the political sphere. The adoption of a strategy of participation through legal channels followed an autocritique and doctrinal change.[11] Taking up a conciliatory position from the regime and opting out of clandestine action, al-Islah condemned violence and redirected its efforts towards greater visibility and public presence. It participated in the 1997 elections and won a number of seats, becoming the legal Islamist opposition party.[12]

The tactical, ideological and doctrinal shifts discussed above should not be interpreted as an indication of the disintegration of Islamist movements. Shifts such as these in a group's position vis-à-vis the state may be understood to involve political processes found in other contestation movements. Charles Tilly has explained the dynamics behind such shifts and redirections in the following terms:

> ...the identities people deploy in political claim-making (including identities of religious affiliation, nationality and citizenship) consist of contingent relationships with other people rather than inbuilt personal traits; they therefore alter as political networks, opportunities and strategies shift.[13]

Islamism as a Socially and Politically Transformative Movement

A more complex picture is revealed when we turn from the geopolitics of Islamist movements to an analysis of the social and political dynamics of Islamism. In geo-strategic terms, Islamists, as Roy observes, have not changed the map of the Middle East. However, it is important to note that their impact at the societal level and in local politics remains significant. My points of contention with Roy's thesis revolve around how we read a number of developments: the Islamists' increasing focus on questions of morality; the Islamists' incorporation of strategies of action developed in spheres other than that of religion; and the relationship between Islamism and re-Islamisation. I will address each in turn.

Roy's assessment of Islamism's failure relates to the Islamists' political project. However, the evidence upon which he builds his case relates to the expansion of activities in the Islamists' religious project of constructing a puritanical society. While there are indeed puritanical tendencies in Islamist movements, exemplified by their moralising views and preoccupation with morality, it would be a mistake to equate them with a religious project. Rather, they should be understood in relation to the Islamists' strategies of insertion into the political field and in terms of modes of societal control involving power relations in the family, neighbourhood and so on. I will return to this point below. At this stage it is important to pause and consider the assumption that Islamism began as an expression of a revolutionary impulse that has faded over time. To this end, I take a detour into the politics of conservative Islamists in order to appreciate the constellation of actors involved in the articulation of Islamist politics and the role played by morality in the dynamic of their interaction.

If we look at the different components of the Islamist configurations in Egypt, Algeria, Morocco and Turkey, we find that a conservative trend was there from the beginning. Conservative Islamists developed as an important force and have long served as a counterbalance to the militants in Egypt, Algeria, Morocco and Turkey.[14] In Iran, where the labels 'conservative,' 'radical' and 'moderate' are more elusive and problematic, the conservatives have constituted a major force and enjoyed the upper hand at particular periods of time. In countries where they constitute a minority within the power hierarchy, the conservatives' political strategy is characterised by a willingness to work within the status quo. Their political project is formulated in cultural, social and moral terms without necessarily entailing a change in the form of government.

Conservative Islamists tend to pursue characteristic patterns of action. They commonly articulate patriarchal views on gender relations and the position of women in society, and their leaders often seek rapprochement, if not a *modus vivendi*, with the state. It is important to note, further, that the conservatives favour a market economy and have managed to become players in the context of liberalisation and privatisation. In spaces ranging from private schools and clinics to shopping malls and investment companies, they have found opportunities to construct an 'Islamic' economy. According to Deborah Harrold, Islamist discourse in Algeria even articulates a vision of a new economy fuelled by trafficking and speculation.[15]

In a number of cases, links have been forged between the militants and the conservatives. In fact, through the dynamic of their interaction there has emerged, as my discussion of conservative Islamism in Egypt (chapter two) demonstrates, a particular structuring of the political field. One outcome of this structuring is that conservative

Islamism operates as a counterbalance to the militants. In Algeria, the leader of Hamas was incorporated into the power elite with direct participation in government and representation in parliament. A temporary alliance between the political elite and the Nurcu leader served to counter the Refah challenge in Turkey. In Morocco, parallel patterns may be noted. The participation of the group al-Islah in the 1997 elections signalled the integration of the 'moderate' Islamists into the power structure and drew attention away from the more oppositional group, al-'Adl wa'l-Ihsan, and its leader Shaykh Yacine.[16]

Islamist interventions in the public sphere on the grounds of morality should be understood in relation to the dynamics of interaction involving the state and other political actors. The interplay among these forces is shaped by their relational position in the political field. The state continues to endeavour to control, regulate and manage religious authority and the production of religious knowledge, and, to this end, is aided by the representatives of official Islam, namely the state-affiliated *shaykhs*. The state may also call on independent or semi-independent religious authorities, while its opponents may call on the public authorities, from whose sympathy and support they sometimes benefit. This suggests a degree of fluidity in the positions of religious authority and in the alliances formed at moments of contestation and conflict. At the same time, there are rules to the contest that the actors try to either preserve or challenge. *Raison d'état* is an ultimate stake in the battle over the definition of orthodoxy and the enforcement of public morality.[17] For the state, re-Islamisation, the defence of Islam and claims to orthodoxy are admissible. But if its legitimacy is challenged by the Islamists' rhetoric, it will wield its repressive capacity against them.[18]

In view of the relations of power involving the various actors and the dynamics of their interaction, interventions in the public sphere on the grounds of morality constitute strategies of insertion into the political field within the scope of limitations on political critique and competition.[19] These limitations shape the politics of morality. Jean-Noël Ferrié argues that the rhetoric of morality allows for the formation of a public sphere that does not alter the non-competitive nature of the political field. It invokes the obligations of each and all, and it speaks of the collectivity, solidarity and the common interest in a manner which eschews questions of government such as representation. Thus, the morality-based critique articulated in the public sphere betrays and sustains the limitations characterising the political sphere. In Ferrié's words, 'il s'agit, dans tous les cas, de la constitution d'un sphère publique ou les questions collectives sont evaluées et discutées (et, bien sur, instrumentalisées) sans (pouvoir) donner lieu à une appropriation partisane.' However, the pursuit of morality as a modality of insertion into the public sphere embodies power practices, in particular dictating the norm. Islamist interventions raise questions about the basis of the frames of reference of public morality, the boundaries of the private and the public, and, ultimately, about who controls the public sphere.

Questions arise as to whether Islamist activities in the moral sphere are apolitical and whether the move to the social field represents an internalisation of crisis and a confirmation of the blocked road to state power. Roy's limited conception of the political, in which politics is equated with government and the state, leads him to answer in the affirmative. Yet, activism in the social sphere allows for a consolidation of Islamist power and for an Islamist contestation of state power. In the domain of social relations, the application of rules of conduct that are not state sanctioned confirms the Islamists' influence not merely as social actors but as political contestants. As such, Islamist movements are assessed differently when politics is understood in terms of practices of power and control and not only in terms of state and government.

At the forefront of Islamist activism in the area of morality are what some scholars call 'the small entrepreneurs of morality' – that is actors seeking to enforce norms in the public domain.[20] They do this, in part, by investing the public sphere with a particular mode of categorising objects and actions; one in which the predominant categories are those of *halal* and *haram* (licit and illicit) and the Islamic and the un-Islamic. There arises, in conjunction, a perpetual demand for producing the 'Islam position' on one issue or another. Rules concerning the mode of operation and the boundaries of activism – for instance, framing public rhetoric in terms of 'true Islam' – are also defined. Thus, Islamists and their opponents invoke Islamic history and call on symbols and signs from Islamic traditions. In the process, they rewrite and reconstruct these traditions. The state, the Islamists and the secularists all engage in producing the 'true Islam' position. This should not be understood to mean that religion dominates but rather that religious signs and symbols are transcribed and inserted into other domains. The operative logic is not that of religion in the abstract, but of the construction of religious traditions in their interaction with the social and the political.

Interpreting the political implications of Islamist interventions on the ground of morality and in the social sphere entails an understanding of politics in its broad sense In this vein, Asef Bayat has concluded that moderate Islamists in Egypt, namely the Muslim Brotherhood, through the occupation of social spaces and the creation of alternative institutional settings to that of the state, have succeeded in developing as a social movement.[21] The Brotherhood established Islamic charitable organisations as well as Islamic schools and clinics, all of which form the basis of a new society. Its success in building institutional networks gives the movement durability and creates channels through which social change may occur. In Gramscian terms, Bayat argues that this type of movement 'focuses on the gradual capture and possession of society by exerting moral and intellectual leadership over civil institutions and processes.'[22] In other words, as a social movement, moderate Islamism's aim is to capture society, not just the state. In this respect, it has succeeded. The factual basis of Bayat's contention may be disputed, but analytically he is right to broaden the understanding of the Islamist movements beyond the field of formal power.

Bayat incorporates the important dimension of hegemony into his analysis of Islamism, thus transcending the limitations found in Roy's thesis. Indeed, the Islamists' struggle for control and hegemony goes beyond the sphere of the state. Moreover, it is in relation to their role at the societal level that we should assess their potential and limitations. Not unlike Roy, my assessment entails normative considerations. Roy arrives at a verdict of failure because he associates early-phase Islamism with socialist ideals and the attendant revolutionary transformations, neither of which have been realised. My concern with the dimension of hegemony, meanwhile, incorporates the issues of domination and resistance, raising the question of the extent to which Islamist politics contribute to sustaining or transforming existing relations of power and domination.

A key dimension to Roy's assessment of failure is the deployment of Islamist idiom and grammar to express strategies and practices such as notabilisation (assignation of the status of notability) that are not necessarily Islamic. This assumes that there are practices that are inherently Islamic and practices that must be intrinsically un-Islamic. What this ignores, however, is that meanings are not given, but are invested socially and historically. Thus, if we consider historical examples of notabilisation on the grounds of religion we find that the processes involved are socially and historically conditioned. For example, the *sayyids* (religious notables) were constituted as notability not out of a religious injunction, but out of specific socio-historical processes of notabilisation. Yet *sayyids* were invested with all the trappings of a privileged social stratum through the deployment of religious referents (linkage to the Prophet, divine blessing, etc.). I want to suggest that the deployment of Islamist idiom and grammar to articulate any given practice and strategy represents an effort of Islamisation that is part of the struggle over signs and the fixing of meanings. The investment of religious signs in domains of social practices, and the redefinition of norms in reference to a constructed orthodoxy, constitute strategies of action and mobilisation.

The Islamists' ability to link up with societal forces, in particular the popular sector, depends on their success in appropriating existing practices and building on spaces of contestation. In a number of countries, the Islamist movement originated in universities with students as the main base of support. However, in later phases, Islamist activism became inscribed in the urban neighbourhoods. Islamists moved into spaces of cooperation and solidarity like the mosque, the sports association and the neighbourhood society. Islamist activism in popular neighbourhoods developed in relation to existing practices – for example, they stepped in to occupy the role of arbiters in disputes. Further, they appropriated the role of protecting women and safeguarding their chastity through the monitoring of gender relations and enforcement of mores governing sexuality. In this type of social outreach, Islamists deployed their own idiom to describe activities that are not necessarily Islamic. Translated into the Islamic idiom practices of arbitration were called *tahakum* (arbitration to God). Similarly, The Islamists' involvement in social services – formalised in terms of *zakat* (alms giving) – built on practices of self-help and mutual aid. In this light, the alternative polity is not to be achieved through a takeover of the state but through societal investment.

Islamist activism and modes of mobilisation in the new popular areas were shaped by the socio-spatial dimensions of the areas. They also articulated with modes of interaction and organisation in everyday life. In the case of the new neighbourhoods, the basis of their positioning was laid out in the process of community spatial implantation. In this process, practices of mutual aid, self-help and autonomy developed. These are resources that can provide a basis of activism and afford a particular positioning from the state. The fundamental argument here is that the strategies used by Islamists intertwine with existing forms of social organisation. The modalities of constituting power and authority are articulated internally, out of the structural arrangements and the strategic choices of the actors. Inasmuch as they are part of the social fabric, it is natural that many of the Islamists have adopted strategies that are the same as those pursued by the communities in which they have been active.[23] Further, the roles occupied by actors within the movement express network ties embedded in the social formation. For instance, in Algeria, the process of notabilisation, involving the construction of a religious identity, expressed relations of power that emerged with economic liberalisation and the accompanying societal disengagement from the state.[24] Here, entrepreneur-notables who emerged with the growth of informal economic activities, in particular those who were active in the *trabendo* networks affirmed their position as social and economic patrons by funding the construction of mosques. The mosques provided services that extended beyond the religious needs of the community, permitting the development of solidarity and social relations based on allegiance and clientelism. In both the Egyptian and Algerian cases, we find political processes that parallel those found in political claim-making, such as the deployment of identities that, in Tilly's terms, 'consist of contingent relationships with other people.' These identities alter with changes in political and social configurations.

The orientations of Islamism as a contestation movement have changed in the course of action and in relation to the setting. Changes in the basis of activism and expansion in the ranks of supporters have been accompanied by a degree of decentralisation in organisational leadership and overall direction. As Gehad Auda notes, the widening of the scope of participation results in a weakening of centralised control over activities and over the articulation of doctrinal matters.[25] It would appear that a localisation of efforts and the establishment of mini principalities or fiefdoms, as opposed to national republics, became the goal of some of the local emirs in certain urban neighbourhoods in Cairo and Algiers. As such, by becoming rooted at the local level, Islamist activism intertwines with local politics (e.g. engaging in historical feuds between local families or splintering into armed factions). The change in orientation may be explained in terms of opportunity structures and changing political configurations.

Finally, Roy interprets re-Islamisation as a sign of both the crisis and failure of Islamism. Re-Islamisation, as used by Roy, refers to the process by which signs and symbols having an Islamic referent are deployed in other spheres of social life. Understood in these terms, the ways in which re-Islamisation has unfolded are viewed as evidence of its banalisation. This banalisation is also taken as a sign of the weakening of the Islamic referent. Part of the argument is that religious signs and symbols are reinscribed in social fields to articulate personal and political strategies that are not necessarily Islamic. Beyond this, hybrid significations emerge, exemplified by the wearing of *hijab* with jeans or tights, or by belly dancers setting up charity meal stands during the month of Ramadan (known as *mawa'id al-rahman*, the Merciful's tables). As such, the insertion, into social life, of markers of re-Islamisation such as the *hijab* does not guarantee a genuine 'Islamicity.' This understanding of re-Islamisation assumes that some signs are more authentically Islamic than others, and that some allow for the dominance of religion better than others. In a caricatured manner, Islamists appear to come in a limited range of shapes and forms: bearded men in *jallabiya*, veiled women in unattractive dress. Hybrid significations signal Islamist failure and the victory of the global market with its mass communication weapons and homogenising commodities.

This understanding of re-Islamisation also assumes that there are inherently Islamic ideas that are part of a closed system. This assumption entails the idea of static and timeless beliefs and practices. However, if religion is conceived as social and historical, then it must also be understood to be subject to change and transformation. In its interaction with social institutions, it undergoes redefinition. Gregory Starrett's study of the changes in the Egyptian educational system underscores the process through which new understandings, uses and terms of religion come about.[26] With the establishment of the modern educational system in Egypt, the production of religious knowledge was transferred to a new sphere, and new authorities of religion emerged. According to Starrett, a new Islam was created by the integration of religious education into the public education system and by the functionalisation of religion as an accessory of public policy.[27] The education system, along with other public institutions, created the need for religious information and for the utilisation of religion as a frame of reference for certain things. This development involved 'the creation of certain compartments in a conceptual order that can only be filled by something, regardless of its specific content, labelled "Islamic."'[28] Within this perspective, Starrett makes the point that re-Islamisation preceded, and provided the ground for, Islamism.

A similar process is noted in the widening of the scope of the 'Islamic' through the transfer and transcription of signs and symbols from religion to other spheres. This process must be understood in terms of the interaction of religion with the social as entailed in the mobilisation of particular religious traditions and their reworking and re-insertion into new domains. The implications of this process are not one-sided, producing either a dilution of religion or its domination over other spheres. Rather, the movement of symbols and signs between the various spheres represents a reordering of the different systems of meaning. For example, veiling is a sign that is articulated within a number of sign systems and, accordingly, its meaning emerges in relation to the signs particular to these systems. By virtue of its articulation in the discourse and practices of Islamist activists, veiling carries particular significations such as adherence to religion, piety and the moral rectitude of the female wearer. However, in its positioning in the world of fashion, it acquires new meanings linked to changing aesthetic sensibilities. The new aesthetic sensibilities shaped by the design houses of the international fashion industry are represented in the fashion magazines that claim a puritanical identity.[29] Co-ordinated with other items of clothing, whether jeans or form-fitting dresses, the new veiling is integrated into international fashion.[30] This insertion of a sign from the field of religion into another system of signs anchored in the profane and determined by considerations derived from trends in marketing, design and taste, contributes to a recasting of the meaning of the veil. Ferrié contends that this recasting has to do more with an aesthetic ensemble designed to promote self-valorisation than with the propagation of a specific brand of feminine modesty.[31] At the same time, by virtue of its association with modesty in Islamist articulations, the veil activates other, perhaps un-intended, meanings. As Starrett points out, 'the act of veiling, whatever its individual motivation and spiritual consequences, is a ritual act that contributes to de-facto Islamisation of public space, altering the social and cultural universe in which subsequent perceptions arise and subsequent choices are made.'[32]

The multiplicity and indeterminacy of meaning extends to religious commodities. Shelved next to other consumer items, religious objects containing Qur'anic verses or transcriptions of the Prophet's sayings are market commodities first and foremost. As Starrett underlines, the religious sign is retrieved once the object leaves the shop.[33] Pursuing the social life of these same commodities, Ferrié points to their incorporation into the domain of decoration.[34] The multiplicity, ambiguity and hybridity of meanings should not be dealt with in terms of the genuine and the not-so-genuine. We may, and should, note innovations in practice. However, treating such innovations as *bida'* in the classical sense (innovation that equates with heresy or the abandonment of religion), implies taking sides in the struggle over what constitutes orthodoxy and ignoring the fact that innovation is a part of all living traditions.

In the articulation of religion with the social, actors are guided by a diversity of registers and a multiplicity of frames of reference. The question that arises is where do we situate Islamism in the diverse expressions of this articulation? The failure thesis proceeds from the view that Islamism is lacking if it does not represent a homogenous and homogenising register. Yet, the premise that the articulation of religion with the social expresses diversity in matters of identity construction and symbolism applies to Islamism. From this perspective, re-Islamisation does not necessarily mean that the rug is pulled out from under the Islamists' feet. Rather than emphasising the negative pull between Islamism and re-Islamisation, we should adopt a grid of reading that allows us to see the ways in which they overlap, converge and diverge.

Re-Islamisation, as one facet of the articulation of religion with the social, is not a uniform process. The social imbrication of religion means that it is shaped by the structural positions and the strategies of the actors. At the micro-level, this translates into a differentiated articulation of religion and diverse modes of everyday community life. Comprehending contemporary Islamist mobilisations does not consist merely in opposing quietism to militancy or distinguishing the political from the a-political in social mobilisations formed around Islam.[35] Rather than relying on these oppositions, we should, as Iman Farag suggests, identify the multiple levels of action and of identity formation co-existing within the same movement.[36]

Withering Islamism?

Before declaring the advent of post-Islamism, we should question the assumption that Islamism was ever coherent and homogeneous. As a political project aiming at establishing the Islamic state, Islamism involved a variety of actors pursuing different modes of action. In the course of their activism, many have repositioned themselves to take advantage of changing political opportunities or to adjust to new constraints. In the process, Islamist goals and objectives have been redefined. Further, the Islamist fact is cumulative: it does not vanish without a trace.

Recent developments in Iran illustrate the cumulative nature of Islamism. Both the Islamist feminist movement and the new theology of the reformists have developed in dialogue with those claiming divine authority. It is against this background that the rights of women in such matters as divorce and child custody have been articulated and won. Iranian women, having negotiated concrete gains from an Islamic government, saw little reason to regard the system as innately opposed to their interests. Surveying these changes and the shifts in the arguments and style of feminist writers, Ziba Mir-Hosseini points out that '[o]ne neglected and paradoxical outcome of the rise of political Islam in the 1970s has been to help create a space within which Muslim women can reconcile their faith with their feminism.'[37] In other words, the course of re-Islamisation itself is interlinked with the Islamist movements and the different positionings of the actors. Mir-Hosseini's view that 'feminist readings of the Shari'a became possible and even inevitable when Islam is no longer an oppositional discourse in national politics' provides further evidence for the argument.[38]

In conclusion, the fortunes of Islamism as a political movement are conditioned by the structures of opportunities, and by political configurations and contingent identities. In their interaction with the state, and other political and social actors, Islamists have adopted a multitude of strategies, ranging from outright confrontation and violent action to agitation in the public sphere to infiltration of societal spaces. Following doctrinal rethinking, some militant groups sought accommodation with the state. Their experience shows that by engaging in hands-on activist work in popular neighbourhoods, they have learned the informal language of politics spoken by the people. Islamism, as a process, and not just a project, is thus not static. Its relation to re-Islamisation should not be reduced to that of a contradictory impulse. The distinction between Islamism and re-Islamisation on the basis of the coherence of one and the fragmentation of the other, or in terms of the political nature of one and the depoliticised nature of the other, may only serve to cloud the fundamental issues at stake: those of domination and resistance. These are not exhausted in Islamism and re-Islamisation discourses and practices. Yet, these two interlinked forces have had much to do with the attempts by divergent social forces to either transform or preserve power relations in society. How they fare in this regard cannot be determined *a priori*. Rather, our assessment must be subject to contextual analysis, so that any outcome is contingent on opportunity structures, strategies of action and dynamics of interaction.

Notes

1: The Study of Islamism Revisited

1. The labels and classifications have been subject to much debate and disagreement among scholars. In particular, the term 'fundamentalism' has been the subject of dissertations dealing with its appropriateness for understanding dynamics in Muslim societies. See Bruce Laurence, 'Muslim Fundamentalist Movements: Reflections toward a New Approach,' in *The Islamic Impulse*, ed. Barbara Stowasser (London: Croom Helm, 1987), 15–36. In more recent works, the term has been recast in comparative studies treating communalist and political movements with a religious reference drawn from both monotheistic and non-monotheistic traditions. See Martin Marty and Scott Appleby, *Fundamentalism Observed* (Chicago: Chicago University Press, 1991).

2. In some ways, my usage of 'Islamist politics' parallels Dale Eickelman and James Piscatori's use of the term 'Muslim Politics' in their book *Muslim Politics*. Eickelman and Piscatori use 'Muslim politics' to refer to the process whereby signs and symbols derived from Islamic traditions are invoked in the political sphere. They recognise and stress that traditions are reworked and that they do not embody inherent or unchanging meanings. However, as used in their work, this process appears to be exhaustive of the political field and to be associated with anything Muslims do. Thus, Cairo urban networks of solidarity are subsumed under Muslim politics when they are better understood in terms of urban politics. Eickelman and Piscatori's *Muslim Politics* hinges on what they term the process of objectification. By

this they mean Muslims' coming to consciousness of their identity as Muslims and their reflection on that identity. Though they link this process to changes in forms of cultural production and structural social transformations, objectification is accorded heavy explanatory weight, rendering the analysis contingent on subjectivist developments – i.e. changes in Muslims' perceptions – rather than on structural or infrastructural conditions. See *Muslim Politics* (Princeton N.J. Princeton University Press, 1996).

3. Ferrié defines re-Islamisation as the declared desire to re-establish a moral order based on austerity. This moral order is a contemporary production seeking to organise social relations on the basis of the control of individual conduct. In this sense, Ferrié sees re-Islamisation as preceding Islamism and presenting a vocabulary that is used by both the partisans and adversaries of Islamism. Jean-Noël Ferrié, 'Les Paradoxes de la réislamisation en Égypte,' *Maghreb-Machrek* 151 (January–March 1996), 4.

4. The Weberian influence on this writing is significant. For an insightful discussion of Weber's views of Islam and its role in society see Bryan S. Turner, *Weber and Islam* (London: Routledge, 1974).

5. See Bobby S. Sayyid, *A Fundamental Fear* (London: Zed Books, 1997).

6. Bryan S. Turner, 'Orientalism and the Problem of Civil Society in Islam,' in his *Orientalism, Postmodernism and Globalism* (London: Routledge, 1994). See also Simon Bromley, *Rethinking Middle East Politics* (London: Polity Press, 1994).

7. I am merely sketching the main contours of the arguments here; they, are usually more complex than this. Of course this is a structuring framework for works adopting the master-narrative perspective such as those of John Esposito and John Voll examined below.

8. Ernest Gellner, *Muslim Society* (Cambridge: Cambridge University Press, 1981). For an excellent critique of Gellner's construction of a totalised Islam and a singular Muslim society see Sami Zubaida, 'Is There a Muslim Society?: Ernest Gellner's sociology of Islam,' *Economy and Society* 24, 2 (1995):151–88.

9. Bruce B. Laurence, *Defenders of God* (London: I.B. Tauris, 1990), 40–4, 229.

10. Sayyid, *A Fundamental Fear*, 120.

11. Several editions of these works have now been published. They have served as general introductory works and standard undergraduate textbooks for courses dealing with the politics of the Middle East and Muslim societies. References in my discussion are to Esposito, *Islam and Politics*, 3rd edition (Syracuse: Syracuse University Press, 1991); Voll, *Islam: Continuity*

and Change in the Modern World, 2nd edition (Syracuse: Syracuse University Press, 1994).

12. Other works pursuing similar lines of investigation and analysis include Hrair R. Dekmejian, *Islam in Revolution: Fundamentalism in the Arab World* (Syracuse: Syracuse University Press, 1985); William Shepard, 'Islam and Ideology: Towards a Typology,' *International Journal of Middle East Studies* 19 (1987): 307–36; Yvonne Haddad, *Contemporary Islam and the Challenge of History* (Albany, New York: State University of New York Press, 1982). Although Haddad does not provide the total Islamic history panorama, her perspective on the role of 'Islam' in contemporary Middle Eastern societies has strong parallels with that of Esposito and Voll. Both Esposito and Voll have elaborated on their positions in later works. See, in particular John Obert Voll, 'The Revivalist Heritage,' in *The Contemporary Islamic Revival: A Critical Survey and Bibliography*, ed. Yvonne Haddad, John Obert Voll and John L. Esposito (New York: Greenwood Press, 1991), 23–36, and John L. Esposito, 'Trailblazers of the Islamic Resurgence,' in ibid., 37–56.

13. I gained this insight through an exchange with Professor Muhammad Ayub during a BRISMES conference.

14. Historical studies of social life in Muslim societies during the medieval and early modern periods show us that understandings and practices of moral purity were subject to contestation. See Abd al-Karim Rafeq, 'Public Morality in 18th-Century Ottoman Damascus,' *Revue d'études de Monde Musulman et de la Méditerranée* 55–56 (1990), 180–96. See also, Hoda Lutfi, 'Manners and Customs of Fourteenth-Century Cairene Women: Female Anarchy versus Shar'i Order in Muslim Prescriptive Treaties,' in *Women in Islamic Middle Eastern History*, ed. Nikki R. Keddie and Beth Baron (New Haven: Yale University Press), 99–121.

15. This tautological formulation is the subject of deconstruction by Aziz Al-Azmeh. In his critique of the Orientalist imagination, Al-Azmeh notes that 'no Islamic subject matter can therefore exist without Islam in its full tautological power, in which things are Islamic because they are constituted by Islam, because it is in their nature to be Islamic.' 'The Articulation of Orientalism,' in *Orientalism, Islam and Islamists*, ed. Asaf Hussein, Robert Olson and Jamil Qureshi (Vermont: Amana Books, 1984), 104.

16. Al-Azmeh, 'The Articulation of Orientalism,' 102.

17. Voll, 'The Revivalist Heritage,' 24–7.

18. Eric Davis, 'The Concept of Revival,' in *The Islamic Impulse*, ed. Barbara Stowasser (London: Croom Helm, 1987), 37–58.

19. Saad Eddin Ibrahim, 'Anatomy of Egypt's Militant Islamic Groups:

180   RETHINKING ISLAMIST POLITICS

Methodological Note and Preliminary Findings,' *International Journal of Middle East Studies* 18 (1980), 448.

20. Charles Tilly, 'Useless Durkheim,' in his *As Sociology Meets History* (New York, Academic Press, 1981).

21. Ibid., 106

22. Charles Tilly, *Big Structures, Large Processes, Huge Comparisons* (New York: Russel Sage Foundation, 1984), 53.

23. See Mark Tessler, 'The Origins of Popular Support for Islamist Movements: A Political Economy Analysis,' In *Islam, Democracy and the State in North Africa*, ed. John P. Entelis (Indianapolis: Indiana University Press, 1997), 93–126.

24. 'Ideology, Social Class and Islamic Radicalism in Modern Egypt,' in *From Nationalism to Revolutionary Islam*, ed. Said Amir Arjomand (Albany: State University of New York, Press, 1984), 134–47.

25. Ibid., 139–40.

26. Ibid., 147.

27. Michael Fischer, 'The Revolt of the Petite Bourgeoisie,' *Deadlus* (Winter 1982): 101–22.

28. Nazih Ayubi, *Political Islam*, (London: Routledge, 1991), 179.

29. Lisa Anderson, 'Fulfilling Prophecies: State Policy and Islamist Radicalism,' in *Political Islam: Revolution, Radicalism or Reform*, ed. John Esposito, (Boulder, Colorado: Lynne Reinner, 1997), 17–31.

30. Ibid., 20.

31. Ibid., 24.

32. Ibid., 23.

33. Gregory Starrett, *Putting Islam to Work: Education, Politics and Religious Transformation in Egypt* (Los Angeles: University of California Press, 1998).

34. Peter Gran, *The Islamic Roots of Capitalism*: Egypt, 1760–1840 (Cairo: American University in Cairo Press, 1999).

35. Jean-Noël Ferrié, 'Remarques sur l'islamisation des espaces modernes au Caire,' *Maghreb-Machrek* 151 (Jan-March 1996): 6–12. See also, Gregory Starrett, 'The Political Economy of Religious Commodities in Cairo,' *American Anthropologist* 97, 1 (Spring 1995): 51–68.

36. Zubaida, 'Is there a Muslim Society?,' 153.

37. Ibid., 153

38. Sami Zubaida, *Islam, the People and the State* (London: I.B. Tauris, 1993), 123.

39. Talal Asad, *The Idea of an Anthropology of Islam*, Center for Con-

temporary Arab Studies, Occasional Paper Series (Washington D.C: Center for Contemporary Arab Studies, 1985).

40. Eickelman and Piscatori's emphasis on contest over meaning and authority points to the power play at stake in producing and defining traditions. However, they pay insufficient attention to questions of domination and resistance embodied in the contention over symbolic power. This downplaying of domination and resistance is linked to the fact that they gloss over structural factors at the local level (e.g. local forms of social organisation and Islamist modes of interaction with them).

41. Asad, *The Idea of an Anthropology of Islam*.

42. Jean-Noël Ferrié, 'Solidarité islamique sans consensus en Égypte: un cadre d'analyse,' *Les Annales de l'autre Islam* 4 (1997), 77.

43. Ibid., See also Beaudoin Dupret, 'Représentations de répertoires juridiques en Égypte: limites d'un consensus,' *Maghreb-Machrek* 151 (January-March 1996): 32–40.

44. Ibid.

45. I developed this point following an exchange with Beaudoin Dupret.

46. See Nabil 'Abd al-Fatah and Diya' Rashwan, ed., *Taqrir al-Hala al-Dinniya fi Misr 1996* [Report on the Religious Condition in Egypt, 1996] (Cairo: al-Ahram Center for Strategic Studies, 1997).

47. Nadia Abu Zahra, *The Pure and the Powerful: Comparative Studies in Contemporary Muslim Societies* (Reading: Ithaca Press, 1997).

48. Jean Noël Ferrié, 'Prier pour disposer de soi: Le sens et la fonction de la prière de demande dans l'Islam marocain actuel,' *Annuaire de l'Afrique du Nord* XXXIII (1994), 123–4.

49. Ibid., 125.

50. Nikki Keddie, 'The New Religious Politics: Where, When and Why Do 'Fundamentalisms' Appear?' *Comparative Studies in Society and History* 40 (1998), 702.

51. See Jean-Noël Ferrié, 'Vers une anthropologie deconstructiviste des sociétés musulmanes du Maghreb,' *Peuples méditérranéens* 54–55 (January-June 1991): 229–45.

52. Ibid.

53. Ferrié, 'Prier pour disposer de soi.'

54. Ibid., 125.

55. Ibid.

56. These questions are formulated in light of the issues raised by Ferrié, 'Prier pour disposer de soi,' 116–17.

57. Beaudoin Dupret and Jean-Noël Ferrié, 'Participer au pouvoir, c'est

édicter la norme: Sur l'affaire Abu Zayd (Égypte, 1992–1996),' *Revue française de science politique* 47, 6 (1997): 762–75.

58. Olivier Roy, *The Failure of Political Islam*, tr. Carol Volk (Cambridge, Massachusetts: Harvard University Press, 1994).

59. Olivier Roy and Patrick Haenni ed., *Le Post-islamisme, Revue du Monde musulman et de la Méditerranée* 85/86 (1999).

60. See Olivier Roy 'Le Post-Islamisme,' in ibid., 12–30, and Patrick Haenni 'Ils n'en ont pas finis avec l'Orient: de quelques islamisations non islamistes,' in ibid., 121–47.

61. Edmund Burke, III, 'Islam and Social Movements: Methodological Reflections,' in *Islam, Politics and Social Movements*, ed. Edmund Burke III and Ira Lapidus (Los Angeles: University of California Press, 1988), 28.

62. Zubaida, *Islam, the People and the State*, 123.

63. The points made in this discussion draw on my analysis in subsequent chapters, especially chapters four and five.

64. Zubaida, *Islam, the People and the State*, 146.

2: Confronting the Other

1. Al-Ahrar (the Liberal Party) emerged out of one of the three platforms of the Arab Socialist Union formed at the beginning of President Sadat's political liberalisation experiment. The leader of the party, Mustafa Kamal Murad, was a second-rank free officer. The party proclaims a liberal identity. However, it articulates a conservative Islamist line in reference to morality and the social sphere. In 1987, it entered an election alliance with the al-'Amal (Labour) Party and the Muslim Brotherhood and was allocated 20 per cent of the seats won. Among its better-known figures were Shaykh Salah Abu Isma'il and Yusuf al-Badri. See Mona Makram Ebeid, 'Le Rôle de l'opposition officielle en Égypte,' *Maghreb-Machrek* 119 (February-March 1988): 5–24.

2. This partly corresponds to Yahya Sadowski's distinction between radicals and legalists. Yahya Sadowski, 'Egypt's Islamic Movement: A New Political and Economic Force,' *Middle East Insight* 25 (1987): 37–45.

3. For an analysis of the radical Islamist discourse in Egypt, see Salwa Ismail, *Radical Islamism in Egypt: Discursive Struggle*, Montreal Studies on the Contemporary Arab World (Montreal: Inter-University Consortium for Arab Studies, 1994); also Hamied Ansari, 'The Islamic Militants in Egyptian Politics,' *International Journal of Middle East Studies* 16 (1984): 123–44.

4. On petro-Islam, or the Islam of riches, see Fu'ad Zakariyya, *Al-Haqiqa*

wa al-Wahm fi al-Haraka al-Islamiya al-Mu'asira [Truth and Illusion in the Contemporary Islamist Movement] (Cairo: Dar al-Fikr lil-Dirasat, 1986).

5. A thoughtful analysis of the dynamics of interaction among these various players is provided by Alain Roussillon in 'Entre al-Jihad et al-Rayyan: Phenomenologie de l'islamisme égyptien,' *Maghreb-Machrek* 127 (January–March 1990): 17–50.

6. This is an informal group of lawyers active in initiating court cases in the name of safeguarding morality and religious values.

7. Differences on matters of doctrinal interpretations have come to the fore recently and revolved around the position of Copts in Egypt. Mustafa Mashhur, the Spiritual Guide of the Muslim Brotherhood, classifies Copts as *dhimmiyyun* (protected subjects) who must pay the *jizya* (tribute, close in nature to a poll tax) and be excluded from military service. See *al-Ahram Weekly*, 3 April 1997. Other figures with links to the movement critiqued this view, asserting that Copts are citizens with full national rights; Muhammad Salim al-'Awwa, 'Bal al-Jizya fi Dhimat al-Tarikh' [But Jizya is in the Realm of History], *al-Wafd*, 18 April 1997. For other examples of responses to Mashhur, see *al-Musawwar*, 25 April 1997.

8. On the role of the Islamist current in the syndicates, see Mustapha K. al-Sayyid,' Le Syndicat des ingenieurs et le courant islamique,' *Maghreb-Machrek* 146 (October-December 1995): 27–39.

9. On Islamic PVOs, see Sarah Ben Nafissa, 'Le Mouvement associatif égyptien et l'Islam: Elements d'une problématique,' *Maghreb-Machrek* 135 (January–March 1992): 19–36. On the social and charitable organisations affiliated with the Brotherhood and the Jihad, see Hala Mustafa, *al-Nizam al-Siyasi wa al-Mu'arada al-Islamiya fi Misr* [The Political System and the Religious Opposition in Egypt] (Cairo: Dar al-Mahrusa, 1996).

10. In 1988 and 1989, in clashes with the Jihad militants, the police laid siege to the Adam mosque in 'Ayn Shams.

11. In the censorship campaign waged against writers and artists, popular preachers such as 'Umar 'Abd al-Kafi used Friday prayer sermons to issue *fatawi* (rulings) condemning various scholarly and artistic works.

12. Emmanuel Sivan, *Radical Islam: Medieval Theology and Modern Politics* (New Haven: Yale University Press, 1985).

13. Ibid., 137.

14. On the development of this concept of ideology, see John B. Thompson, *Studies in the Theory of Ideology* (Los Angeles: University of California Press, 1985), particularly chap. 3.

15. Here I am drawing on Talal Asad's notion of discursive tradition. Asad defines an Islamic discursive tradition as 'simply a tradition of Muslim dis-

courses that addresses itself to conceptions of the past and future, with reference to a particular present.' Talal Asad, *The Idea of an Anthropology of Islam* (Washington, D.C.: Centre for Contemporary Arab Studies, 1986), 14.

16. For a critique of the revivalist explanation, see Eric Davis, 'The Concept of Revival and the Study of Islam and Politics,' in *The Islamic Impulse*, ed. Barbara F. Stowasser (London: Croom Helm, 1987), 37–58.

17. Social violence has been used in attempts to enforce the *hijab* (veil) and to prohibit the sale of alcohol. This comes under the rubric of *al-amr bil ma'ruf wa al-nahy 'an al-munkar* (enjoining good and forbidding evil).

18. Despite the wide-scale arrests that followed the assassination of President Sadat by Jihad members, the group was reconstituted several times under different names, such as the Vanguard of Conquest. Al-Jama'a al-Islamiya is made up of numerous cells active on university campuses. In the last two years, out of seventeen trials of Islamist groups, fifteen involved cells of al-Jama'a. The nature of the structure of this group and the links between the various cells are not clearly established. See 'Abd al-Fatah and Rashwan, ed., *Taqrir al-Hala al-Dinniya*.

19. On state violence, see Ahmed Abdalla, 'Egypt's. Islamists and the State: From Complicity to Confrontation,' *Middle East Report* 183 (July–August 1993): 28–31; see also, The Egyptian Organisation for Human Rights, *Difa 'an Huquq al-Insan* [In Defense of Human Rights] (Cairo: al-Munazama al-Misriya li-Huquq al-Insan, 1997). For an overview of the clashes between the state and the militants over the last two years, see 'Abd al-Fatah and Rashwan, ed., *Taqrir al-Hala al-Dinniya*.

20. For an analysis of the mufti's report, see Ansari, 'Islamic Militants,' and Ismail, *Radical Islamism in Egypt*.

21. The positioning of the state in relation to the cultural politics of the Islamists is dealt with in chapter three. On al-Azhar's expanding role in censorship, see, The Egyptian Organisation for Human Rights, *Hurriyat al-Ra'y wa al-'Aqida: Qiyud wa Ishkaliyat, Riqabat al-Azhar 'ala al-Musannafat al-Fanniya* [Freedom of Thought and Belief: Constraints and Problems; al-Azhar's Censorship of Artistic Productions] (Cairo: al-Munazama al-Misriya li-Huquq al-Insan, 1994).

22. Eric Davis, 'Ideology, Social Class and Islamic Radicalism,' in *From Nationalism to Revolutionary Islam*, ed. Said Amir Arjomand (Albany: State University of New York Press, 1984), 133–47.

23. William Shepard, 'Islam and Ideology: Towards a Typology,' *International Journal of Middle East Studies* 19 (1987): 307–36.

24. Hrair Dekmejian, 'Islamic Revival, Catalysts, Categories and Conse-

quences,' in *The Politics of Islamic Revivalism*, ed. Shireen Hunter (Bloomington: Indiana University Press, 1988), 3–22.

25. Works by state-affiliated and independent shaykhs as well as selected reports on economic and financial affairs from the official press make up the corpus of texts used to study the discourses on morals, rituals, and usury.

26. The texts cover the period 1978 to 1989 and are representative of conservative Islamist writings. Jindi's early writings fall within the field of literary criticism. His later works, beginning in the 1960s: deal with issues surrounding Arab and Islamic civilisation, Islam's relation to the West, and contemporary Arab intellectual writings. For a critical examination of Jindi's writings as representative of contemporary Islamist thought, see Muhammad Arkun, *Tarikhiya t al-Fikr al-'Arabi al-Islami* [The Historicity of Arab Islamic Thought] (Beirut: Markaz al-Inma' al-Qawmi, 1987).

27. The method used for analysing the writings under study benefits from certain concepts developed in the field of discourse analysis, particularly those of A.J. Greimas. In particular, A.J. Greimas, *On Meaning: Selected Writings in Semiotic Theory*, trans. Paul J. Perron and Frank H. Collins (Minneapolis: University of Minnesota Press, 1987); and A.J. Greimas, *The Social Sciences: A Semiotic View*, trans. Paul Perron and Frank H. Collins (Minneapolis: University of Minnesota Press, 1990). Some of the technical terminology common to this methodology, and to the presentation of its findings, has been omitted or modified in this text. However, the meanings, concepts, and themes found in the conservative Islamist discourse, as well as the elements identified as being part of its organisation and structure, are distilled through detailed textual analysis.

28. Anwar al-Jindi, *Shubuhat al-Taghrib* [The Suspect Claims of Westernisation] (Beirut: al-Maktab al-Islami, 1978), 15.

29. 'Al-Islam la Yatalawwan abdan … Ya Duktur' (Islam Does not Change Colors … O Doctor), *al-Nur*, 30 March 1988.

30. al-Jindi, *Shubuhat*, 17. It is interesting to compare these formulations with the following lament of a prominent member of the Muslim Brotherhood organisation: 'Marxism and secularism are being propagated openly and publicly. The contemporary 'Crusaders' plan and act to infiltrate everywhere without fear; the media, in addition to clubs and theatres, spread obscenities and misconduct.' Yusuf al-Qaradawi, *Islamic Awakening Between Rejection and Extremism* (Washington, D.C.: The American Trust Publication, n.d.).

31. 'Hamalat Waqiha Min Wara' al-Hudud' [Rude Campaigns from Across the Border], *al-Nur*, 14 December 1988.

32. 'Al-Fikr al-Dini al-Mustanir' [Enlightened Islamic Thought], *al-Mukhtar al-Islami*, 73 (February 1989): 72–7.

33. 'Hamalat Waqiha,' *al-Nur*.

34. 'Al-Shaykh al-Sha'rawi Yuwajih Du'at al-'Ilmaniya ' [Shaykh al-Sha'rawi Confronts the Preachers of Secularism], *al-Ahram*, 12 January 1986.

35. 'Mustaqbal al-Tabshir fi Misr wa al-Amal fi Makka' [The Future of Proselytisation is in Egypt and the Hope is in Mecca], *al-Nur*, 22 June 1988.

36. al-Jindi, *Shubuhat*

37. 'Mustaqbal al-Tabshir fi Misr,' *al-Nur*.

38. Anwar al-Jindi, 'Marahil al-Mukhattat al-Marsum li-Iqtiham al-Islam Min al-Kharij' [The Stages of the Planned Plot to Invade Islam from the Outside], *al-Nur*, 3 November 1988.

39. 'Mustaqbal al-Tabshir fi Misr,' *al-Nur*.

40. 'Ulama al-Islam Yuhaddidun Mafhum wa Mazahir wa 'Ilaj al-Tatarruf ' [The Ulama of Islam Define the Concept, Symptoms, and Remedy of Extremism], *al-Nur*, 2 March 1988.

41. Al-Jindi, 'Marahil.'

42. 'Hamalat Waqiha,' *al-Nur*.

43. 'Mustaqbal al-Tabshir fi Misr,' *al-Nur*.

44. Al-Jindi, *Shubuhat*, 16–17.

45. 'Al-Shaykh al-Sha'rawi Yuwajih Du'at al-'Ilmaniya ' [Shaykh al-Sha'rawi Confronts the Preachers of Secularism], *al-Ahram*, 12 December 1986.

46. Al-Jindi, *Shubuhat*, 120.

47. The term for 'instinct' used in the original Arabic text is '*ghariza*.' It is argued that 'religiosity is an instinct' *(al-tadayyun ghariza)*. 'Al-Islam la Yatalawwan,' *al-Nur*, 30 March 1988.

48. Al-Jindi, *Shubuhat*, 107.

49. Anwar al-Jindi, *Suqut al-'Ilmaniya* [The Collapse of Secularism] (Beirut: Dar al-Kitab al-Lubnani, 1980), 175.

50. Fu'ad Zakariyya, 'al-Muslim al-Mu'asir wa al-Bahth 'an al-Yaqin' [The Contemporary Muslim and the Search for Certainty], in *al-Haqiqa wa al-Wahm fi al-Haraka al-Islamiya al-Mu'asira* (The Truth and the Illusion in the Contemporary Islamic Movement) (Cairo: Dar al-Fikr lil-Dirasat, 1986), 5–20:

51. Muhammad 'Abid al-Jabiri, *al-Khitab al-'Arabi al-Mu'asir* [On Contemporary Arab Discourse] (Beirut: al-Tali'ah, 1982).

52. Sayyid Qutb, *Ma'rakat al-Islam wa al-Ra'smaliya* [The Battle of Islam and Capitalism] (Cairo: Dar al-Shuruq, 1987), 101–2.

53. Ibid.

54. 'Hamalat Waqiha,' *al-Nur.*

55. Ibid.

56. Al-Jindi, 'Marahil.'

57. Anwar al-Jindi, 'al-Tayyar al-Islami Haqiqa Thabita' [The Islamic Current is a Rooted Fact] *al-I'tisam,* 1 December 1988.

58. 'Al-Islam la Yatalawwan,' *al-Nur.*

59. Vladimir Propp's analysis of Russian folk tales posited the presence of underlying narrative structures organised in terms of a basic trajectory: the quest by the subject or hero for the realisation of an object of value. Greimas's model of narrative as the organising principle of discourse is inspired by the Proppian schema.

60. Al-Jindi, 'Marahil.'

61. Al-Jindi, *Suqut,* 136.

62. 'Hamalat Waqiha,' *al-Nur.*

63. Ibid.

64. Al-Jindi, 'al-Tayyar al-Islami.'

65. 'Al-Islam la Yatalawwan,' *al-Nur.*

66. Discursive organisation refers to the communication process, or how the message is communicated to a locutee. In this process, the sender of the message makes use of and manipulates discursive tools to ensure the good reception of the message.

67. 'Hamalat Waqiha,' *al-Nur.*

68. 'Mustaqbal al-Tabshir fi Misr,' *al-Nur.*

69. Al-Jindi, 'al-Tayyar al-Islami.'

70. Ibid.

71. In debates with the secularists, thinkers associated with the Muslim Brotherhood, such as Yusuf al-Qaradawi and Muhammad al-Ghazali, have used this strategy of argumentation. See Nancy E. Gallagher, 'Islam vs. Secularism in Cairo: An Account of the Dar al-Hikma Debate,' *Middle Eastern Studies* 25, 2 (April 1989): 208–15.

72. Al-Jindi, 'al-Tayyar al-Islami.'

73. 'Al-Shaykh al-Sha'rawi,' *al-Ahram.*

74. Ibid.

75. Ibid.

76. Ibid.

77. Al-Jindi, 'Marahil.'

78. 'Wa Islamah!' (o Islam!), *al-Ahrar,* 24 August 1987.

79. Al-Jindi, 'al-Tayyar al-Islami.'

80. Albert Hourani, *Arabic Thought in the Liberal Age: 1798–1939* (London: Oxford University Press, 1976), 144.

81. lbid., 138–44.

82. This position was expressed by nationalists such as Ahmad Lutfi al-Sayyid, who voiced concern that Egypt pay its debts in order to regain national independence. See Hourani, *Arabic Thought*, 180.

83. Al-Jindi, *Shubuhat*.

84. Shaykh Kishk is an al-Azhar graduate who studied *usul al-din* (the fundamentals of religion). He was an *imam* (leader of the prayer) at a government mosque and a preacher in 'Ayn al-Hayat mosque. He was arrested in 1966. His recorded sermons gained wide distribution in the early 1970s. He also contributed a column in the government-sponsored *al-Liwa' al-Islami*. See Gilles Kepel, *The Prophet and the Pharaoh: Muslim Extremism in Egypt* (London: al-Saqi Books, 1985), 174–6. See also Johannes G. Jansen, *The Neglected Duty* (New York: Macmillan Publishing Company, 1986), chap. 4.

85. Shaykh Sha'rawi is recognised as the star of television preachers. He is an al-Azhar graduate of no scholarly distinction. He worked as a religious teacher in the state educational system. In 1976, he was appointed minister of religious endowments by Sadat. Prior to this, he had spent some time teaching in Saudi Arabia. Shaykh Sha'rawi is a central figure by virtue of the multiple positions he occupies. He is a popular preacher whose Friday sermons are televised. He has worked as a consultant to the Islamic Societies for the Placement of Funds. In addition, he has been engaged in various attempts to broker peace between the government and the militant Islamists. For a critical reading of Sha'rawi's discourse and his rise to prominence, see Zakariyya, *al-Haqiqa wa al-Wahm*. See also Hava Lazarus-Yafeh, 'Muhammad Mutawalli al-Sha'rawi – A Portrait of a Contemporary 'Alim in Egypt,' in *Islam, Nationalism and Radicalism in Egypt and the Sudan*, ed. Gabriel R. Warburg and Uri M. Kupferschmidt (New York: Praeger, 1983), 281–97, and Jansen, *The Neglected Duty*, chap. 5.

86. 'Abd al-Kafi belongs to the younger generation of preachers who have gained a large following. His sermons are said to be behind the decision of many middle-class women to don the veil. He is also known for *a fatwa* stipulating that Muslims should not be the first to greet non-Muslims.

87. Zakariyya, ''al-Muslim al-Mu'asir.'

88. Court proceedings initiated by the head of a Sufi order sought to ban the film from Egyptian cinemas. An earlier version of the screenplay had been deemed 'blasphemous' in an al-Azhar ruling. In addition, conservative Islamist figures such as Yusuf al-Badri have been involved in initiating court cases against movie billboards charging theatre owners with transgression against the moral code.

89. Intervention carried out in the name of the public good.

90. In March 1993, Abu Zayd's candidacy for promotion to professor in the Arabic Language department of Cairo University's Faculty of Arts was denied. This decision was based on an apostasy charge made against his writings in the report of Shaykh 'Abd al-Sabur Shahin, a member of the promotion committee. Shaykh Shahin used the pulpit of 'Amr ibn al-'As mosque, where he is the Friday preacher, to denounce Abu Zayd and his works. The 'offensive' works include a semiotic study of the Qur'anic text and a critique of contemporary Islamist discourses. The court case seeking the annulment of his marriage was brought by the Islamist lawyer Muhammad Samida Abu Samad.

91. one should keep in mind the role of the rector of al-Azhar in influencing the direction of the institution. Under the late Shaykh Jad al-Haq, al-Azhar was more aligned with the conservatives and came into conflict with the mufti, Shaykh Sayyid Tantawi, who was considered a liberal figure. Following the death of Shaykh Jad al-Haq, Shaykh Tantawi succeeded to the position of rector of al-Azhar. Conservatives within al-Azhar have organised in the form of the Ulema of al-Azhar Front, issuing statements denouncing the International Conference on Population and Development (ICPD), held in Cairo in September 1994. The text of the statement appeared in *al-Wafd*, 7 August 1994. On al-Azhar's position on the ICPD, see Donna Lee Brown, 'Abortion, Islam and the 1994 Cairo Population Conference,' *International Journal of Middle East Studies* 29 (1997): 161–84. The front has been active in declaring liberal and secular intellectuals as infidels. The latest target of this charge is the Egyptian thinker Hasan Hanafi; Richard Engel, 'Apostate Ruling Endangers Professor,' *Middle East Times*, 11 May 1997.

92. See the text of the ruling; *Mahkamat Isti'naf al-Qahira, al-Da'ira 14, Isti'naf 278*, 1995 (Cairo Court of Appeal, District 14, Appeal Case 278, 1995).

93. Islamic authority figures from the 'moderate' camp were party to *takfir*. For example, at the trial of the assassin of Faraj Fuda, Shaykh Muhammad al-Ghazali, a prominent Islamic figure identified with the Muslim Brotherhood, testified that it was permissible for a Muslim to apply *hadd al-ridda* (the ordinance of apostasy) to an apostate.

94. Mustafa Ali Ahmad, 'Les intérêts bancaires sont illicites,' *al-Ahram al-Iqtisadi*, 2 June 1986, in *Islam et déregulation financière*, ed. and tr. Jean François Rycx (Cairo: CEDEJ, 1988), 60–7.

95. Ibid., 61.

96. On the activities of the Islamic banks and companies, see Nazih Ayubi, *Political Islam* (London: Routledge, 1991), 178–95.

97. On the links between the religious establishment and the ISPF, see 'Abd al-Qadir Shuhayb, *al-Ikhtiraq: Qisat Sharikat Tawzif al-Amwal* [The Infiltration: The Story of the Islamic Societies for the Placement of Funds] (Cairo: Dar Sina, 1989).

98. 'Les Banques islamiques et les sociétés islamiques de placement sont-elles une reaction de l'Islam des riches ou une reaction de l'Islam politique?' *al-Ahram al-Iqtisadi*, 12 May 1986, in *Islam et déregulation financière*, 92–3.

99. Fathi Mohammed Tawfik, 'C'est leur succes qui attire des attaques contre les investissements islamiques,' *Middle East Times*, 23–29 November 1986, in *Islam et deregulation financière*, 227.

100. John Frow, 'Discourse and Power,' *Economy and Society* 14 (May 1985): 204.

101. For more on these, see Muhammad Nur al-Din, 'Tatawwur Ra's al-Mal al-Masrafi fi Misr' [The Development of Finance Capital in Egypt], *Qadaya Fikriya* (August-October 1986), 136–64; Malak Zalouk, *Power, Class and Foreign Capital in Egypt* (London: Zed Books, 1989).

102. This idea is drawn from Frow, 'Discourse and Power.'

103. 'Taqrir Mufti al-Jumhuriya 'an Kitab al-Farida al-Gha'iba' [The Mufti's Report on the Book 'The Missing Precept'], appendix in Ni'mat Junayna, *Tanzim al-Jihad: Hal Huwa al-Hal al-Badil fi Misr* [The Jihad Organisation: Is it the Alternative in Egypt?] (Cairo: Dar al-Hurriya , 1988).

104. 'Ba'd Musalsal al-Sidam bayn al-Shurta wa al-Jama'a al-Islamiya ' [After the Episode of Confrontation between the Police and the Islamic Jama'a], *al-Nur*, 18 January 1989; 'Kalafu Anfusahum bi-Tatbiq Hudud Allah wa Jaladu al-Nas fi al-Shawari'' [They Abrogated the Right of Applying the Religious Ordinances and They Flogged the People in the Streets], *al-Ahrar*, 26 December 1988.

105. According to Alain Roussillon, Egypt has witnessed a rearrangement of the political scene, with new lines of division between the secularists and the Islamists replacing the left/right division. Alain Roussillon, 'al-Jama'at al-Islamiya fi al-Siyasa al-Misriya ' [The Islamist Groups in Egyptian Politics], *al-Mawqif al-'Arabi* 94 (February-March 1988): 74–102.

106. Faraj Fuda, *al-Haqiqa al-Gha'iba* [The Missing Truth] (Cairo: Dar al-Fikr lil-Dirasat wa al-Nashr wa al-Tawzi', 1988).

107. 'Abd al-Salam Faraj, 'al-Farida al-Gha'iba' (The Missing Precept), appendix in *Tanzim al-Jihad*.

108. Fuda, *al-Haqiqa*, 22.

109. There have been a number of recent works devoted to a re-reading of the early Islamic period. Among these writings are Sayyid Mahmud al-Qimmani, *Hurub Dawlat al-Rasul* [The Wars of the Prophet's State] (Cairo: Dar Sina, 1993); Khalil 'Abd al-Karim, *Mujtama' Yathrib* [The Society of Yathrib] (Cairo: Dar Sina, 1997); and Khalil 'Abd al-Karim, *Shadw al-Rababa bi-'Ahwal Mujtama' al-Sahaba* [The Fiddle's Chants on the Ways of the Society of the Companions] (Cairo: Dar Sina, 1997). 'Abd al-Karim's works deny any puritanical pretension to the society of Madina and to the Companions. Profane concerns governed much of the actions of the members of the model society. Again, an underlying message is that the sexual code and practices of the period are far removed from their idealised representation by the Islamists.

110. Fuda, *al-Haqiqa*, 86.

111. Ibid., 100.

112. Ibid., 130.

113. A more detailed analysis of the discourse can be found in Salwa Ismail, 'Discourse and Ideology in Contemporary Egypt,' (Unpublished Ph.D thesis, McGill University, 1992). The findings are based on an examination of thirty articles covering the party's weekly seminars and the leaders' speeches given on different occasions, such as religious celebrations, memorial anniversaries, and party conventions. The survey looked at issues covered in a three-month sample for each year between 1980 and 1984.

114. The Labour Party traces ideological and membership roots to Young Egypt, a pre-Revolutionary political organisation.

115. A position taken by the Muslim Brotherhood and the 'independent' *'ulama* who condemn violence as a weapon of opposition while maintaining a critical view of the government for its delay in applying the Shari'a in a comprehensive manner.

116. The party paper's position on the International Conference on Population and Development was articulated in moral terms. It termed the conference *'mu'tamar al-ibahiya wa al-shudhudh'* (the conference of promiscuity and deviance). See *al-Sha'b*, July and August 1994.

117. Roussillon, 'al-Jama'at al-Islamiya .'

118. Ibid., 86.

119. Ibid.

120. Differences between the Labour Party and the Muslim Brotherhood developed in the early 1990s. They were largely tactical rather than ideological in nature. For instance, the Muslim Brothers' acquisition of a weekly publication in 1993 reflected an internal competition for leverage over common political and doctrinal positions. In the Labour Party's Sixth National

Conference, executive-committee positions were filled predominantly by party members, while the Muslim Brothers' presence was marginal. The continued alliance between the party and the Brothers was, however, affirmed by party leader Ibrahim Shukri in his speech at the conference; *al-Ahali*, 12 May 1993.

121. 'Hamalat Waqiha,' *al-Nur*.

3: Religious 'Orthodoxy' as Public Morality

1. For a discussion of conservative Islamism see chapter two of this volume.

2. While the term orthodoxy has no equivalent in the Arabic language, the semantic and semiotic fields associated with it have their parallels in Islamic traditions. The term itself is used in reference to the founding Islamic traditions by such scholars as Talal Asad and Muhammad Arkoun. The latter has delineated in a systematic manner the process of formulating the elements of Islamic orthodoxy. See Arkoun, *Tarikhiyat al-Fikr al-'Arabi al-Islami* [The Historicity of Arab Islamic Thought] (Beirut: Markaz al-Inma' al-Qawmi, 1986), chapter two. Nasr Hamid Abu Zayd describes this process in terms of 'a battle over the production of the laws of collective memory' and the establishment of 'knowledge-producing mechanisms.' See Abu Zayd, *Al-Nas, al-Sulta, al-Haqiqa: al-Fikr al-Dini Bayna Iradat al-Ma'rifa wa Iradat al-Haymana* [The Text, Power, Truth: Religious Thought between the Will to Knowledge and the Will to Power] (Al-Dar al-Bayda': al-Markaz al-Thaqafi al-'Arabi, 1995), 18.

3. Talal Asad, 'The Limits of Religious Criticism in the Middle East: Notes on Islamic Public Argument,' in his *Genealogies of Religion* (Baltimore: Johns Hopkins University Press, 1993), 200–36.

4. Muhammad Arkoun, *Tarikhiyat al-Fikr*, 74–81.

5. This view of ethics, developed in Ash'ari theology, came close to Shafi'i jurisprudence, merging rules governing ethical action with divinely sanctioned legal justice. George F. Hourani, 'Ethics in Islam: A Conspectus,' in *Reason and Tradition in Islamic Ethics* (Cambridge: Cambridge University Press, 1985), 15–22.

6. The *muhtasib* was the person officially entrusted with the application of *hisba* in the regulation of market activities and moral behaviour. *Hisba* refers to the duty of every Muslim to enjoin good and forbid evil. See *hisba* in *The Encyclopaedia of Islam*, New Edition (Leidin: E.J. Brill, 1979), 485–93. See also Ahmad Abd al-Raziq, 'La Hisba et le muhtasib en Égypte au temps des Mamlouks,' *Annales Islamologiques* 13 (1977): 165–78.

7. Asad, 'The Limits of Religious Criticism,' 211–12.

8. Sayyid Qutb, *Ma'alim fi al-Tariq* [Signposts] (Cairo: Dar al-Shuruq, 1987), 162–77.

9. Ibid., 135–48.

10. Cited in Ghali Shukri, 'Hukuma Khafiya fi Misr Did al-Thaqafa' [A Hidden Government in Egypt Against Culture], *Ruz al-Yusuf*, 3 January 1994, 28.

11. *al-Sha'b*, 14 January 1994.

12. In 1994, Islamist lawyers sued a large number of theatre owners in various districts of Cairo, including al-Azbakiya, Zamalek, and Rud al-Farag.

13. Shaykh Yusuf al-Badri is a high school Arabic language teacher. In the 1970s, he became a preacher in South Cairo. In the mid-1980s he was a member of al-Ahrar Party and won a parliamentary seat on the Alliance ticket in 1987. In the early 1990s, he was appointed to the High Council of Islamic Affairs.

14. Judges used Article 3 of the Civil Procedures Code and Article 12 of the State Council Law which require that a plaintiff have an interest in any lawsuit he/she is initiating. See Centre for Human Rights Legal Aid (CHLRA), *Hisba: Is Egypt a Civil or Religious State?* (Cairo: CHRLA, January 1996), 6–8.

15. Dar al-Ifta' is an institution in charge of providing Islamic opinion and, in a sense, ruling on any issue of concern to Muslims.

16. *Ruz al-Yusuf*, 10 July 1995.

17. Ibid.

18. *al-Ahali*, 5 July 1995.

19. In my discussions with colleagues and friends in Egypt immediately following the broadcast of the high profiled interview with 'Abd al-Baqi, I found that they considered the revelations regarding sexual improprieties to be the most damning and the ones most likely to attract the attention of the viewers.

20. Torture in the grave is a favourite subject of many popular preachers.

21. Shaykh Shahin is a professor of Arabic at the College of Sciences, Cairo University as well as a preacher at 'Amr Ibn al-'As mosque. He is also a member of the governing National Democratic Party. From the pulpit of his mosque, Shaykh Shahin attacked both Abu Zayd and the writers who defended his right to intellectual freedom.

22. This practice is permitted under Article 280 of the Shari'a Court Regulations. Centre for Human Rights Legal Aid, *Hisba: Is Egypt a Civil or a Religious State?*, 10.

23. Mahkamat Ist'inaf al-Qahira, al-Da'ira 14, Ahwal Shakhsiya, Ist'inaf

278, 1995. (Cairo Court of Appeal, District 14, Personal Status, Appeal Case 278, 1995), 23.

24. Ibid., 4.

25. According to the articles of the new law, plaintiffs are to direct their cases to the Public Prosecutor who is to decide whether or not to proceed with the case. Centre for Human Rights Legal Aid, *Saying What we Think* (Cairo: CHRLA, February 1996), 47–50.

26. Cited in Muhammad Sa'id al-'Ashmawi, 'al-Irhab al-Fikri wa al-Hisba,' [Intellectual Terrorism and *hisba*], *October*, 26 May 1996, 17.

27. On the formalisation of *fatwa*-giving in Islamic history see Muhammad Khalid Masud, Brinkley Messik and David S. Powers 'Muftis, Fatwas and Islamic Legal Interpretation,' in *Islamic Legal Interpretation: Muftis and their Fatwas*, ed. Muhammad Khalid Masud, Brinkley Messik and David S. Powers (Cambridge: Harvard University Press, 1996), 5–23.

28. At the time, the Mufti was Shaykh Jad al-Haqq who was appointed Shaykh of al-Azhar in 1982 and held the position until his death in 1996.

29. See 'Taqrir Mufti al-Jumhuriya 'an Kitab al-Farida al-Gha'iba' [The Report of the Mufti of the Republic on the Text of the Missing Precept] in Ni'mat Guinayna, *Tanzim al-Jihad: Hal Huwa al-Badil al-Islami fi Misr* [The Jihad Organisation: Is it the Islamic Alternative in Egypt?] (Cairo: Dar al-Huriya, 1988). See also Salwa Ismail, *Radical Islamism in Egypt: Discursive Struggle*. Montreal Papers on the Contemporary Arab World (Montreal: Inter-University Consortium for Arab Studies, 1994) and Johannes J.G. Jansen, *The Neglected Duty* (New York: MacMillan Publishing Company, 1986), 54–60.

30. For example see his letter of support to Fahmi Huwaydi, 'Risalat Min Shaykh al-Azhar,' [A Message from the Shaykh of al-Azhar] *Al-Ahram*, 16 February 1988.

31. In banning recommendations, these are the most common formulations appearing in the reports of the Majma'. For the title of works on the recommendation list in 1996, see 'Abd al-Fatah and Rashwan ed., *Taqrir al-Hala al-Dinniya*, 32–4.

32. I have examined five reports concerning items appearing in weekly and monthly publications and two reports on Khalil-'Abd al-Karim's *Mujtama' Yathrib* [The Society of Yathrib] (Cairo: Dar Sina, 1996) and *Shadw al-Rababa bi Ahwal Mujtama' al-Sahaba: Muhammad wa al-Sahaba* [The Fiddle's Chants on the Ways of the Society of the Companions: Muhammad and the Companions] (Cairo: Dar Sina, 1997). In these books, 'Abd al-Karim undertakes a critical re-reading of the founding period of Islam.

33. I learnt of the shaykh's recommendation in an exchange with the

Public Relations director of his office. The position of the Majma' was stated in a meeting with Mr Shukri Muhammad, a general director in the Research and Publication Department of al-Majma', April 29, 1998. In fact, the Majma' had refused my request to examine copies of the reports and recommended that I get permission from the grand shaykh. I met with the grand shaykh and made my request directly to him. During my brief visit to his office, the grand shaykh contacted the office of Shaykh Sami al-Sha'rawi, the Majma' director, and gave instructions that my inquiries be handled 'with honesty and truth.' Nonetheless, when I visited the Majma' following this, the officials in the Majma' director's office continued to deny me access to the reports. The shaykh's instructions were ignored and I was advised to return with written permission. As I had managed to secure some copies from human rights organisations involved in some of the censorship cases, I did not persist with the Majma'. However, I reported the results of my efforts to the grand shaykh's office director and to the al-Azhar public relations director. Both recommended that I meet with the shaykh again. The position of both sides indicated that they were gearing up for a confrontation. The clash came soon after with the al-Azhar Reform Bill introduced in June 1998.

34. The Egyptian Human Rights Organisation, *Hurriyat al-Ra'y wa al-'Aqida: Qiyud wa Ishkaliyat, Riqabat al-Azhar 'ala al-Musannafat al-Fanniya* [Freedom of Thought and Belief, Constraints and Problems: al-Azhar's Censorship of Artistic Productions] (Cairo: al-Munazzama al-Misriya li-Huquq al-Insan, 1994).

35. 'Wisdom of the Mosque,' *Index on Censorship* 23, nos. 1–2 (1994), 123.

36. On these differences see Malika Zeghal, 'La Guerre des fatwas: Gad al-Haqq et Tantawi: Les cheikh-s à l'épreuve du pouvoir,' *Cahiers de l'Orient* 45 (1997): 81–95.

37. 'Wisdom of the Mosque,' p. 125; The Egyptian Human Rights Organisation, *Hurriyat al-Ra'y wa al-'Aqida*.

38. Richard Engel, 'Apostate Ruling Endangers Professor,' *Middle East Times*, 11 May 1997.

39. Qimani was charged under Article 198 of the criminal code with propagating ideas that denigrate Islam. The Majma''s report contested his use of the Old Testament as a source on events in Abraham's life, judging it to be a distortion of what is known from Qur'anic truths. Among other issues of contention, the Majma' objected to Qimani's recounting of historical episodes involving the third caliph, 'Uthman.

40. A summary of the report by the Majma' on al-Qimani is given in the

text of the ruling issued by the North Cairo Lower Court. See, Mahkmat Shamal al-Qahira al-Ibtida'iya, Jalsat 15–09–1997 (North Cairo Lower Court, 15 September 1997).

41. Yahya Isma'il, 'Introduction,' in Umar 'Abd Allah Kamil, *al-Ayat al-Bayinat lima fi Asatir al-Qimani min al-Dalal wa al-Khurafat* [The Proven Verses about the Myths and Deviations in Qimani's Legends] (Cairo: Dar al-Turath al-Islami, 1997), 5–9.

42. For a report on the divisions between the Front and the grand shaykh see *al-Musawwar*, 12 June 1998.

43. 'Wisdom of the Mosque,' 126.

44. *al-Ahali*, 11 January 1995.

45. Ibid.

46. Ibid.

47. In the area of military security, the Censorship Board defers to the General Security Apparatus.

48. *al-Musawwar*, 7 January 1995.

49. Ibid.

50. Ali E. Hillal Dessouki, 'Official Islam and Political Legitimation in the Arab Countries,' in *The Islamic Impulse*, ed. by Barbara F. Stowasser (London: Croom Helm, 1987), 135–141; Ibrahim Ibrahim, 'Religion and Politics under Nasser and Sadat 1952–1981,' in ibid., 121–34.

51. Hala Mustafa, *al-Dawla wa al-Harakat al-Islamiya al-Mu'arida: Bayna al-Muhadana wa al-Muwajaha fi 'Ahday al-Sadat wa Mubarak* [The State and Oppositonal Islamist Groups: Between Cooptation and Confrontation in the Eras of Sadat and Mubarak] (Cairo: Kitab al-Mahrusa, 1996), 241.

52. 'Abd al-Fatah and Rashwan, ed., *Taqrir al-Hala al-Dinniya*, 49.

53. Mustafa, *al-Dawla wa al-Harakat al-Islamiya al-Mu'arida*, 394–5.

54. Aziz al-Azmeh, 'Ba'idan 'an Sutwat al-Qawl al-Dini' [Stepping Away From the Authority of the Religious Utterance], *al-Naqid* 16 (October 1989): 78.

55. Nazih Ayubi, *Political Islam: Religion and Politics in the Arab World* (London: Routledge, 1991), 35.

56. Valerie J. Hoffman-Ladd, 'Polemics on the Modesty and Segregation of Women in Contemporary Egypt,' *International Journal of Middle East Studies* 19 (1987), 29.

57. See Leila Ahmad's discussion of counter-cultural traditions in Islamic history in *Women and Gender in Islam: Historical Roots of a Modern Debate* (New Haven: Yale University Press, 1992), 95–101.

58. See Adil Mustafa Ahmad, 'The Erotic and the Pornographic in Arabic Literature,' *Journal of British Aesthetics* 34, no. 3 (July 1994): 278–84.

59. Ahmed, *Women and Gender in Islam*, 92.

60. Muhammad Galal Kishk, *Khawatir Muslim fi al-Mas'ala al-Jinsiya* [A Muslim's Thoughts on the Sexual Question]. (Cairo: Maktabat al-Turath al-Islami, 1992).

61. See al-Azmeh, 'Ba'idan 'an Sutwat al-Qawl al-Dini,' 78.

62. *al-Nur*, 18 January 1989; *al-Ahrar*, 26 December 1988.

63. Janet Abu Lughod, 'The Islamic City-Historic Myth, Islamic Essence and Contemporary Relevance,' *International Journal of Middle East Studies* 19 (1987): 155–76. On the role of the *futuwwa* in the neighbourhood see Sawsan al-Messiri, 'The Changing Role of the Futuwwa in the Social Structure of Cairo,' in *Patrons and Clients in Mediterranean Societies*, ed. by Ernest Gellner and John Waterbury (London: Duckworth, 1977), 239–53. I have dealt with the question of how Islamist oppositional activities are inscribed in the spatial organisation of the informal housing communities of Cairo in 'The Politics of Space in Urban Cairo: Informal Communities and the State,' *Arab Studies Journal* 4, no. 2 (Fall 1996): 119–32.

4: Militant Islamism as a Popular Movement

1. The 1990s have seen an intensification of violent clashes between the Islamists and the government, claiming over 1,000 lives. The Islamist attacks have been aimed particularly at the tourism sector and the police. More than a hundred police officers and soldiers have been killed. For more details see the annual reports of *al-Taqrir al-Istratiji al-'Arabi* [The Arab Strategic Report]. See also 'Abd al-Fatah and Rashwan, ed., *Taqrir al-Hala al-Dinniya*.

2. The rise of al-Jama'a al-Islamiya in the Upper Egypt governorates of Qena, Asyut, Suhaj, Minya and Aswan must be examined in relation to the social fabric and spatial organisation of their cities and towns. The complexity of social organisation based on tribe and family and the hierarchies characterising social, economic and political positions in the various provinces, have yet to be studied in a comprehensive manner, and are beyond the scope of this essay. See Nazih Ayubi, *Political Islam* (London: Routledge, 1991), and Mamun Fandy, 'Egypt's Islamic Group: Regional Revenge,' *Middle East Journal* 48, 4 (1994): 607–25.

3. This formulation is borrowed from Sami Zubaida, 'Class and Community in Urban Politics,' in *État et ville, et mouvements sociaux au Maghreb et au Moyen-Orient*, ed., Kenneth Brown et al. (Paris: L'Harmmattan, 1989), 70.

4. On the first two groups see Saad Eddin Ibrahim, 'Islamic Militancy as a Social Movement: The Case of Two Groups in Egypt,' in *The Islamic Resurgence in the Arab World*, ed. Ali E. Hillal al-Dessouki (New York: Praeger, 1982), 117–37. The Jihad and the Jama'a groups formed an alliance in 1980 which was forged by 'Abd al-Salam Faraj of Jihad and Karam Zuhdi of al-Jama'a. The alliance was responsible for the assassination of President Sadat. In 1984, the alliance broke down. More recently, leading Jihad figures such as Abud al-Zumur were reconciled with the Jama'a and rejoined its ranks. The Jihad originated in Cairo and carried out most of its activities there. The Jama'a's roots are in Upper Egypt. The two groups differ in modes of operation. The Jihad's membership is smaller, its activities more concentrated and its violence more targeted. The Jama'a is more diffuse at each of these levels. For more details, see 'Abd al-Fatah and Rashwan ed., *Taqrir al-Hala al-Dinniya*, 183–6.

5. For a discussion of the militant groups' ideological discourse, see Salwa Ismail, *Radical Islamism in Egypt*.

6. See Yvonne Haddad and John L. Entelis, *The Islamic Revival Since 1988: A Critical Survey and Bibliography* (London: Greenwood Press, 1997).

7. For examples of this approach see Emmanuel Sivan, *Radical Islam: Medieval Theology and Modern Politics* (New Haven: Yale University Press, 1985) and P.J. Vatikiotis, *Islam and the State* (London: Croom Helm, 1987), particularly chapter three.

8. See R.H. Dekmejian, 'Islamic Revival, Catalysts, Categories, and Consequences,' in *The Politics of Islamic Revivalism*, ed. Shireen Hunter (Bloomington: Indiana University Press, 1988), 3–22, and John O. Voll, 'Renewal and Reform in Islamic History: Tajdid and Islah,' in *Voices of Resurgent Islam*, ed. John L. Esposito (New York: Oxford University Press, 1983), 32–47.

9. Saad Eddin Ibrahim, 'Islamic Militancy as a Social Movement,' and Hamied Ansari, 'The Islamic Militants in Egyptian Politics,' *International Journal of Middle East Studies* 16 (1984): 123–44.

10. Ansari, 'The Islamic Militants,' 141.

11. Saad Eddin Ibrahim, 'The Changing Face of Egypt's Islamic Activism,' in *Security Challenges in the Mediterranean Region*, ed. Roberto Aliboni, George Joffe and Tim Niblock (London: Frank Cass, 1996), 27–40.

12. Afaf Lutfi al-Sayyid-Marsot, 'Religion or Opposition? Urban Protest Movements in Egypt,' *International Journal of Middle East Studies* 16 (1984): 541–52.

13. Ibid., 55.

14. Guilain Deneoux, 'Religious Networks and Urban Unrest: Lessons

from Iranian and Egyptian Experiences,' in *The Violence Within: Cultural and Political Opposition in Divided Nations*, ed. Kay B. Warren (Boulder: Westview Press, 1993), 123–55.

15. Ibid., 137.

16. Ibid., 145.

17. Edmund Burke III, 'Towards a History of Urban Collective Action in the Middle East: Continuities and Change, 1750–1980,' in *État, ville et mouvements sociaux au Maghreb et au Moyen-Orient*, ed. Kenneth Brown et al., 42–56.

18. Ibid., 44.

19. For a critical introduction to the literature on urban organisation, see R. Stephen Humphreys, *Islamic History: A Framework for Inquiry* (London: I.B. Tauris, 1995), chapter ten. See also Masahi Haneda and Toru Miura ed., *Islamic Urban Studies: Historical Review and Perspectives* (London: Kegan Paul International, 1994).

20. Recent literature on urbanism in Islamic history has questioned Orientalist scholarship on the idea of the Islamic city. The critique of orientalist urban studies is outside the immediate interest of this essay. However, the questions raised in the ongoing debates have a direct bearing on how we view urban society in Middle Eastern countries. See Ibid., and Kenneth Brown, 'The Uses of a Concept: "The Muslim City",' in *Middle Eastern Cities in Comparative Perspective*, ed. Kenneth Brown et al. (London: Ithaca Press, 1987), 73–81.

21. André Raymond, 'Urban Networks and Popular Movements in Cairo and Aleppo End of the 18th Century – Beginning of the 19th Century,' in *The Proceedings of the International Conference on Urbanism in Islam* (ICUTT) vol. 2 (Tokyo: The Middle East Culture Centre, 1989), 219–71.

22. Ibid., 263.

23. See Gabriel Baer, ' Decline and Disappearance of Guilds,' in *Studies in the Social History of Modern Egypt* (Chicago: The University of Chicago Press, 1982), 149–60. For a more nuanced approach drawing on extensive archival sources, see Juan R. I. Cole, *Colonialism and Revolution in the Middle East: The Social and Cultural Origins of the Urabi Revolution* (Princeton N.J.: Princeton University Press, 1993). See also, Ehud Toledano, *State and Society in mid-Nineteenth-Century Egypt* (Cambridge: Cambridge University Press, 1990).

24. Sawsan El-Messiri, 'The Changing Role of the Futuwwa in the Social Structure of Cairo,' in *Patrons and Clients in Mediterranean Societies*, ed. Ernest Gellner and John Waterbury (London: Duckworth, 1977), 239–53. On these groups in Cairo and Aleppo see Raymond, 'Urban Networks.' On

the *zu´r* in Damascus see Miura Toru, 'The Structure of the Quarter and the Role of the Outlaws: The Salihiya Quarter and the Zu´r Movement in Mamluk Period,' in *The Proceedings of the International Conference on Urbanism in Islam* (ICUTT) vol. 3 (Tokyo: The Middle East Culture Centre, 1989), 402–37.

25. Afaf Loutfi El Sayed, 'The Role of the *'Ulama'* in Egypt during the Nineteenth Century,' in *Political and Social Change in Modern Egypt*, ed. P.M. Holt, (London: Oxford University Press, 1968), 264–80.

26. Abu Lughod, 'The Islamic City.'

27. André Raymond, 'Quartiers et mouvements populaires au Caire au xviiième siècle,' in *Political and Social Change in Modern Egypt*, ed. P.M. Holt (London: Oxford University Press, 1968), 111.

28. Ibid.

29. Although dealing with an earlier period, it is instructive to read Boaz Shoshan's study of the moral contract between ruler and ruled on the provision of subsistence goods. Shoshan, 'Grain Riots and the "Moral Economy": Cairo 1350–1517,' *Journal of Interdisciplinary History* 10, 3 (Winter 1980): 459–78.

30. Raymond, 'Quartiers Populaires.'

31. Juan Cole's study of the Urabi revolution crystallises the character of urban social organisation and the ways in which it framed collective action from the 1850s on, culminating in the eruption of the events of 1881–82. Cole, *Colonialism and Revolution.*

32. El-Messiri, 'The Changing Role of the Futuwwa.'

33. Abu Lughod, 'The Islamic City.'

34. Ibid.

35. Nawal al-Messiri-Nadim, 'The Concept of the Hara: A Historical and Sociological Study of al-Sukkariya,' *Annales islamologiques* 15 (1979): 313–48.

36. Ibid.; see also Diane Singerman, *Avenues of Participation: Family, Politics and Networks in Urban Quarters of Cairo* (Princeton N.J.: Princeton University Press, 1995), and Arlene Elow MacLeod, *Accommodating Protest: Working Women, the New Veiling and Change in Cairo* (New York: Columbia University Press, 1991).

37. Al-Messiri-Nadim, 'The Concept of the Hara.'

38. Georg Stauth, 'Gamaliyya: Informal Economy and Social Life in a Popular Quarter of Cairo,' in *Informal Sector in Egypt*, ed. Nicholas Hopkins, *Cairo Papers in Social Science* (Winter 1991), 78–103.

39. Ibid.

40. The development of neighbourhood along class lines extends back to

the turn of the century, see Robert Ilbert, 'Égypte 1900, Habitat populaire, société coloniale,' in *État, ville et mouvements sociaux au Maghreb et au Moyen-Orient*, ed. Kenneth Brown et al. (Paris: L'Harmmattan, 1989), 266–82.

41. For an overview of state urban planning policies see Galila al-Kadi, 'Trente ans de plannification urbaine au Caire,' *Revue Tiers Monde* 31, 121 (Janvier-Mars 1990): 185–207.

42. Based on files from the Jihad trial, Case 462, 1981. See the summaries of the interrogation statements of the accused Jihad members in Ni'mat Gueineina, *Tanzim al-Jihad: Hal Huwa al-Badil al-Islami fi Misr* [The Jihad Organisation: Is it the Islamic Alternative in Egypt] (Cairo: Dar al-Hurriya, 1988). In his study of the Jihad group, Gilles Kepel partially attributes this spatial distribution to the movements of the group's leader around the city. See *The Prophet and the Pharaoh: Muslim Extremism in Egypt* (London: Al-Saqi, 1985).

43. My evidence of the Islamist presence in these areas is based on reports of state security operations there, arrest records indicating the militants' place of residence, and documented activism. State security operations are carried out with the aim of finding the hideouts of escaped militant defendants and the locations of weapons cashes. The Egyptian press regularly reports on police campaigns which, in many cases, result in shootouts and casualties. Among these, it is worth mentioning the early 1994 attacks on hideouts in Ma'sara and al-Zawiya al-Hamra which resulted in the death of seven Islamists in a flat in al-Zawiya al-Hamra. Annual compilation of data on these events may be found in *al-Taqrir al-Istratiji al-'Arabi* [The Arab Strategic Report] (Cairo: al-Ahram Center for Strategic Studies). In 1990, ten security operations were conducted in Ain Shams, Imbaba, Helwan and Umraniya. The number of operations increased to fifty in 1993, taking place in Imbaba, Boulaq, Haram, Ain Shams, Matariya, Shubra and Zaynhum. Galal 'Abdallah Mu'awad, *al-Hamishiyun al-Hadariyun wa al-Tanmiya fi Misr* [The Urban Marginals and Development in Egypt] (Cairo: Cairo University, Faculty of Economics and Political Science, 1998). Other communities that did not know strong militant formation, witnessed the implantation of organised Islamic voluntary organisations such as al-'Ashira al-Muhammadiya in Manshiyat Nasir.

44. For antecedents of squatter type settlements in Cairo and Alexandria, see Robert Ilbert, 'Égypte 1900.' Ilbert views the 'ishash (huts) development at the turn-of-the-century as an expression of the same phenomenon which appears with squatting. At the base, urban planning policies were directed in the interests of the dominant forces in society.

45. On state housing policies, see Milad Hanna, *al-Iskan wa al-Masyada* [Housing and the Trap] (Cairo: Dar al-Mustaqbal al-'Arabi, 1988).

46. This discussion of the informal housing communities draws on Salwa Ismail, 'The Politics of Space in Urban Cairo: Informal Communities and the State,' *Arab Studies Journal* 4, 2 (Fall 1996): 119–32.

47. For a comprehensive map of the informal housing communities in Egypt see Mamduh al-Wali, *Sukkan al-Ishash wa al-Ashwa'iyat: al-Kharita al-Iskaniya lil-Muhafazat* [The Inhabitants of Huts and Haphazard Communities: A Map of the Governorates] (Cairo: Engineers Syndicate, 1993).

48. Linda Oldham, Haguer al-Hadidi and Hussein Tamaa, 'Informal Communities in Cairo: The Basis of a Typology,' *Cairo Papers in Social Science* 10, 4 (Winter 1987).

49. These studies are discussed in Ismail, 'The Politics of Space.' The main insights for my understanding of the dynamics of community organisation are drawn from Agnes DeBoulet, 'État, squatters et maitrise de l'espace,' *Égypte/Monde Arabe* 1 (1er trimèstre 1990): 79–96; Oldham et. al, 'Informal Communities.'

50. See Nader Fergany, 'A Characterisation of the Employment Problem in Egypt,' in *Employment and Structural Adjustment in Egypt in the 1990s*, ed. Heba Handoussa and Gillian Potter (Cairo: The American University in Cairo Press, 1991), 25–56.

51. Singerman, 'Avenues of Participation,' 22.

52. Belgin Tekçe, Linda Oldham and Frederic Shorter, *A Place to Live: Families and Child Health in a Cairo Neighborhood* (Cairo: The American University in Cairo Press, 1994).

53. Duha al-Maghazi, 'Sukan al-'Ashwa'iyat bayna Thaqafat al-Faqr wa Istratijiyat al-Baqa, Dirasat Anthropologiya ,' [The Residents of Haphazard Communities between the Culture of Poverty and the Strategies of Survival: An Anthropological Study], in The Proceedings of the Conference on *al-Mujtma' al-Misri fi Daw' Mutaghayrat al-Nizam al-'Alami* [Egyptian Society in Light of the Changes in the International System] ed. Ahmad Zayid and Samiya al-Khashab (Cairo: Cairo University, Faculty of Arts, 1995).

54. The results of the report are published in *al-Ahali*, 1 May 1994.

55. Homa Hoodfar, 'Survival Strategies and the Political Economy of Low-Income Households in Cairo,' in *Development, Change and Gender in Cairo: A View from the Household*, ed. Diane Singerman and Homa Hoodfar (Bloomington: Indiana University Press, 1996), 1–26.

56. Iqbal al-Amir al-Samaluti, 'Nahwa Namudhaj Tanmawi li Muwajahat Ihityajat al-Mujtama'at al-Hadariya al-Mutakhalifa bi al-Tatbiq 'ala-Mujtama' al-Munira al-Gharbiya' [Towards a Developmental Model for

Meeting the Needs of Underdeveloped Urban Societies with Application to the Society of Munira al-Gharbiya] cited in al-Wali, *Sukkan al-Ishash*, 79.

57. The presence of university graduates in these markets was brought to my attention by Diya' Rashwan. On the informal labour market see Ragui Assaad, 'Formal and Informal Institutions in the Labor Market, With Applications to the Construction Sector in Egypt,' *World Development* 21, 6 (1993): 925–39.

58. Tekçe et. al. *A Place to Live*.

59. Ibid.

60. Ibid., 55.

61. This is confirmed by Assaad in his studies of the informal labour market in the construction sector and of the garbage collectors. Assaad, 'Formal and Informal Institutions,' and 'L'Informel structuré: Les Zabalin du Caire,' *Peuples méditerranéens* 41–42 (1988): 181–92.

62. On the organisation of squatter markets see Helmi R. Tadros, Mohamed Fateeh and Allen Hibbard, 'Informal Markets in Cairo,' *Cairo Papers in Social Science* 13, 1 (1990). See also Mustafa Kharoufi, 'Du Petit au grand espace urbain: Le Commerce des fruits et légumes à Dar al-Salam,' *Égypte/Monde Arabe* 5 (1er trimèstre 1991): 81–96.

63. It is estimated that by 1986, 500,000 residents of the old quarters had relocated, many moving to informal housing communities. Eric Denis, 'Urban Planning and Growth in Cairo,' *Middle East Report* 27, 1 (Winter 1997): 7–12.

64. Ibid., 10.

65. Ibid.

66. Hisham Mubarak, *al-Irhabiyun Qadimun: Dirasa Muqarana Bayna Mawqif al-Ikhwan al-Muslimin wa Jama'at al-Jihad min Qadiyat al-'Unf, 1938–1994* [The Terrorists are Coming: A Comparative Study of the Position of the Muslim Brotherhood and the Jihad Groups from the Question of Violence 1938–1994] (Cairo: Dar al-Mahrusa, 1995).

67. Ibid., 246.

68. Ibid.

69. Ibid., 247.

70. Ibid., 248

71. Ibid., 256.

72. Ibid., 262.

73. Oldham et. al, 'Informal Communities.'

74. *Al-Ahali*, 1 September 1993, 10.

75. Ibrahim, 'The Changing Face,' 36

76. *Al-Gumhuriya*, 2 September 1988, and *al-Ahram*, 2 September 1988.

77. *Al-Ahrar*, 16 November 1987.

78. *Al-Ahram*, 23 April 1989.

79. *Al-Gumhuriya*, 12 August 1993.

80. This concurs with Hisham Mubarak's age breakdown for the groups he studied.

81. As pointed out by Gregory Starret, young men in particular enjoy opportunities to experience diverse ideological and cultural views in coffee shops, mosques, schools and so on. These opportunities allow them to escape the tight social controls imposed within the family. Gregory Starrett, *Putting Islam to Work: Education, Politics and Religious Transformation in Egypt* (Los Angeles: University of California Press, 1998), 170.

82. In one militant cell, the emir, 'Adel Siyam married Hayam 'Abd al-'Alim, sister of Ahmad and Muhammad 'Abd al-'Alim, two male activists. It was Hayam's brother Muhammad who arranged the marriage. Muhammad's own marriage to wife Huriya 'Abd al-Satar was arranged by his other sister Amal. *Al-Ahram*, 18 June 1994.

83. Marsha Pripstein Posusney qualifies the Egyptian workers' activism as 'defensive and restorative.' See her 'Collective Action and Workers' Consciousness in Contemporary Egypt,' in *Workers and Working Classes in the Middle East: Struggles, Histories, Historiographies*, ed. Zackary Lockman (New York: State University of New York Press, 1994), 211–46.

84. For a chronicle of labour protests in the 1990s see the annual publication of *al-Taqrir al-Istratiji al-'Arabi*.

85. See Joel Beinin, 'Islam, Marxism, and the Shubra al-Khayma Textile Workers: Muslim Brothers and Communists in the Egyptian Trade Union Movement,' in *Islam, Politics, and Social Movements*, ed., Edmund Burke, III and Ira M. Lapidus (Los Angeles: University of California Press, 1988), 207–27.

86. Ellis Goldberg, 'Muslim Union Politics in Egypt: Two Cases,' in *Islam, Politics, and Social Movements*, ed. Edmund Burke III and Ira M. Lapidus (Los Angeles: University of California Press, 1988), 228–43.

87. Personal communication with Diya' Rashwan.

88. *Ruz al-Yusuf*, 30 May 1994.

89. Based on a compilation from seven court cases involving militants between 1991 and 1993 and a larger number of accused, Hisham Mubarak provided a different occupational profile. The occupational distribution which is given puts the total percentage of professionals at 26.2 per cent, students 25 per cent, workers 21 per cent, traders 3 per cent, unemployed 20 per cent and 4 per cent unknown. Although he argues that the ranks of university students have expanded and that this as an indication of the importance of

the university, Mubarak does not indicate the fields of study or of professional training. Also, he does not specify the fields of economic activity for those listed under workers. The data for the four cases used here is more precise, and we know the types of trades the tradesmen are engaged in and the level and field of study of the students.

90. This may not be the case for the Jama'a al-Islamiya which sees in public sector employment a way of infiltrating the system or at least of finding employment for its members.

91. Mostafa Kharoufi, 'The Informal Dimension of Urban Activity in Egypt: Some Recent Work,' in *Informal Sector in Egypt*, ed. Nicholas Hopkins, *Cairo Papers in Social Science* (Winter 1991), 8–20.

92. The figure is provided by Nader Fergany quoted in Soad Kamil Rizq, 'The Structure and Operation of the Informal Sector in Egypt,' in *Employment and Structural Adjustment: Egypt in the 1990s*, ed. Heba Handoussa and G. Potter (Cairo: The American University Press, 1991), 167–85.

93. Singerman, *Avenues of Participation*, 178.

94. Ibid., 187.

95. Ibid.

96. The assumption of the task of religious teaching by the lay emirs suggests an additional dynamic to the changes in the religious educational infrastructure examined by Gregory Starrett. Starrett argues that the modern religious educational system represents an important component of the infrastructural background of the 'Islamic Trend.' He contends that the functionalisation of religious education by the modern state has served to shift the bases of legitimate religious authority from traditional centres of learning to the Western-style school system. The new educated groups are thus able to appropriate claims to legitimate religious knowledge. As part of this structural transformation the need, and hence the market for religious information were created. From this perspective, the Islamisation of public life is part of the long-term change in the social relations of Islamic cultural production that accompanied the establishment of the modern educational system. See Starrett, *Putting Islam to Work*, 227–30.

97. See the responses of Tal'at Qasim, the Jama'a's public relations spokesperson, in interview with Hisham Mubarak, 'Ba'd Indhar al-Suyah wa al-Mustathmirin: al-Ahali Taltaqi fi al-Danmark bi al-Mutahadith al-I'lami li-al-Jama'a al-Islamiya [After the Warning to Tourists and Investors: *al-Ahali* Meets with the Jama'a's Public Relations Spokesperson in Denmark], *al-Ahali*, 9 February 1994.

98. Mubarak, *al-Irhabiyun Qadimun*.

99. Ibid.

100. Ibid.

101. *Al-Mussawar*, 15 December 1988.

102. The main ideological texts are authored by this leadership. These include *al-Farida al-Gha'iba* by 'Abd al-Salam Faraj, *Hatmiya al-Muwajaha*, *Mithaq al-Amal al-Islami* co-authored by the leaders of the Jama'a in prison. There are also research pamphlets such as *Falsafat al-Muwajaha* by Tareq al-Zumur, and *Research on Hakimiya* by Usama Qasim. 'Abd al-Fatah and Rashwan ed., *Taqrir al-Hala al-Dinniya 1996*, 185. Some of these texts can be found in Muhammad Rif'at Sayyid Ahmad, *al-Nabi al-Musalah, al-Tha'irun* [The Armed Prophet, The Rebellious] (London: Riad al-Rayyes Books, 1991).

103. One should bear in mind that there is an ongoing process of cultural Islamisation which involves the state, the popular preachers, and the moderate Islamists. The merging of popular traditions and Islamic traditions is part of this process. See chapter 3 of this volume.

104. I thank Diya' Rashwan for bringing this to my attention. See 'Abd al-Fatah and Rashwan ed., *Taqrir al-Hala al-Dinniya 1996*.

105. *Ruz al-Yusuf*, 19 December 1988.

106. Mubarak, *al-Irhabiyun Qadimun*.

107. The view that the militants are the contemporary manifestations of the *zu'r*, *futuwwa* and other outlaws was put forward by Muhammad Nur Farhat and has influenced a number of analysts. See his 'al-'Unf al-Siyasi wa al-Jama'at al-Hamishiya: Dirasat fi al-Tarikh al-Ijtima'i,' [Political Violence and the Marginal Groups: A Study in Social History] in the Proceedings of the Conference *al-'Unf al-Siyasi fi al-Watan al-'Arabi* [Political Violence in the Arab Nation], ed. Usama al-Ghazali Harab (Amman: Arab Thought Forum, 1987), cited in both Mu'awad, *al-Hamishiyun*, and Mubarak, *al-Irhabiyun Qadimun*.

108. *Ruz al-Yusuf*, 19 December 1988, 13–16.

109. *Al-Taqrir al-Istratiji al-'Arabi 1992* [The Arab Strategic Report 1992] (Cairo: Markaz al-Dirasat al-Siasyiya wa al-Istratijiya, 1993).

110. On the *baltagi* type see El-Messiri, 'The Role of the Futuwwa,' 248.

111. This is the view of some Egyptian commentators and journalists. See for example Salah Muntasir, 'Mas'uliyat al-Makan,' [The Responsibility of Space], *Al-Ahram al-Dawli*, 15 December 1992.

112. On the concept of *Ibn al-Balad* see Sawsan el-Messiri, *Ibn al-Balad: A Concept of Egyptian Idenity* (Leiden: Brill,1979).

113. Hussein Ali Abd al-Salam, 'Violence in Egypt, 1967–1992.' Unpublished Ph.D. thesis (Politics Department, University of Exeter, 1997).

114. The Maadi station which was the target of a 1986 uprising of central

security soldiers has been fortified, and the main street leading to it has a roadblock and police guards. The Helwan station, which is on a main thoroughfare, is surrounded by high walls, with armed soldiers guarding the entrance.

115. Asef Bayat, 'Cairo's Poor: Dilemmas of Survival and Solidarity,' *Middle East Report* 27, 1 (Winter 1997): 2–6, 12.

116. In negotiations with the state, the Jama'a demands tend to centre on the government keeping its hands off their mosques. See Mubarak, 'Ba'd Indhar al-Suyah.'

117. The idea of *satr* is deployed in the face of compromising situations where a person commits a moral indiscretion. Norms of social control necessitate the application of sanctions to such indiscretions. However, the safeguarding of reputation, loyalty and solidarity translate into a common interest among members of a family or group to keep certain indiscretions from becoming public. *Satr*/protection is deployed for this purpose. For a discussion of the rules of sanction and mediation see Andrea B. Rugh, *Family in Contemporary Egypt* (Syracuse: Syracuse University Press, 1984), 157–8.

118. There is dissension within the movement itself with regard to using this level of violence. The historic leadership in prison has called for a truce but has been disregarded. The extreme acts have been perpetrated by members of cells in Upper Egypt who, following the call for a truce, shifted allegiance to the overseas leadership. See Hisham Mubarak, 'The Violence of Despair,' *Cairo Times*, vol. 1, 21 (11–24 December 1997).

119. 'The "Normalization" of the Islamic Movement in Egypt from the 1970s to the Early 1990s,' in *Accounting for Fundamentalism*, ed. Martin W. Marty and R. Scott Appleby (Chicago, University of Chicago Press, 1994).

120. For a discussion of this process see chapter 2 of this volume.

5: Islamist Politics in Algeria and Tunisia

1. Clan distinctions corresponded to the territorialised divisions within the Algerian Liberation Army (ALN), that is, *wilayat* divisions and the interior-exterior bases of operation. The Oujda clan that grouped together the military leaders based in the Oujda town on the Moroccan border, was the one that took control of the state at independence. Episodes of intrigue and rivalry leading to the brutal elimination of contestants marked the first decade of the post-independence period. See Ahmed Rouadjia, 'La Violence et l'histoire du mouvement national Algérien,' *Peuples méditérraneens* 70–71

(January–June 1995): 173–87. Political manoeuvres between clans continued into the post-independence period.

2. Lahouari Addi, 'Violences et systèmes politiques en Algérie,' Les Temps
Modernes 50, 580 (January–February 1995), 59.

3. See Lahouari Addi, L'Algérie et la démocratie: Pouvoir et crise politique
dans L'Algérie contemporaine (Paris: La Découverte, 1994).

4. Ahmed Rouadjia, Grandeur et décadence de l'état algérien (Paris:
Karthala, 1995).

5. Sami Nair, 'Le Peuple exclu,' Les Temps Modernes 50, 580 (January–
February 1995): 34–45.

6. André Nouschi, L'Algérie amère (Paris: Editions de la Maison de Sciences de l'Homme, 1995), 275.

7. Addi, L'Algérie et la démocratie: See also Jean Leca, and J. Claude
Vatin, L'Algérie politique: Institutions et régime (Paris: Presses de la
Fondation Nationale des Sciences Politiques, 1975).

8. On the populism of the Algerian state, see Addi, L'Algérie et la
démocratie.

9. Nouschi, L'Algérie amère, 243.

10. Lahouari Addi, 'La Crise structurelle de l'économie Algérienne,'
Peuples méditérraneens 52–53 (1990), 188.

11. Lucile Provost, 'L'Économie de rente et ses avatares,' Esprit 19 (1995),
87.

12. See Rouadjia, Grandeur et décadence, chap. 5.

13. A. Henni, 'Qui a légalisé quel "trabendo"?' Peuples méditérraneens
52–53 (1990): 233–43.

14. Jacques Fontaine, 'Les Élections locales algériennes du 12 Juin 1990:
Approche statistique et géographiques,' Maghreb-Machrek 129 (July–September 1990), 132.

15. Jacques Fontaine, 'Quartiers défavorisés et vote islamiste en Algérie,'
Revue du Monde Musulman et de la Méditrranée 65 (1993): 141–64.

16. Rabah Saoud, 'Urban Form, Social Change and the Threat of Civil
War in North Africa,' Third World Planning Review 19, 3 (1997): 289–312.

17. Madani Safar-Zitoun, Stratégies patrimoniales et urbanisation, Alger
1962–1992 (Paris: Editions L'Harmattan, 1996).

18. According to the Ministry of Housing, there were 500,000 illicitly
built homes in the country in 1986. Cited in Rabbia Bekkar, 'Les Habitans
batisseurs à Tlemcen,' Les Annales de la recherche urbaine 66 (March 1995),
64.

19. Safar-Zitoun, Stratégies patrimoniales, 134–5.

20. Maurice Guetta and Cyrille Megdiche, 'Le Peuplement des bidonvilles

d'Alger; emplois et mobilité socio-professionnelle,' *Revue Française de Sociologie* 31, 2 (1990): 297–313.

21. Safar-Zitoun, *Stratégies patrimoniales*, 101.

22. Malika Ghanem, 'L'Évolution de deux quartiers d'habitat "illicite" à Constantine (Algérie),' in *Politiques et pratiques urbaines dans les pays en voi de developpement*, vol. 2, ed. Nicole Haumont and Alain Marie (Paris: L'Harmattan, 1987), 44–53.

23. Omar Steele, 'Une Économie piégé entre trabendo et ajustement,' in *L'Algérie dans la guerre*, ed. Remy Leveau (Bruxelles: Editions Complexe, 1995), 36.

24. G. Duvigneau, 'L'Économie clandestin au peril du contrat social en Algérie,' in *Nouvelles logiques marchandes*, ed. Chantal Bernard (Paris: CNRS, 1991), 181–99. See also, Henni, 'Qui a legalisé quel "trabendo"?'

25. Duvigneau, 'L'Économie clandestin,' 197.

26. Luis Martinez, *La Guerre civile en Algérie* (Paris: Karthala, 1998), 50.

27. Ahmed Rouadjia, *Les Frères et la mosquée* (Paris: Karthala, 1990).

28. See Ibid.

29. Naciri, Mohamed 'La Mosquée: Un Enjeu dans la ville,' *Lamalif* 192 (October 1990): 48–52

30. Smail Haj Ali, 'Communication, ville et violences à travers la grève politique du Front Islamique du Salut (FIS): L'Occupation de la ville d'Alger (mai-juin 1991),' *Revue tunisienne des sciences sociales* 29, 110 (1992), 232.

31. Hannah Davies, 'Taking up Space in Tlemcen: Interview with Rabia Bekkar,' *Middle East Report* 179 (November-December 1992), 13.

32. Ibid., 13.

33. Abderrahim Hafiane, 'L'Intermédiation sociale dans le cas des quartiers d'habitat illégal à Guelma et Constantine (Algérie),' in *L'Urbain dans le monde arabe: politiques, instruments et acteurs*, ed. Pierre Signoles, Galila El Kadi, Rachid Sidi Boumedine (Paris: CNRS editions, 1999), 275–80.

34. Smail Haj Ali, 'L'Occupation de la ville.'

35. Safar-Zitoun, *Stratégies*, 248.

36. Youssef Fatès, 'Jeunesse, sport et politique,' *Peuples méditérraneens* 52–53 (1990): 57–71.

37. Miriem Vergès, ' La Qasbah d'Alger: Chronique de survie dans un quartier en sursis,' in *Exiles et royaumes: Les appartenences au monde arabo-musulam aujourd'hui*, ed. Gilles Kepel (Paris: Press de la Fondation des Sciences Politiques, 1994), 78.

38. Ibid., 78.

39. Hocine Benkheira, 'Algérie: La Boisson, la prière et le football,' *Autrement* 95 (December 1987), 59.

40. Fatès, 'Jeunesse, sport,' 65.

41. Benkheira, 'Algérie: La Boisson,' 59.

42. Miriem Vergès, 'Les Jeunes, le stade, le FIS: Vers une analyse de l'action protestataire,' *Maghreb-Machrek* 154 (October-December 1996), 51.

43. Fatès, 'Jeunesse, sport,' 69.

44. Key figures identified with the Islamising tendency within the state included Ahmed Taleb Ibrahimi, Abderrahmane Chibane, and Mouloud Kassim Belcacem. The religious nationalist current in the FLN expressed itself through the *al-Asala* newspaper established in 1970. See Luc-Willy Dehueveles, *Islam et pensée contemporaine en Algérie: La revue al-Asala 1971–1981* (Paris: Éditions du CNRS, 1992).

45. On the articulation of Islamic symbolism and traditions in state apparatuses and policies see Henri Sanson, *Laïcité islamique en Algérie* (Paris: Editions du CNRS, 1983).

46. A theological school was established by the state. At its head, in the position of rector, was Shaykh Muhammad al-Ghazali, the Egyptian theologian known for his Muslim Brotherhood links. Shaykh Ghazali was also featured in religious programmes on Algerian television.

47. See François Burgat and William Dowell, *The Islamic Movement in North Africa* (Austin, Texas: Centre for Middle Eastern Studies, 1993).

48. This wing took over the direction of the FIS at the Congress of Batna in July 1991. Its key figures include Abdelkader Hachani, Mekhloufi, Muhammad Said and Rejjam. Said and Rejjam would later join the armed Islamist groups, but Rejjam soon returned to the ranks of the FIS.

49. For more on these two currents and their mutations within the FIS see Severine Labat, *Les Islamistes algériens entre les urnes et les maquis* (Paris: Éditions du Seuil, 1995).

50. In addition to the FIS, two other Islamist groups formed political parties with the legalisation of multipartism, namely al-Nahda of Abdallah Jabellah and Hamas of Shaykh Nahnah. Both of these groups have adopted legalist positions and attempted compromises and negotiations with the government. See Arun Kapil 'Les partis islamistes en Algérie: Elements de présentation,' *Maghreb-Machrek* 133 (July-September1991), 103–11.

51. Burgat and Dowell, *The Islamic Movement in North Africa*.

52. Safar-Zitoun, *Stratégies*.

53. Ghania Samai-Ouramdane, 'Le Front Islamique du Salut à travers son organe de presse (Al Munqid),' *Peuples méditérraneens* 52–53 (1990): 155–65.

54. Vergès, 'La Qasbah,' 81.

55. In February 1989, the FIS was officially founded in the mosque of al-

Sunna in the Bab el-Oued quarter. Its first general assembly lasted for over five days. The participants included hundreds of Imams active in clandestine groups. Some had links with the militant Bouyali group active in the mid 1980s. Kapil, 'Les partis islamistes en Algérie,' 103–4.

56. Labat, *Les Islamistes algériens*, 132.

57. Ibid., 134.

58. Merrani's ambitions may have propelled him to attack the FIS leaders in a televised statement in June 1991. His dissidence earned him a position in the circle of state power as a religious councillor to the then prime minister, Sid Ahmed Ghozali. Labat, *Les Islamistes*, 135.

59. See Deborah Harrold, 'The Menace and Appeal of Algeria's Parallel Economy,' *Middle East Report* 25, 1 (January-February 1995): 18–22.

60. On Mohamad Abed see Rouadjia, *Les Frères*. On Hadj Sadoq see Martinez, *La Guerre*.

61. Vergès, 'Les Jeunes, le stade.'

62. Vergès, 'La Qasbah,' 81.

63. Ibid., 78.

64. Karim Chergui, 'Novembre 1986: La Révolte des jeunes à Constantine,' *Hérodote* 45 (1987): 61–70.

65. Ibid., 65.

66. Ibid., 66.

67. Ibid., 70.

68. Ibid.

69. Hocine Benkheira, 'Un désir absolu,' *Peuples méditérraneens* 52–53 (1990), 9.

70. Ibid., 11.

71. Naget Khadda, Monique Gadant, 'Mots et gestes de la révolte,' *Peuples méditérraneens* 52–53 (1990): 19–24.

72. Smail Haj Ali, 'L'Islamisme dans la ville: Espace urbain et contre-centralité,' *Maghreb-Machrek* (1994), 69.

73. Ibid., 71.

74. Amine Touati, *Algérie: Les Islamistes à l'assault du pouvoir* (Paris: L'Harmattan, 1995), chapter one.

75. Hamza Kaidi, 'La Démocratie en état de siège,' *Jeune Afrique* 1589, 12–18 June 1991, 4–5.

76. Safar-Zitoun, *Stratégies*, 225.

77. For a discussion of the traditional spatial arrangements of producing and ensuring *horma*, see Djaffar Lesbet, 'Des pièces de la vie: Maisons vernaculaires et pratiques sociales dans la Casbah d'Alger,' in *Politiques et*

pratiques urbaines dans les pays en voi de developpement, vol. 2, ed. Nicole Haumont and Alain Marie (Paris: L'Harmattan, 1987), 284–312.

78. Vergès, 'La Qasbah.'

79. On the transformations taking place in the family, see Lahouari Addi, *Les Mutations de la société algérienne: Famille et lien social dans l'Algérie contemporaine* (Paris: Editions La Découverte, 1998).

80. Nabila Amir, 'Ces familles que la guerre déchire,' *al-Watan*, reprinted in *Le Nouvel Observateur* 1567, 19–25 January 1995, 10–11.

81. Ibid.

82. Davies, 'Taking up Space.'

83. Ibid. The problems of public space and morality are also encountered within the dwellings themselves. In a study of a transitional settlement in Constantine, Boudababa found that preserving privacy and shielding the private from the intrusion of the public were main concerns. One of the challenges faced by the households was dealing with the obscene language used in the housing complex. Young women in their family rooms and in the presence of their fathers had to develop devices to avoid the embarrassment caused by this type of intrusion. The women found symbolic ways of removing themselves from the space. For instance, they would pretend to be engrossed in one thing or another such as sewing, reading or the activities going on outside. Rabah Boudababa, 'The Social Consequences of Resettlement Programs in Algeria: Transitional Settlement in Constantine,' in *Population Displacement and Resettlement: Development and Conflict in the Middle East*, ed. Seteni Shami (New York: Centre for Migration Studies, 1996), 24–46.

84. It should be noted that the adoption of the *hijab* has a territorial association derived from the definition of an inside and an outside space and the positioning of women in these spaces. Thus, women, in the immediate city quarters where they are known, felt the need to wear the *hijab*, while women in villages or small towns considered the intimacy of the immediate space to be a reason for not wearing the *hijab*. For a nuanced view of the spatial dimension of *hijab* wearing see Dahbia Abrous, 'Le voile en Algérie ou la muraille eclatée,' *Maghreb-Machrek* 123 (1989): 202–6. See also Rabia Bekkar, 'Territoires des femmes à Tlemcen: Pratiques et représentations,' *Maghreb-Machrek* (1994): 126–41.

85. Ghania Samai-Ouramdane, 'Le Front Islamique du Salut à travers son organe de presse (Al Munqid),' *Peuples méditérraneens* 52–53 (1990): 155–65.

86. Rouadjia, *Les Frères*, and, 'Discourse and Strategy of the Algerian Islamist Movement,' in *The Islamist Dilemma: The Political Role of Islamist*

Movements in the Contemporary World, ed. Laura Gauzzone (Reading: Ithaca Press, 1995), 69–103.

87. Ibid.

88. Martinez, *La Guerre.*

89. See Abderrahamane Moussaoui, 'La Mosquée au peril de la commune,' *Peuples méditérraneens* 52–53 (1990): 81–9, and Said Belguidoum, 'Citadins en attente de la ville,' *Maghreb-Machrek* (1994): 43–55.

90. Safar-Zitoun, *Stratégies,* 225.

91. Zineb Guerroudj, 'Pratiques des nouveaux logements par les habitants des bidonvilles d'Alger,' in *Politiques et pratiques urbaines dans les pays en voi de developpement,* vol. 2, ed. Nicole Haumont and Alain Marie (Paris: L'Harmattan, 1987), 269–83.

92. The use of violence as a means to establish the Islamic state had been advocated by an armed group active in the 1980s and headed by Mustafa Bouyali. Bouyali was gunned down in 1987. See Burgat and Dowell, *The Islamic Movement in North Africa.*

93. Martinez, *La Guerre,* 158.

94. On the *zu'r* in Damascus and Cairo see Ira M. Lapidus, *Muslim Cities in Middle Ages* (Cambridge: Cambridge University Press, 1988). See also Toru Miura 'The Structure of the Quarter and the Role of the Outlaws: The Sahiliya Quarter and the Zu'r Movement in the Mamluk Period,' in *The Proceedings of the International Conference on Urbanism in Islam* (ICUTT) vol. 3 (Tokyo: The Middle East Culture Centre, 1989), 402–37.

95. Martinez, *La Guerre,* 161.

96. Labat, *Les Islamistes algériens,* 264–5.

97. Ibid., 265.

98. On the history of the two groups see Aissa Khelladi, 'Algérie: Les Groupes islamistes armés,' *Confluences* 12 (Fall 1994): 63–76, and François Burgat, 'Algérie: l'AIS et le GIA itineraires de constitution et relations,' *Maghreb-Machrek* 149 (1995): 105–13.

99. In line with this, the AIS announced a cease-fire in 1997.

100. Aissa Khelladi, 'Esquisse d'une géographie des groupes islamistes en Algérie,' *Hérodote* 77 (April–June 1995), 33.

101. Ibid., 37.

102. This does not mean that only the militant Islamists are the authors of the assassinations of intellectuals and journalists. François Burgat raises doubts about the accusations levelled against Islamists in certain cases, for instance, the murders of M. Boucebci and of Malek Alloula. Burgat, 'L'Islamisme contre les intellectuels?,' *Peuples méditérraneens* 70–71(1995): 57–76.

103. In 1997, 100 people were massacred in a town in Ain Delfa, an area under the control of the GIA. The inhabitants had been on good terms with the armed men, some of whom had married women from the town. As such, it is difficult to attribute the act to the GIA. Abed Charef, *Algérie, Autopsie d'un massacre* (Editions de l'Aube, 1998). See Djillali Hadjadj, *Corruption et démocratie en Algérie* (Paris: La Dispute, 1999). In some instances, the massacres of villagers are blamed on former landlords who aimed to terrorise members of the rural population into abandoning their land.

104. See Ahmad Rouadjia, 'La Violence et l'histoire du mouvement national algérien,' *Peuples méditérraneens* 70–71 (1995): 173–86, and Burgat 'L'Islamisme contre les intellectuels?.'

105. This is the conclusion of a fact-finding commission. See Hadjadj, *Corruption et démocratie en Algérie.*

106. Martinez points to links existing between the notables-entrepreneurs and the armed groups. The latter provided protection for businesses and destroyed public sector competitors. This also supports the regime's liberalisation policy objectives of redrawing the economic map, with thousands of jobs liquidated as a result of the destruction of the public enterprises. Martinez, *La Guerre,* 192–5, and 311–30.

107. Elbaki Hermassi, 'Montée et declin du mouvement islamiste en Tunisie,' *Confluences méditerranée* 12 (Automne 1994): 33–50

108. Abdelkader Zghal, 'Repenser les mouvements islamistes dans un perspective comparative trans-historique et trans-culturelle,' mimeo, n.d.

109. Abdelkader Zghal 'Le Retour du sacré et la nouvelle demande idéologique des jeunes scolarisé: le cas de la Tunisie,' *Annuaire de l'Afrique du Nord* XVIII 1979 (Paris: Editions CNRS, 1981), 41–64.

110. Elbaki Hermassi, 'La Société tunisienne au miroir islamiste,' *Maghreb-Machrek* 103 (January-March 1984): 39–56.

111. Zghal, 'Le Retour du sacré'; Hermassi, 'La Société tunisienne.'

112. Michel Camau, 'L'État tunisien: de la tutelle au désengagement,' *Maghreb-Machrek* 103 (January-March 1984): 8–38.

113. On the structure of the party, see Lars Rudenbeck, *Party and People: A Study of Political Change in Tunisia* (London: C. Hurst and Company, 1969).

114. Interview with S. Jurshi, Tunis July 1999.

115. Hermassi, 'La Société tunisienne,' and Zghal, 'Le Retour du sacré.'

116. Yadh Ben Achour, 'Islam perdu, Islam retrouvé,' *Annuaire de l'Afrique du Nord* xviii 1979 (Paris: Editions CNRS, 1981), 65–75.

117. Souhayr Belhassen, 'L'Islam contestaire en Tunisie,' *Jeune Afrique* no. 949, 14 March 1979, 82–4.

118. Hermassi, 'La Société tunisienne.' See Mohamed Talbi, 'L'Expression religieuse dans la presse et les revues tunisiennes aujourd'hui (1984–85),' *The Maghreb Review* 11, 1 (1986): 1–18, and Nikki R. Keddie 'The Islamist Movement in Tunisia,' *The Maghreb Review* 11, 1 (1986): 26–39.

119. Hermassi, 'La Société tunisienne,' 41.

120. Ibid., 43.

121. Ibid., 44; Zghal, 'Le Retour du sacré.'

122. Abdellatif Hermassi, 'Société, Islam et islamisme en Tunisie,' *Cahiers de la méditeranée* 49 (1994), 80.

123. Ibid.

124. Souhayr Belhassen, 'Femmes tunisiennes islamiste,' *Annuaire de l'Afrique du Nord 1979* (Paris: Editions CNRS, 1981), 77–94.

125. See Ibid. Compare Tunisian women's constructions of why they adopted the veil with those of Egyptian women. See Arlene Elow Macleod, *Accommodating Protest: Working Women, the New Veiling and Change in Cairo* (New York: Columbia University Press, 1991).

126. Belhassen, 'Femmes tunisiennes,' 79–80.

127. Ibid., 80.

128. Ibid., 83.

129. Ibid., 84.

130. Antoine Sfeir, 'Voyage au sein de l'islamisme tunisien,' *Les Cahiers de l'Orient* 7 (1987), 30.

131. Emad Eldin Shahin, *Political Ascent: Contemporary Islamic Movements in North Africa* (Boulder, Colorado: Westview Press, 1997), 95.

132. Interview with leftist and secular intellectuals, Tunis, July 1999.

133. Interview with S. Jurshi, Tunis, July 1999.

134. *La Presse* May 1991, and September 1991.

135. Leader Rachid Ghanoushi sent a message on cassette encouraging popular participation in the events. Hermassi, 'Montée et declin,' and Mohamed Elhachmi Hamdi, *The Politicisation of Islam: A Case Study of Tunisia* (Boulder: Westview Press, 1998).

136. Hassine Dimassi, 'La Crise économique en Tunisie: une crise de régulation,' *Maghreb-Machrek* 103 (January-March 1984): 57–69.

137. Eva Bellin, 'Tunisian Industrialists and the State,' in *Tunisia: The Political Economy of Reform*, ed. I. William Zartman (Boulder: Lynne Rienner Publishers, 1991), 45–65.

138. Christopher Alexander, 'State, Labor and the New Global Economy in Tunisia,' in *North Africa: Development and Reform*, ed. Dirk Vandewalle (London: MacMillan, 1996), 177–202.

139. See Souhayr Belhassen, 'Le Procès des syndicalistes embarrassent le pouvoir,' *Jeune Afrique* no. 917, August 2, 1978, 18–19.

140. Paul Lowy, 'Espace idéologique et quadrillage policier: Le 26 janvier 1978 à Tunis,' *Hérodote* 13 (1979), 109.

141. Ibid., 111.

142. Sophie Bessi, ' Tunisie: L'Explosion,' *Jeune Afrique* no. 1201 (January1984), 30.

143. Jim Paul, 'States of Emergency: The Riots in Tunisia and Morocco,' *MERIP Reports* 14, 8 (October 1984): 3–6.

144. Jean-Philip Bras, 'Tunisie,' *Annuaire de l'Afrique du Nord XXIII, 1984* (Paris: Editions CNRS, 1986), 961.

145. David Seddon, 'Popular Protest and Political Opposition in Tunisia, Morocco and Sudan,' in *Etat, ville et mouvements Sociaux au Maghreb et au Moyen Orient*, ed. Kenneth Brown et al. (Paris: L'Harmattan, 1989), 179.

146. Abdelkader Zghal [and Mouldi Lahmar], 'The "Bread Riot" and the Crisis of the One-Party System in Tunisia,' in *African Studies in Social Movements and Democracy*, ed. Mahmood Mamdani and Ernest Wambadia-Wamba (Dakar: Codersia Book Series, 1995), 99–132.

147. Asma Larif-Beatrix, 'Tunisie,' *Annuaire de l'Afrique du Nord XXV 1986* (Paris: Editions CNRS, 1988), 798.

148. Hermassi, 'Montée et declin.'

149. Ibid.

150. Asma Larif-Beatrix, 'Tunisie,' *Annuaire de l'Afrique du Nord 1987* (Paris: Edition CNRS 1989), 649.

151. Zakiya Daoud, 'Chronique tunisienne,' *Annuaire de l'Afrique du Nord XXVIII 1989* (Paris: Editions CNRS, 1991), 691.

152. *Réalites* 299, 3/5–30/5 1991, 7.

153. *La Presse* 7 May 1991.

154. The UGTE is the Union of Islamist Students.

155. *La Presse* 10 May 1991.

156. Ibid., 22 May 1991.

157. There are cases of clear socio-professional spatialisation. For instance, in the north, certain quarters are inhabited mainly by doctors (Hilton north), by teachers of higher education (Manar) or by judges. Abdellatif Baltagi, 'Système d'habitat et ségrégation sociale dans l'agglomération de Tunis,' *Peuples méditerranéens* 43 (April-June 1986), 79–80.

158. These can be identified in a schematic manner: the Medina (dating to the seventh century), the colonial city (1881), the suburban extensions in the north (1930), the gourbivilles in the west and north-west (1930). The post-independence period saw the further development of residential hous-

ing in the north, middle-standing homes in the south and west and rehousing and spontaneous quarters in the west of the city. Morched Chabbi, 'Evolution du grand Tunis: Territorialités et centralité,' Conference 'Sciences Sociales et Phenomènes urbains dans le Monde Arabe,' Casablanca, 30 November–2 December, 1994. See also Pierre Signoles, J.M. Miossec and H. Dlala, *Tunis: Evolution et fonctionnement de l'espace urbain*, Fascicule de recherches, no. 6, Tours, Urbama, 1980.

159. Habib Abichou, 'Les habitants des gourbis dans le district de Tunis,' in l'Entré dans la ville, seminar organised by the district of Tunis, Hamamat 1986.

160. Morched Chabbi, 'Une nouvelle forme d'urbanisation à Tunis: L'habitat spontanée peri-urbaine,' Ph.D. thesis, Université de Paris, Val De Marne, Institut d'urbanisme de Paris-Creteil, 1986, 271–2.

161. Ibid.

162. In fact, the sale prices of the new homes proved beyond the means of many of the residents of the old shanty-towns. See Chehab Tekari, 'Habitat et dépassement du droit en Tunisie: Les constructions spontanées,' *Annuaire de l'Afrique du Nord XXV1986* (Paris: Editions CNRS, 1988), 165–73.

163. Chabbi, *Une nouvelle forme*, 392.

164. This discussion draws on Chabbi, *Une nouvelle forme*. See, also, his 'The Pirate Sub-developer: A new Form of Land Developer in Tunis,' *International Journal of Urban and Regional Research* 12, 1 (1988): 8–21.

165. Chabbi, *Une nouvelle forme*, 376.

166. Ibid., 346.

167. Elizabeth Vasile, 'Devotion as Distinction, Piety as Power: Religious Revival and the Transformation of Space in the Illegal Settlements of Tunis,' in *Population, Poverty and Politics in Middle Eastern Cities*, ed. Michael E. Bonine (University of Florida Press, 1997), 135.

168. Ibid.

169. Ibid., 127.

170. Ibid., 128.

171. *La Presse* May 11, 1991.

172. Ibid., June 7, 1991.

173. In a study of a planned 'city' in Tunis, Isabelle Berry Chikhaoui observes that the social system in the area recalls past arrangements in old quarters of Cairo, associating elections and co-optation. This system assures both the incorporation of the residents and their involvement in quarter life. Chikhaoui 'Le lien social et politique dans un quartier en formation à Tunis: allegeance et/ou clientelisme?' Paper presented to the Conference

Villes et territoires au Maghreb: mode d'articulation et formes de territorialisation, Tunis, 17–19 September 1998, p. 8.

174. Chikhaoui, 'Le lien sociale.'

175. Michel Camau, 'D'une République à l'autre: Refondation politique et aléas de la transition libérale,' *Maghreb-Machrek* 157 (July-September 1997), 5.

176. Karen Pfeifer, 'How Tunisia, Morocco, Jordan and even Egypt Became IMF "Success Stories" in the 1990s,' *Middle East Report* 29, no. 1 (Spring 1999): 23–7.

177. See Jean-Philip Bras, 'Tunisie: Ben Ali et sa classe moyenne,' *Poles* (April-June 1996): 174–95.

178. Guilain Deneoux, 'Tunisie: Les élections presidentielles et législatives 20 mars 1994,' *Maghreb-Machrek,* 145 (June-September 1994), 59.

179. See *La Presse* 1991 and 1992

180. *La Presse* May 18, 1991.

181. Ibid.

182. Deneoux, 'Tunisie: Les élections.'

183. *La Presse,* June 7, 1991.

184. Deneoux, 'Tunisie: Les élections,' 66.

185. For more on the relationship between the women's movement and the Ben Ali regime see Laurie Brand, *Women, the State and Political Liberalization,* (Columbia University Press, 1998), chapters 8 & 9. See also, Zakiya Daoud, 'Les Femmes tunisiennes: Gains juridiques et statut économique et social,' *Maghreb-Machrek* 145 (June-September 1994): 27–48.

186. Hamed Ibrahimi, 'Les Libertés envolées de la Tunisie,' *Le Monde Diplomatique* February 1997, 4–5, and Louza Toscane and Olfa Lamloun, 'Les Femmes, alibi du pouvoir tunisien,' *Le Monde Diplomatique* June 1998, 3.

187. Ibid.

188. Daoud, 'Chronique tunisienne,' 950.

6: The Paradox of Islamist Politics

1. Olivier Roy, *The Failure of Political Islam.* Translated by Carol Volk, (Cambridge, Massachusetts: Harvard University Press, 1994).

2. See David Hirst, 'Time for the Temporal,' *al-Ahram Weekly,* 10–16 February 2000, 6–7. See also, Max Rodenbeck, 'Is Islamism Losing its Thunder?' *The Washington Quarterly* 21, 2 (Spring 1998): 177–93.

3. Olivier Roy, 'Le Post-Islamisme,' in Olivier Roy and Patrick Haenni, ed. *Le Post-Islamisme, Revue du Monde Musulman et de la Méditerannée* 85–86 (1999), 12–30.

4. Ibid., 9.

5. The term refers to former opponents of the Prophet Muhammad who were reconciled to Islam during its founding period by grants and gifts. See *The Encyclopaedia of Islam*, New Edition. Vol. VII, Leidin: Brill, 1993, 254. The Iranian government's aid policies to other Muslim countries came under this rubric.

6. See *Al-Hayat*, 31–07–1998.

7. See Abu al-Ila Madi, 'Ba'd Hadith al-Uqsur: al-'Unf wa Kayfiyat 'Ilajuh fi al-Hala al-Misriya al-Rahina,' [After the Luxor Event: Violence and how to Remedy it in the Egyptian Case], *al-Hayat*, 25 December 1997. See also Idem in *al-Ahram*, 11–2–1998 and 18–2–1998.

8. See Isam Sultan, *al-Jil*, 7–2–1999.

9. See *Ruz al-Yusuf* 1–2–1999, p. 16. See also *al-Hayat* 7–7–1998.

10. *Ruz al-Yusuf*, 1–2–1999.

11. Mohamed Tozy, *Monarchie et Islam Politique au Maroc* (Paris: Presses de la Fondation Nationale des Sciences Politiques, 1999), 235.

12. Ibid.

13. Charles Tilly, 'Social Movements and (all Sorts) of Other Political Interactions – Local, National and International – Including Identities,' *Theory and Society* 27 (1998), 457.

14. The Nurcu movement in Turkey shares certain features in common with Conservative Islamism in Egypt and Algeria. See Hakan Yavuz, 'Towards an Islamic Liberalism? The Nurcu Movement of Fethullah Gulen.' *Middle East Journal* 53, 4 (Autumn 1999): 584–605.

15. See Deborah Harrold, 'The Menace and Appeal of Algeria's Parallel Economy,' *Middle East Report* 25, 1 (January-February 1995), 21.

16. Mohamed Tozy, 'Reformes politiques et transitions démocratique,' *Maghreb-Machrek* 164 (April-June 1999), 84.

17. See Saadia Radi, 'De la toile au voile,' *Maghreb-Machrek* 151 (January-March 1996):13–17.

18. Ibid., 17.

19. Jean-Noël Ferrié, 'Les politiques de la morale en Égypte et au Maroc,' (mimeo).

20. Jean-Noël Ferrié, 'Solidarité islamique sans consensus en Égypte: Un Cadre d'analyse,' *Les Annales de l'autre Islam*, 4 (1997): 73–83.

21. Asef Bayat, 'Revolution Without Movement, Movement Without Revolution: Comparing Islamic Activism in Iran and Egypt,' *Comparative Studies in Society and History* 40, 1 (1998): 136–69.

22. Ibid., 141.

23. A non-Islamist activist from Imbaba indicated to me in an interview

in April 2000 that his activism paralleled that of Shaykh Jabir, the emir leader arrested by the police in 1992. The activist viewed his interventions in the social sphere – mobilising to extend aid to needy families, resolving conflicts in the quarter, and so on – as similar in nature to Shaykh Jabir's. He also acknowledged differences in method. Jabir used force in some instances. However, on the whole, his role was that of a mediator following established social practices and conventions, with the added investment of Islamic frames of reference.

24. Luis Martinez, *La Guerre civile en Algérie* (Paris: Karthala, 1998).

25. Gehad Auda, 'The Normalization of the Islamic Movement in Egypt from the 1970s to the Early 1990s,' in *Accounting for Fundamentalism*, ed. Martin Marty and Scott Appleby (Chicago: Chicago University Press, 1994), 374–412.

26. Gregory Starrett, *Putting Islam to Work: Education, Politics and Religious Transformation in Egypt* (California: California University Press, 1998).

27. Ibid., 229.

28. Ibid.

29. Jean Noël-Ferrié, 'Remarques sur l'islamisation des espaces modernes au Caire,' *Maghreb-Machrek* 151 (January-March 1996), 10–11.

30. Ibid.

31. Ibid.

32. Starrett, *Putting Islam to Work*, 245.

33. Gregory Starrett, 'The Political Economy of Religious Commodities in Cairo,' *American Anthropologist* 97, 1 (Spring 1995): 51–68.

34. Ferrié, 'Remarques sur l'Islamisation,' 12.

35. Iman Farag, 'Croyance et interêt: reflexion sur deux associations islamiques égyptiennes,' in *Modernisation et nouvelles formes de mobilisation sociale* II, *Dossiers CEDEJ* (Cairo: CEDEJ, 1992), 127–40.

36. Ibid.

37. Ziba Mir-Hosseini, 'Rethinking Gender: Discussions with Ulama in Iran,' *Critique* 12 (Fall 1998), 48.

38. Ibid., 49.

Bibliography

Abdalla, Ahmad. 'Egypt's Islamists and the State: From Complicity to Confrontation.' *Middle East Report* 183 (July-August 1993): 28–31.

'Abd al-Fatah, Nabil and Rashwan, Diya', ed. *Taqrir al-Hala al-Dinniya fi Misr 1996* (Report on the Religious Condition in Egypt, 1996). Cairo: Markaz al-Ahram lil-Buhuth al-Istratijiya , 1997.

Abd al-Raziq, Ahmad. 'La Hisba et le muhstasib en Égypte au temps des Mamlouks.' *Annales Islamologiques* 13 (1977): 165–78.

Abd al-Salam, Hussein Ali. 'Violence in Egypt, 1967–1992.' Unpublished Ph.D. thesis, Politics Department, University of Exeter, 1997.

Abichou, Habib. 'Les habitants des gourbis dans le district de Tunis.' In l'Entré dans la ville, seminar organised by the district de Tunis, Hamamat, 1986.

Abrous, Dahbia. 'Le voile en Algérie ou la muraille eclatée.' *Maghreb-Machrek* 123 (1989): 202–6.

Abu Lughod, Janet. 'The Islamic City – Historic Myth, Islamic Essence and Contemporary Relevance.' *International Journal of Middle East Studies* 19 (1987): 155–76.

Abu Zahra, Nadia. *The Pure and the Powerful: Comparative Studies in Contemporary Muslim Societies*. Reading: Ithaca Press, 1997.

Abu Zayd, Nasr Hamid. *Al-Nas, al-Sulta, al-Haqiqa: al-Fikr al-Dini Bayna Iradat al-Ma'rifa wa Iradat al-Haymana* [The Text, Power, Truth: Religious Thought between the Will to Knowledge and the Will to Power]. Al-Dar al-Bayda': al-Markaz al-Thaqafi al-'Arabi, 1995.

Addi, Lahouari. *Les Mutations de la société algérienne: Famille et lien social dans l'Algérie contemporaine*. Paris: Editions la Découverte, 1998.

—— *L'Algérie et la démocratie: Pouvoir et crise dans l'Algérie contemporaine*.

Paris: La Découverte, 1994.

—— 'Violences et systèmes politiques en Algérie.' *Les Temps Modernes* 50, 580 (1995): 46–70.

—— 'La Crise structurelle de l'économie Algérienne.' *Peuples méditérraneens* 52–53 (1990): 187–93.

Adelkhah, Fariba. *Being Modern in Iran*. London: Hurst, 1999.

Ahmad, Muhammad Rif'at Sayyid. *Al-Nabi al-Musalah, al-Tha'irun* [The Armed Prophet, the Rebellious]. London: Riad al-Rayyes Books, 1991.

Ahmad, Mustafa Adil. 'The Erotic and the Pornographic in Arabic Literature.' *Journal of British Aesthetics* 34, 3 (July 1994): 278–84.

Ahmed, Leila. *Women and Gender in Islam: Historical Roots of a Modern Debate*. New Haven: Yale University Press, 1992.

Alexander, Christopher. 'State, Labor and the New Global Economy in Tunisia.' In *North Africa: Development and Reform*, ed. Dirk Vandewalle, 177–202. Gainsville: MacMillan, 1996.

Amir, Nabila. 'Ces familles que la guerre déchire.' *al-Watan*, reprinted in *Le Nouvel Observateur* 1567, 19–25 January, 10–11.

Anderson, Lisa. 'Fulfilling Prophecies: State Policy and Islamist Radicalism.' In *Political Islam: Revolution, Radicalism or Reform*, ed. John Esposito, 17–31. Boulder, Colorado: Lynne Reinner, 1997.

Ansari, Hamied. 'The Islamic Militants in Egyptian Politics.' *International Journal of Middle East Studies* 16 (1984): 123–44.

Arkoun, Muhammad. *Tarikhiya t al-Fikr al-'Arabi al-Islami* [The Historicity of Arab Islamic Thought]. Beirut: Markaz al-Inma' al-Qawmi, 1987.

Asad, Talal. *The Idea of an Anthropology of Islam*. Center for Contemporary Arab Studies Occasional Papers. Washington, DC: Center for Contemporary Arab Studies, 1985.

—— 'The Limits of Religious Criticism in the Middle East: Notes on Islamic Public Argument.' In *Genealogies of Religion*, 200–36. Baltimore: Johns Hopkins University Press, 1993.

Assaad, Ragui. 'Formal and Informal Institutions in the Labor Market, With Applications to the Construction Sector in Egypt.' *World Development* 21, 2 (1993): 935–35.

—— 'l'Informel structuré: Les Zabain du Caire.' *Peuples méditérraneens* 41–42 (1988): 181–92.

Auda, Gehad. 'The Normalization of the Islamic Movement in Egypt from the 1970s to the Early 1990s.' In *Accounting for Fundamentalism*, ed. Martin Marty and Scott Appleby, 374–412. Chicago: Chicago University Press.

Ayubi, Nazih. *Political Islam*. London: Routledge, 1991.

Al-Azmeh, Aziz. 'The Articulation of Islamism.' In *Orientalism, Islam and Islamists*, ed. Asaf Hussein, Robert Olson and Jamil Qureshi, 89–124. Vermont: Amana Books, 1984.

—— 'Bai'dan an Sutwat al-Qawl al-Dini' [Away from the Authority of the Religious Utterance]. *al-Naqid* 16 (October 1989).

Baer, Gabriel. 'Decline and Disappearance of Guilds.' In *Studies in the Social History of Modern Egypt*, 149–60. Chicago: The University of Chicago Press, 1982.

Baltagi, Abdellatif. 'Système d'habitat et ségrégation sociale dans l'agglomération de Tunis.' *Peuples méditérraneens* 43 (April-June 1986): 79–86.

Bayat, Asef. 'Cairo's Poor: Dilemmas of Survival and Solidarity.' *Middle East Report* 27, 1 (Winter 1997): 2–6 &12.

Bayat, Asef. 'Revolution without Movement, Movement without Revolution: Comparing Islamic Activism in Iran and Egypt.' *Comparative Studies in Society and History* 40, 1 (1998): 136–69.

Beatrix, Asma Larif. 'Tunisie.' *Annuaire de l'Afrique du Nord* XXV 1986. Paris: Editions CNRS, 1988.

—— 'Tunisie.' *Annuaire de l'Afrique du Nord* XXVI 1987. Paris: Editions CNRS, 1989.

Beinin, Joel. 'Islam, Marxism and the Shubra al-Khayma Textile Workers: Muslim Brothers and Communists in the Egyptian Trade Union Movement.' In *Islam, Political and Social Movements*, ed. Edmund Burke III and Ira Lapidus, 207–27. Los Angeles: University of California Press, 1988.

Beinin, Joel and Joe Stork, ed. *Political Islam*. London: I.B. Tauris, 1998.

Bekkar, Rabia. 'Territoires des femmes à Tlemcen: Pratiques et représentations.' *Maghreb-Machrek* (1994): 155–65.

—— 'Les Habitants batisseurs à Tlemcen.' *Les Annales de la recherche urbaine* 66 (March 1995): 60–71.

Belhassen, Souhayr. 'L'Islam contestaire en Tunisie.' *Jeune Afrique* 949 (14 March 1979): 82–4.

—— 'Femmes tunisiennes islamiste.' *Annuaire de l'Afrique du Nord* 1979. Paris: Editions CNRS 1981, pp 77–94.

—— 'Le Procès des syndicalistes embarrassent le pouvoir.' *Jeune Afrique* 917 (August 2, 1978): 18–9.

Belguidoum, Said. 'Citadins en attente de la ville.' *Maghreb-Machrek* (1994): 43–55.

Bellin, Eva. 'Tunisian Industrialists and the State.' In *Tunisia: The Political Economy of Reform*, ed. William Zartman, 45–65. Boulder: Lynne Rienner Publishers, 1991.

Ben Achour, Yadh. 'Islam perdu, Islam retrouvé.' *Annuaire de l'Afrique du Nord* XVIII 1979. Paris: Editions CNRS, 1981, pp 65–75.

Benkheira, Hocine. 'Un désir absolu.' *Peuples méditérraneens* 52–53 (1990): 7–18.

—— 'Algérie: La Boisson, la prière et le football.' *Autrement* 95 (1987): 56–69.

Ben Nafissa, Sarah. 'Le Mouvement associatif égyptien et l'Islam: Elements d'une problématique.' *Maghreb-Machrek* 135 (1992): 19–36.

Bessi, Sophie. 'Tunisie: l'Explosion.' *Jeune Afrique* 1201 (January 1984): 30.

Boudababa, Rabah. 'The Social Consequences of Resettlement Programs in Algeria: Transitional Settlement in Constantine.' In *Population Displacement and Resettlement: Development and Conflict in the Middle East*, ed. Seteni Shami, 24–46. New York: Center for Migration Studies, 1996.

Brand, Laurie. *Women, the State and Political Liberalization*. New York: Columbia University Press, 1998.

Bras, Jean Philip. 'Tunisie: Ben Ali et sa classe moyenne.' *Poles* (April-June 1996): 174–95.

—— 'Tunisie.' *Annuaire de l'Afrique du Nord* XXIII, 1984. Paris: Editions CNRS, 1986.

Bromley, Simon. *Rethinking Middle East Politics*. London: Polity Press, 1994.

Brown, Donna Lee. 'Abortion, Islam and the 1994 Cairo Population Conference.' *International Journal of Middle East Studies* 29 (1997): 161–84.

Brown, Kenneth. 'The Uses of a Concept: "The Muslim City".' In *Middle Eastern Cities in Comparative perspective*, ed. Kenneth Brown et al., 73–81. London: Ithaca Press, 1986.

Burgat, François, and William Dowell. *The Islamic Movement in North Africa*. Austin, Texas: Center for Middle Eastern Studies, 1993.

Burgat, François. 'Algérie: l'AIS et le GIA itinéraires de constitutions et relations.' *Maghreb-Machrek* 149 (July-September 1995): 105–13.

—— l'Islamisme contre les intellectuels?' *Peuples méditérraneens* 70–71 (1995): 57–76.

Burke III, Edmund. 'Towards a History of Urban Collective Action in the Middle East: Continuities and Change 1750–1980.' In *État, ville, et mouvements sociaux au Maghreb et au Moyen-Orient*, ed. Kenneth Brown et al., 42–56. Paris: l'Harmmattan, 1989.

Burke III, Edmund. 'Islam and Social Movements: Methodological Reflections.' In *Islam, Political and Social Movements*, ed. Edmund Burke III and Ira Lapidus, 17–35. Los Angeles: University of California Press, 1988.

Camau, Michel. 'D'une République à l'autre: Refondation politique et aléas de la transition libérale.' *Maghreb-Machrek* 157 (July-September 1997):

3–16.

—— 'L'État tunisien: de la tutelle au désengagement.' *Maghreb-Machrek* 103 (January-March 1984): 8–38.

Center for Human Rights Legal Aid (CHLRA). *Hisba: Is Egypt a Civil or Religious State.* Cairo: CHRLA, 1996.

—— *Saying What we Think.* Cairo:CHLRA, 1996.

Chabbi, Morched. 'Une nouvelle forme d'urbanisation à Tunis: L'habitat spontanée peri-urbaine.' Ph.D thesis, Université de Paris, Vale de Marne, Institut d'urbanisme de Paris-Creteil, 1986.

—— 'The Pirate Sub-Developer: A New Form of Land Developer in Tunis.' *International Journal of Urban and Regional Research* 12, 1 (1988): 8–21.

—— 'Evolution du grand Tunis: Territorialités et centralité.' Conference *Sciences sociales et phenomènes urbains dans le Monde Arabe,* Casablanca 30 November–2 December 1994.

Charef, Abed. *Algérie, Autopsie d'un massacre.* Paris: Editions de l'Aube, 1998.

Chergui, Karim. 'Novembre 1986: La Révolte des jeunes à Constantine.' *Hérodote* 45 (1987): 61–70.

Chikhawi, Isabelle Berry. 'Le Lien social et politique dans un quartier en formation à Tunis: Allegeance et/ou clientelisme?' Paper presented to the Conference *Villes et territoires au Maghreb: Modes d'articulation et formes de territorialisation,* Tunis 17–19 September 1998.

Cole, Juan R. I. *Colonialism and Revolution in the Middle East: The Social and Cultural Origins of the Urabi Revolution.* New Jersey: Princeton University Press, 1990.

Daoud, Zakiya. 'Les Femmes tunisiennes: Gains juridques et statut économique et social.' *Maghreb-Machrek* 145 (June-September 1994): 27–48.

—— 'Chronique tunisienne.' *Annuaire de l'Afrique du Nord* XXVIII 1989. Paris: Editions CNRS, 1991.

—— 'Chronique tunisienne.' *Annuaire de l'Afrique du Nord* XXX 1991. Paris: Editions CNRS, 1993.

Davis, Eric. 'Ideology, Social Class and Islamic Radicalism in Modern Egypt.' In *From Nationalism to Revolutionary Islam,* ed. Said Arjomand, 134–47. Albany: State University of New York Press, 1984.

—— 'The Concept of Revival and the Study of Islam and Politics.' In *The Islamic Impulse,* ed. Barbara Stowasser, 37–58. London: Croom Helm, 1987.

Davies, Hannah. 'Taking up Space in Tlemcen: Interview with Rabia Bekkar.'

Middle East Report 179 (November-December 1992): 11–5.

DeBoulet, Agnes. 'État, squatters et maitrise de l'espace.' *Égypte/Monde Arabe* 1 (1er trimestre 1990): 70–96.

Deheuveles, Luc-Willy. *Islam et pensée contemporaine en Algérie: La revue al-asala 1971–1981.* Paris: Éditions du CNRS, 1992.

Dekmejian, Hrair. *Islam in Revolution: Fundamentalism in the Arab World.* Syracuse: Syracuse University Press, 1985.

—— 'Islamic Revival, Catalysts, Categories and Consequences.' In *The Politics of Islamic Revivalism,* ed. Shireen Hunter, 3–22. Bloomington; Indiana University Press, 1988.

Deneoux, Guilain. 'Religious Networks and Urban Unrest; Lessons from Iranian and Egyptian Experiences.' In *The Violence Within: Cultural and Political Opposition in Divided Nations,* ed. Kay B. Warren, 123–55. Boulder: Westview Press, 1993.

—— 'Tunisie: Les élections présidentielles et législatives 20 mars 1994.' *Maghreb-Machrek* 145 (June-September 1994): 49–72.

Denis, Eric. 'Urban Planning and Growth in Cairo.' *Middle East Report* 27, 1 (Winter 1997): 7–12.

Dessouki, Ali E. Hillal. 'Official Islam and Political Legitimation in the Arab Countries.' In *The Islamic Impulse,* ed. Barbara Stowasser, 135–41. London: Croom Helm, 1987.

Dimassi, Hassine. 'La Crise économique en Tunisie: Une crise de régulation.' *Maghreb-Machrek* 103 (January-March 1984): 57–69.

Dupret, Beaudoin. 'Représentations de répretoires juridiques en Égypte: limites d'un consensus.' *Maghreb-Machrek* 151 (January-March 1996): 32–40.

Dupret, Beaudoin, and Jean-Noël Ferrié. 'Participer au pouvoir, c'est édicter la norme: Sur l'Affaire Abu Zayd (Égypte 1992–1996).' *Revue française de science politique* 47 (1997): 762–75.

Duvigneau, G. 'l'Économie clandestin au peril du contrat social en Algérie.' In *Nouvelles logiques marchandes,* ed. Chantal Bernard, 181–99. Paris: CNRS, 1991.

Ebeid, Mona Makram. 'Le rôle de l'opposition officielle en Égypte.' *Maghreb-Machrek* 119 (Februray-March 1988): 5–24.

Egyptian Human Rights Organisation. *Hurriyat al-Ra'y wa al-'Aqida: Qiyud wa Ishkaliyat Riqabat al-Azhar 'ala al-Musannafat al-Fanniya* [Freedom of Thought and Belief, Constraints and Problems: al-Azhar's Censorship of Artistic Productions]. Cairo: al-Munazzama al-Misriya li Huquq al-Insan, 1994.

—— *Difa'a an Huquq al-Insan* (In Defense of Human Rights). Cairo: al-

Munazzama al-Misriya li Huquq al-Insan, 1997.

Eickelman, Dale F. and James Piscatori. *Muslim Politics*. New Jersey: Princeton University Press, 1996.

Engel, Richard. 'Apostate Ruling Endangers Professor.' *Middle East Times* 11 May 1997.

Esposito, John. *The Islamic Threat: Myth or Reality*. New York: Oxford University Press, 1992.

—— *Islam and Politics*. 3rd ed. Syracuse: Syracuse University Press, 1991.

—— 'Trailblazers of the Islamic Resurgence.' In *The Contemporary Islamic Revival: A Critical Survey and Bibliography*, ed. Yvonne Haddad, John Obert Voll and John L. Esposito, 37–56. New York: Greenwood Press, 1991.

Fandy, Mamoun. 'Egypt's Islamic Group: Regional Revenge.' *Middle East Journal* 48, 4 (1994): 607–25.

Farag, Iman. 'Croyance et intérêt: reflexion sur deux associations islamiques égyptiennes.' In *Modernisation et nouvelles formes de mobilisation sociale* II, 127–40. Cairo: CEDEJ, 1992.

Faraj, 'Abd al-Salam. 'Al-Farida al-Gha'iba' (The Missing Precept). Appendix in Ni'mat Junayna, *Tanzim al-Jihad, hal huwa al-hal al-Badil fi Misr* (The Jihad Organization: Is it the Alternative in Egypt). Cairo: Dar al-Hurriya , 1988.

Fatès, Youssef. 'Jeunesse, sport et politique.' *Peuples méditérraneens* 52–53 (1990): 57–71.

Fergany, Nader. 'A Characterisation of the Employment Problem in Egypt.' In *Employment and Structural Adjustment in Egypt in the 1990s*, ed. Heba Handoussa and Gillian Potter, 25–56. Cairo: The American University in Cairo Press, 1991.

Ferrié, Jean-Noël. 'Remarques sur l'islamisation des espaces modernes au Caire.' *Maghreb-Machrek* 151 (January–March 1996): 6–12.

—— 'Solidarité islamique sans consensus en Égypte: Un Cadre d'analyse.' *Les Annales de l'autre Islam* 4 (1997): 73–83.

—— 'Prier pour disposer de soi: Le sens et la fonction de la prière de demande dans l'Islam marocain actuel.' *Annuaire de l'Afrique de Nord* XXXIII (1994), 113–27.

—— 'Les paradoxes de la réislamisation en Égypte,' *Maghreb-Machrek* 151 (January-March 1996).

—— 'Vers une anthropologie deconstructiviste des sociétés musulmanes du Maghreb.' *Peuples méditérraneens* 54–55 (January-June 1991): 229–45.

—— 'Les Politiques de la morale' (mimeo).

Fischer, Michael. 'The Revolt of the Petite Bourgeoisie.' *Deadlus* (Winter

1982): 101–22.

Fontaine, Jacques. 'Les Éléctions locales algériennes du 12 Juin 1990: Approche statistique et géographiques.' *Maghreb-Machrek* 129 (July-September 1990): 121–40.

—— 'Quartiers défavorisés et vote islamiste en Algérie.' *Revue du monde musulman et de la Méditerranée* 65 (1993): 141–64.

Frow, John. 'Discourse and Power.' *Economy and Society* 14 (1985): 193–214.

Fuda, Faraj. *Al-Haqiqa al-Gha'iba* (The Missing Truth). Cairo: Dar al-Fikr lil-Dirasat wa al-Nashr wa al-Tawzi', 1988.

Gallagher, Nancy E. 'Islam vs. Secularism in Cairo: An Account of Dar al-Hikma Debate.' *Middle Eastern Studies* 25, 2 (1989): 208–15.

Gellner, Ernest. *Muslim Society*. Cambridge: Cambridge University Press, 1981.

Ghanem, Malika. 'l'Évolution de deux quártier d'habitat illicite à Constantine (Algérie).' In *Politiques et pratiques urbaines dans les pays en voi de developpement*, vol. 2, ed. Nicole Haumon and Alain Marie, 44–53. Paris: L'Harmmattan, 1987.

Goldberg, Ellis. 'Muslim Union Politics in Egypt: Two Cases.' In *Islam, Political and Social Movements*, ed. Edmund Burke III and Ira Lapidus, 228–43. Los Angeles: University of California Press, 1988.

Gran, Peter. *The Islamic Roots of Capitalism: Egypt, 1760–1840*. Cairo: American University in Cairo Press, 1999.

Greimas, A. J. *On Meaning: Selected Writings in Semiotic Theory*, trans. Paul J. Peron and Frank H. Collins. Minneapolis: University of Minnesota Press, 1987.

—— *The Social Sciences: A Semiotic View*, trans. Paul J. Peron and Frank H. Collins. Minneapolis: University of Minnesota Press, 1990.

Guetta, Maurice, and Cyrille Megdiche. 'Le Peuplement des bidonvilles d'Alger: emplois et mobilités socio-professionelle.' *Revue Française de Sociologie* 31, 2 (1990): 297–313.

Guerroudj, Zineb. 'Pratiques des nouveaux logements par les habitants des bidonvilles d'Alger.' In *Politiques et pratiques urbaines dans les pays en voi de developpement*, vol. 2, ed. Nicole Haumon and Alain Marie, 269–83. Paris: L'Harmmattan, 1987.

Haddad, Yvonne. *Contemporary Islam and the Challenge of History*. Albany, New York: State University of New York Press, 1982.

Haddad, Yvonne, John Obert Voll, and John L. Esposito, ed. *The Contemporary Islamic Revival: A Critical Survey and Bibliography*. New York: Greenwood Press, 1991.

Haddad, Yvonne, and John L. Esposito. *The Islamic Revival since 1988: A Critical Survey and Bibliograpy.* London: Greenwod Press, 1997.

Hadjadj, Djillali. *Corruption et démocratie en Algérie.* Paris: La Dispute, 1999.

Haj Ali, Smail. 'Communication, ville et violences à travers la grève politique du Front Islamique du Salut (FIS): l'Occupation de la ville d'Alger (mai-juin 1991).' *Revue tunisienne des sciences sociales* 29, 110 (1992): 219–34.

—— 'l'Islamisme dans la ville; Espace urbain et contre-centralité.' *Maghreb-Machrek* (1994): 69–74.

Haenni, Partick. 'Ils n'en ont pas fini avec l'Orient: de quelques islamisations non islamistes.' In Olivier Roy and Patrick Haenni, ed., *Le Post-Islamisme, Revue du Monde Musulman et de la Méditerranée* 85–86 (1999): 121–47.

Hafiane, Abderrahim. 'L'Intermédiation sociale dans le cas des quarties d'habitat illégal à Guelma et Constantine (Algérie).' In *L'Urbain dans le monde arabe: politiques, instruments et acteurs,* ed. Pierre Signoles, Galila al-Kadi, and Rachid Sidi Boumediene, 275–80. Paris: CNRS Editions, 1999.

Hamdi, Mohamed Elhachmi. *The Politicisation of Islam: A Case Study of Tunisia.* Boulder: Westview Press, 1998.

Haneda, Masahi, and Toru Miura, ed. *Islamic Urban Studies: Historical Review and Perspectives.* London: Kegan Paul, 1994.

Hanna, Milad. *Al-Iskan wa al-Masyada* (Housing and the Trap). Cairo: Dar al-Mustaqbal al-'Arabi, 1988.

Harrold, Deborah. 'The Menace and Appeal of Algeria's Parallel Economy.' *Middle East Report* 25, 1 (January-Februrary 1995): 18–22.

Henni, A. 'Qui a legalisé quel "trabendo"?' *Peuples méditérraneens* 52–53 (1990): 233–43.

Hermassi, Abdellatif. 'Société, Islam et islamisme.' *Cahiers de la méditerranée* 49 (1994): 61–82.

Hermassi, Elbaki. 'Montée et declin du mouvement islamiste en Tunisie.' *Confluences méditerranée* 12 (Fall 1994): 33–50.

Hermassi, Elbaki. 'La Société tunisienne au miroir islamiste.' *Maghreb-Machrek* 103 (January-March 1984): 39–56.

Hirst, David. 'Time for the Temporal.' *al-Ahram Weekly* 10–16 February 2000, pp 6–7.

Hoodfar, Homa. 'Survival Strategies and the Political Economy of Low-Income Households in Cairo.' In *Development, Change and Gender in Cairo: A View from the Household,* ed. Diane Singerman and Homa Hoodfar, 1–26. Bloomington: Indiana University Press, 1996.

Hoffman-Ladd, Valerie J. 'Polemics on the Modesty and Segregation of Women in Contemporary Egypt.' *International Journal of Middle East*

Studies 19 (1987): 23–50.

Hourani, Albert. *Arabic Thought in the Liberal Age: 1798–1939*. London: Oxford University Press, 1976.

Hourani, George F. 'Ethics in Islam: A Conspectus.' In *Reason and Tradition in Islamic Ethics*. Cambridge: Cambridge University Press, 1985, 15–22.

Humphreys, Stephen R. *Islamic History: A Framework for Inquiry*. London: I.B. Tauris, 1995.

Ibrahim, Ibrahim. 'Religion and Politics under Nasser and Sadat 1952–1981.' In *The Islamic Impulse*, ed. Barbara Stowasser, 121–34. London: Croom Helm, 1987.

Ibrahim, Saad Eddin. 'The Changing Face of Egypt's Islamic Activism.' In *Security Challenges in the Mediterranean Region*, ed. Robert Aliboni, George Joffe and Tim Niblock, 27–40. London: Frank Cass, 1996.

—— 'Islamic Militancy as a Social Movement: The Case of Two Groups in Egypt.' In *The Islamic Resurgence in the Arab World*, ed. Ali E. Hillal al-Dessouki, 117–37. New York: Praeger, 1982.

—— 'Anatomy of Egypt's Militant Islamic Groups: Methodological Note and Preliminary findings.' *International Journal of Middle East Studies* 12 (1980): 423–53.

Ibrahimi, Hamed. 'Les Libertés envolées de la Tunisie.' *Le Monde Diplomatique*, February 1997, pp 4–5.

Ilbert, Robert 'Égypte 1900, habitat populaire, société coloniale.' In *État, ville et mouvements sociaux au Maghreb at au Moyen-Orient*, ed. Kenneth Brown et al., 266–82. Paris: L'Harmmattan, 1989.

Ismail, Salwa. 'The Politics of Space in Urban Cairo: Informal Communities and the State.' *Arab Studies Journal* 4, 2 (Fall 1996): 119–32.

—— *Radical Islamism in Egypt: Discursive Struggle*, Montreal Papers on the Contemporary Arab World, Montreal: Inter-University Consortium for Arab Studies, 1994.

—— 'Discourse and Ideology in Contemporary Egypt.' Unpublished Ph.D thesis, Political Science Department, McGill University, 1992.

Isma'il, Yahya. Introduction to *al-Ayat al-Bayinat lima fi Asatir al-Qimani min al-Dalal wa Khurafat* [The Proven Verses about the Myths and Deviations in Qimani's Legends] by Omar Abdallah Kamil. Cairo: Dar al-Turath al-Islami, 1997.

al-Jabiri, Muhammad 'Abid. *Al-Khitab al-'Arabi al-Mu'asir* [Contemporary Arab Discourse]. Beirut: al-Tali'ah, 1982.

Jansen, Johannes J.G. *The Neglected Duty*. New York: MacMillan Publishing Company, 1986.

al-Jindi, Anwar. *Suqut al-I'lmaniya* [The Collapse of Secularism]. Beirut:

Dar a-Kitab al-Lubnani, 1980.

—— *Shubuhat al-Taghrib* [The Suspect Claims of Westernisation]. Beirut: al-Maktab al-Islami, 1978.

al-Kadi, Galila. 'Trente ans de plannification urbaine au Caire.' *Revue Tiers Monde* 31, 121 (Janvier-Mars 1990): 185–207.

Kaidi, Hamza. 'La Démocratie en état de siège.' *Jeune Afrique* 1589 (12–18 June 1991): 4–5.

Kapil, Arun. 'Les partis islamistes en Algérie: Elements de présentation.' *Maghreb-Machrek* 133 (July-September 1991): 103–11.

Keddie, Nikki. 'The Islamist Movement in Tunisia.' *The Maghreb Review* 11, 1 (1986): 26–39.

—— 'The New Religious Politics: Where, When and Why Do 'Fundamentalisms' Appear?' *Comparative Studies in Society and History* 40, 4 (1998): 696–723.

Kepel, Gilles. *The Prophet and the Pharaoh: Muslim Extremism in Egypt.* London: Al-Saqi, 1985.

Khadda, Naget and Gadant Monique. 'Mots et gestes de la révolte.' *Peuples méditérraneens* 52–53 (1990): 19–24.

Kharoufi, Mustafa. 'Du Petit au grand espace urbain: Le Commerce des fruits et légumes à Dar al-Salam.' *Égypte/Monde Arabe* 5 (1er trimestre 1991): 81–96.

—— 'The Informal Dimension of Urban Activity in Egypt: Some Recent Work.' In Nicholas Hopkins (ed.), *Informal Sector in Egypt. Cairo Papers in Social Science* (Winter 1991), pp 8–20.

Khelladi, Aissa. 'Algérie: Les Groupes islamistes armés.' *Confluences* 12 (Fall 1994): 63–76.

—— 'Esquisse d'une géographie des groupes islamistes en Algérie.' *Hérodote* 77 (April-June 1995): 28–42.

Kishk, Muhammad Jalal. *Khawatir Muslim fi al-Mas'ala al-Jinsiya* [A Muslim's Thoughts on the Sexual Question]. Cairo: Maktabat al-Turath al-Islami, 1992.

Labat, Severine. *Les Islamistes algériens entre les urnes et les maquis.* Paris: Editions du Seuil, 1995.

Lapidus, Ira M. *Muslim Cities in the Middle Ages.* Cambridge: Cambridge University Press, 1988.

Laurence, Bruce B. *Defenders of God.* London: I.B. Tauris, 1990.

—— 'Muslim Fundamentalist Movements: Reflections toward a New Approach.' In *The Islamic Impulse*, ed. Barbara Stowasser, 15–36. London: Croom Helm, 1987.

Lazarus-Yafeh, Hava. 'Muhammad Mutawalli al-Sha'rawi – A Portrait of a

Contemporary 'Alim.' In *Islam, Nationalism and Radicalism in Egypt and the Sudan*, ed. Gabriel R. Warburg and Uri M. Kupferschmidt, 281–97. New York: Praeger, 1983.

Leca, Jean, and Jean-Claude Vatin. *L'Algérie politique: Institutions et régime*. Paris: Presse de la Fondation Nationale des Sciences Politiques, 1975.

Lesbet, Djaffar. 'Des pièces de la vie: Maisons vernaculaires et pratiques sociales dans la Casbah d'Alger.' In *Politiques et pratiques urbaines dans les pays en voi de developpement*, vol. 2, ed. Nicole Haumon and Alain Marie, 284–312. Paris: L'Harmmattan, 1987.

Lowy, Paul. 'Espace idéologique et quadrillage policier: Le 26 janvier 1978 à Tunis.' *Hérodote* 13 (1979): 103–14.

Lutfi, Hoda. 'Manners and Customs of Fourteenth Century Cairene Women: Female Anarch versus Shar'i Order in Muslim Prescriptive Treaties.' In *Women in Islamic Middle Eastern History*, ed. Nikki Keddie and Beth Baron, 99–121. New Haven: Yale University Press, 1991.

MacLeod, Arlene Elow. *Accommodating Protest: Working Women, the New Veiling and Change in Cairo*. New York: Columbia University Press, 1991.

al-Maghazi, Duha. 'Sukan al-'Ashwa'iyat bayna Thaqafat al-Faqr wa Istratijiyat al-Baqa': Dirasa Anthropologiya' [The Residents of Haphazard Communities between the Culture of Poverty and Survival Strategies: An Anthropological Study]. In Proceedings of the Conference on *al-Mujtama' al-Misri fi Daw' Mutaghayrat al-Nizam al-'Alami* (Egyptian Society in Light of the Changes in the International System), ed. Ahmad Zayid and Samiya al-Khashab. Cairo: Cairo University, Faculty of Arts, 1995.

Marsot, Afaf Lutfi al-Sayyid. 'Religion or Opposition? Urban Protest Movements in Egypt.' *International Journal of Middle East Studies* 16 (1984): 541–52.

Martinez, Luis. *La Guerre civile en Algérie*. Paris: Karthala, 1998.

Marty, Martin and Scott Appleby, ed. *Fundamentalism Observed*. Chicago: Chicago University Press, 1991.

Masud, Muhammad Khalid, Brinkley Messik and David S. Powers, 'Muftis, Fatwas and Islamic Legal Interpretation.' In *Islamic Legal Interpretation: Muftis and their Fatwas*, ed. Muhammad Khalid Masud, Brinkley Messik and David S. Powers, 5–23. Cambridge: Harvard University Press, 1996.

al-Messiri, Sawsan. 'The Changing Role of the Futuwwa in the Social Structure of Cairo.' In *Patrons and Clients in Mediterranean Society*, ed. Ernest Gellner and Johan Waterbury, 230–53. London: Duckworth, 1977.

—— *Ibn al-Balad: A Concept of Egyptian Identity*. Leiden: Brill, 1979.

Mir-Hosseini, Ziba. 'Rethinking Gender: Discussions with Ulama in Iran.' *Critique* 12 (Fall 1998): 45–59.

Moussaoui, Abderrahamane. 'La Mosquée au peril de la commune.' *Peuples méditérraneens* 52–53 (1990): 81–9.

Mu'awad, Galal 'Abdallah. *Al-Hamishiyun al-Hadariyun wa al-Tanmiya fi Misr* [Urban Marginals and the Development in Egypt]. Cairo: Cairo University, Faculty of Economics and Political Science, 1998.

Mubarak, Hisham. *Al-Irhabiyun Qadimun: Dirasa Muqarana Bayna Mawqif al-Ikhwan al-Muslimin wa Jama'at al-Jihad min Qadiyat al-'Unf, 1938–1994* [The Terrorists are Coming: A Comparative Study of the Position of the Muslim Brotherhood and the Jihad Groups from the Question of Violence]. Cairo: Dar al-Mahrusa, 1995.

—— 'The Violence of Despair.' *Cairo Times* 1, 21 (11–24 December 1997).

Mustafa, Hala. *Al-Nizam al-Siyasi wa al-Mu'arada al-Islamiya fi Misr* [The Political System and Islamist Opposition in Egypt]. Cairo: Dar al-Mahrusa, 1996.

—— *Al-Dawla wa al-Harakat al-Islamiya al-Mu'arida: Bayna al-Muhadana wa al-Muwajaha fi 'Ahday al-Sadat wa Mubarak* [The State and Oppositional Islamist Groups: Between Cooptation and Confrontation in the Eras of Sadat and Mubarak]. Cairo: Dar al-Mahrusa, 1996.

Naciri, Mohamed. 'La Mosquée: Un Enjeu dans la ville.' *Lamalif* 192 (October 1992): 48–52.

Nadim, Nawal al-Massiri. 'The Concept of the Hara: A Historical and Sociological Study of al-Sukkariya.' *Annales islamologiques* 15 (1979): 313–48.

Nair, Sami. 'Le peuple exclu.' *Les Temps Modernes* 50, 580 (January-Februrary 1995): 34–45.

Nouschi, André. *L'Algérie amère 1914–1994*. Paris: Editions de la maison de sciences de l'homme, 1995.

Nur al-Din, Muhammad. 'Tatawwur Ra's al-Mal al-Masrafi fi Misr' [The Development of Finance Capital in Egypt]. *Qadaya Fikriya* (August-October 1986): 136–64.

Oldham, Linda, Haguer al-Hadidi, and Hussein Hussein. 'Informal Communities in Cairo: The Basis of a Typology.' *Cairo Papers in Social Science* 10, 4 (Winter 1987).

Paul, Jim. 'States of Emergency: The Riots in Tunisia and Morocco.' *MERIP Reports* 14, 8 (October 1984): 3–6.

Pfeifer, Karen. 'How Tunisia, Morocco, Jordan and even Egypt Became IMF "Success Stories" in the 1990s.' *Middle East Report* 29, 1 (1999): 23–7.

Posusney, Marsha Pripstein. 'Collective Action and Workers' Consciousness in Egypt.' In *Workers and Working Classes in the Middle East: Strug-*

gles, Histories, Historiographies, ed. Zackary Lockman, 211–46. New York: State University of New York Press, 1994.

Provost, Lucile. 'l'Économie de rente et ses avatares,' Esprit 19 (1995): 82–95.

al-Qaradawi, Yusuf. Islamic Awakening between Rejection and Extremism. Washington D.C: The American Trust Publication, n.d.

Qutb, Sayyid. Ma'rakat al-Islam wa al-Ra'smaliya [The Battle of Islam and Capitalism]. Cairo: Dar al-Shuruq, 1987.

—— Ma'alim fi al-Tariq [Signposts]. Cairo: Dar al-Shuruq, 1987.

Radi, Saadia. 'De la toile au voile.' Maghreb-Machrek 151 (January–March 1996): 13–17.

Rafeq, Abd al-Karim. 'Public Morality in 18th-Century Ottoman Damascus.' Revue d'études de Monde Musulman et de la Méditerranée 55–56 (1990): 180–96.

Raymond, André. 'Urban Networks and Popular Movements in Cairo and Aleppo at the End of the 18th Century – Beginning of the 19th Century.' In The Proceedings of the International Conference on Urbanism in Islam (ICUTT), vol. 2. Tokyo: The Middle East Culture Centre, 1989, 219–71.

—— 'Quartiers et mouvements populaires au Caire au xviiième siècle.' In Political and Social Change in Modern Egypt, ed. P.M. Holt, 104–16. London: Oxford University Press, 1968.

Rizq, Soad Kamil. 'The Structure and Operation of the Informal Sector in Egypt.' In Employment and Structural Adjustment in Egypt in the 1990s, ed. Heba Handoussa and Gillian Potter, 167–85. Cairo: The American University in Cairo Press, 1991.

Rodenbeck, Max. 'Is Islamism Losing its Thunder?' The Washington Quarterly 21, 2 (Spring 1998): 177–93.

Rouadjia, Ahmed. Grandeur et décadence de l'Etat Algérien. Paris: Karthala, 1995.

Roudjia, Ahmed. Les Frères et la mosquée. Paris: Karthala, 1990.

—— 'La Violence et l'histoire du mouvement national Algérien.' Peuples méditérraneens 70–71 (January–June 1995): 13–87.

—— Grandeur et décadence de l'état algérien. Paris: Karthala, 1995.

—— 'Discourse and Strategy of the Algerian Islamist Movement.' In The Islamist Dilemma: The Political Role of Islamist Movements in the Contemporary World, ed. Laura Gauzzone, 69–103. (Reading: Ithaca Press, 1995).

Roussillon, Alain. 'Entre al-Jihad et al-Rayan: Phenomenologie de l'islamisme égyptien.' Maghreb-Machrek 127 (January–March 1990): 17–50.

—— 'al-Jama'at al-Islamiya fi al-Siyasa al-Misriya ' (The Islamist Groups in Egyptian Politics). *al-Mawqif al-'Arabi* 94 (February-March 1988): 74–102.

Roy, Olivier. *The Failure of Political Islam*. Translated by Carol Volk. Cambridge, Massachusetts: Harvard University Press, 1994.

—— 'Le Post-Islamise.' In Olivier Roy and Haenni, Patrick, ed. *Le Post-islamisme, Revue du Monde Musulman et de la Méditerranée* 85–86 (1999): 11–30.

Roy, Olivier, and Patrick Haenni, ed. *Le Post-islamisme, Revue du Monde Musulman et de la Méditerranée* 85–86 (1999).

Rudenbeck, Lars. *Party and People: A Study of Political Change in Tunisia*. London: C. Hurst and Company, 1969.

Rugh, Andrea. *Family in Contemporary Egypt*. Syracuse: Syracuse University Press, 1984.

Rycx, Jean-François, ed. & trans. *Islam et déregulation financière*. Cairo: CEDEJ, 1988.

Sadowski, Yahya. 'Egypt's Islamic Movement: A New Political and Economic Force.' *Middle East Insight* 25, 8 (1987): 37–45.

Safar-Zitoun, Madani. *Stratégies patrimoniales et urbanisation, Alger 1962–1992*. Paris: Editions L'Harmmattan, 1996.

Samai-Ouramdane, Ghania. 'Le Front Islamique du Salut à travers son organe de presse (Al Munqid).' *Peuples méditérraneens* 52–53 (1990): 155–65.

Sanson, Henri. *Laicité islamique en Algérie*. Paris: Editions du CNRS, 1983.

Saoud, Rabah. 'Urban Form, Social Change and the Threat of Civil War in North Africa.' *Third World Planning Review* 19, 3 (1997): 289–312.

Sayed, Afaf Loutfi el. 'The Role of the *'ulama'* in Egypt during the Nineteenth Century.' In *Political and Social Change in Modern Egypt*. P.M. Holt, ed. London: Oxford University Press, 1968, 264–80.

Sayyid, Boby S. *A Fundamental Fear*. London: Zed Books, 1997.

al-Sayyid, Mustapha Kamil. 'Le Syndicat des ingénieurs et le courant islamique.' *Maghreb-Machrek* 146 (October-December 1995): 27–39.

Scott, James C. *Domination and the Arts of Resistance*. New Haven: Yale University Press, 1990.

Seddon, David. 'Popular Protest and Political Opposition in Tunisia, Morocco and Sudan.' In *État, ville et mouvements sociaux au Maghreb et au Moyen-Orient*, ed. Kenneth Brown et al., 179–97. Paris: L'Harmmattan, 1989.

Sfeir, Antoine. 'Voyage au sein de l'islamisme tunisien.' *Les Cahiers de l'Orient* 7 (1987): 23–32.

Shahin, Emad Eldin. *Political Ascent: Contemporary Islamic Movements in*

North Africa. Boulder, Colorado: Westview Press, 1997.

Shepard, William. 'Islam and Ideology: Towards a Typology.' *International Journal of Middle East Studies* 19 (1987): 307–36.

Shoshan, Boaz. 'Grain Riots and "the Moral Economy": Cairo 1350–1517.' *Journal of Interdisciplinary History* 10, 3 (Winter 1980): 459–78.

Shuhayb, 'Abd al-Qadir. *Al-Ikhtirak: Qisat Sharikat Tawzif al-Amwal* [The Infiltration: The Story of Societies for the Placement of Funds]. Cairo: Dar Sina, 1989.

Signoles, Pierre, J.M. Miossec, and M. Dlala. *Tunis: Evolution et fonctionnement de l'espace urbaine.* Fasicule de recherches 6. Tours, Urbama, 1980.

Singerman, Diane. *Avenues of Participation: Family, Politics and Networks in Urban Quarters of Cairo*. Princeton N.J.: Princeton University Press, 1995.

Sivan, Emmanuel. *Radical Islam: Medieval Theology and Modern Politics*. New Haven: Yale University Press, 1985.

Starrett, Gregory. *Putting Islam to Work: Education, Politics and Religious Transformation in Egypt*. California: California University Press, 1998.

—— 'The Political Economy of Religious Commodities in Cairo.' *American Anthropologist* 97, 1 (Spring 1995): 51–68.

Stauth, Georg. 'Gamaliyya: Informal Economy and Social Life in a Popular Quarter of Cairo.' In *Informal Sector in Egypt*. Nicholas Hopkins, ed. *Cairo Papers in Social Science* (Winter 1991), 78–103.

Steele, Omar. 'Une économie piégé entre trabendo et ajustement.' In *L'Algérie dans la guerre*, ed. Remy Leveau, 25–38. Bruxelles: Editions Complex, 1995.

Tadros, Helmi R., Mohamed Fateeh and Allen Hibbard. 'Informal Markets in Cairo.' *Cairo Papers in Social Science* (1990).

Talbi, Mohamed. 'L'Expression religieuse dans la presse et les revues tunisiennes d'aujourd'hui (1984–1985).' *The Maghreb Review* 11, 1 (1986): 1–18.

Al-Taqrir al-Istratiji al-'Arabi 1992 [The Arab Strategic Report]. Cairo: al-Ahram Center for Strategic Studies, 1993.

'Taqrir Mufti al-Jumhuriya an Kitab al-Farida al-Gha'iba [The Mufti's Report on the Book 'The Missing Precept'].' Appendix in Ni'mat Junayna, *Tanzim al-Jihad: Hal Huwa al-Hal al-Badil fi Misr* [the Jihad Organization: Is it the Alternative in Egypt?]. Cairo: Dar al-Hurriya , 1988.

Tekari, Chehab. 'Habitat et dépassement du droit en Tunisie: Les constructions spontanées.' *Annuaire de l'Afrique du Nord* XXVI 1986. Paris: CNRS Editions, 1988, 165–73.

Tekçe, Belgin, Linda Oldahm and Fredric Shorter. *A Place to Live: Families and Child Health in a Cairo Neighborhood*. Cairo: The American University in Cairo Press, 1994.

Tessler, Mark. 'The Origins of Popular Support for Islamist Movements; A Political Economy Analysis.' In *Islam, Democracy and the State in North Africa*, ed. John P. Entelis, 93–126. Indianapolis: Indiana University Press, 1997.

Thompson, John B. *Studies in the Theory of Ideology*. Los Angeles: University of California Press, 1985.

Tilly, Charles. 'Social Movements and (all Sorts) of Other Political Interactions – Local, National and International – Including Identities.' *Theory and Society* 27 (1998): 453–80.

—— *Big Structures, Large Processes, Huge Comparisons*. New York: Russel Sage Foundation, 1984.

—— 'Useless Durkheim.' In *As Sociology Meets History*. New York: Academic Press, 1981.

Toledano, Ehud. *State, and Society in mid-Nineteenth-Century Egypt*. Cambridge: Cambridge University Press, 1990.

Toru, Miura. 'The Structure of the Quarter and the Role of the Outlaws: The Salilhiya Quarter and the Zu'r Movement in Mamluk Period.' In *The Proceedings of the International Conference on Urbanism in Islam* (ICUTT), vol. 2. Tokyo: The Middle East Culture Center, 1989, 402–37.

Touati, Amin. *Algérie: Les Islamistes à l'assault du pouvoir*. Paris: Editions L'Harmmattan, 1995.

Toscane, Louza and Lamloun, Olfa. 'Les Femmes, alibi du pouvoir tunisien.' *Le Monde Diplomatique*, June 1998, 3.

Tozy, Mohamed. *Monarchie et Islam politique au Maroc*. Paris: Presses de la Fondation Nationale des Sciences Politiques, 1995.

—— 'Reformes politiques et transitions démocratiques.' *Maghreb-Machrek* 164 (April–June 1999): 67–84.

Turner, Bryan S. *Orientalism, Postpodernism and Globalism*. London: Routledge, 1994.

—— *Weber and Islam*. London: Routledge, 1974.

al-Wali, Mamduh. *Sukkan al-Ishash wa al-Ashwa'iyat: al-Kharita al-Iskaniya lil Muhafazat* (The Inhabitants of Huts and Haphazard Communities: A Map of the Governorates). Cairo: Engineers Syndicate, 1993.

'Wisdom of the Mosque.' *Index on Censorship* 23, 1–2 (1994).

Vasile, Elizabeth. 'Devotion as Distinction, Piety as Power: Religious Revival and the Transfromation of Space in the Illegal Settlements of Tunis.'

In *Population, Poverty and Politics in Middle Eastern Cities*, ed. Michael E. Bonine. 113–40. University of Florida Press, 1997.

Vatikiotis, P.J. *Islam and the State*. London: Croom Helm, 1987.

Vergès, Miriem. 'La Qasbah d'Alger: Chronique de survie dans un quartier en sursis.' In *Exils et royaumes: Les appartenences au monde arabo-musulman d'Aujourd'hui*, ed. Gilles Kepel, 69–88. Paris: Presse de la Fondation des sciences politiques, 1994.

—— 'Les jeunes, le stade, le FIS: Vers une analyse de l'action protestataire.' *Maghreb-Machrek* 154 (October-December 1996): 48–54.

Voll, John Obert. *Islam, Continuity and Change in the Modern World*. 2nd edition. Syracuse: Syracuse University Press, 1994.

—— 'The Revivalist Heritage.' In *The Contemporary Islamic Revival: A Critical Survey and Bibliography*, ed. Yvonne Haddad, John Obert Voll and John L. Esposito, 23–36. New York: Greenwood Press.

—— 'Renewal and Reform in Islamic History: Tajdid and Islah.' In *Voices of Resurgent Islam*, ed. John L. Esposito, 32–47. New York: Oxford University Press, 1983.

Yavuz, Hakan. 'Towards an Islamic Liberalism? The Nurcu Movement of Fethullah Gulen.' *Middle East Journal* 53, 4 (Autumn 1999): 584–605.

Zakariyya, Fu'ad. *Al-Haqiqa wa al-Wahm fi al-Haraka al-Islamiya al-Mu'asira* [Truth and Illusion in the Contemporary Islamist Movement]. Cairo: Dar al-Fikr lil Dirasat, 1986.

Zalouk, Malak. *Power, Class and Foreign Capital in Egypt*. London: Zed Books, 1989.

Zeghal, Malika. 'La Guerre des fatwa-s: Gad al-Haqq et Tantawi: Les Sheikhs à l'epreuve du pouvoir.' *Cahiers de l'Orient* 45 (1997); 81–95.

Zghal, Abdelkader. 'Repenser les mouvements islamistes dans un perspective trans-historique et trans-culturelle.' mimeo, n.d.

—— 'Le retour du sacré et la nouvelle demande idéologique des jeunes scolarisé: Le cas de la Tunisie.' *Annuaire de l'Afrique du Nord* XVIII 1979. Paris; Editions CNRS, 41–64.

Zghal, Abdelkader [and Lahmar, Mouldi]. 'The "Bread Riot" and the Crisis of the One-Party System in Tunisia.' In *African Studies in Social Movements and Democracy*, ed. Mahmood Mamdani and Ernest Wamba-dia-Wamba, 99–132. Dakkar: Codersia Book Series, 1995.

Zubaida, Sami. *Islam, the People and the State: Political Ideas and Movements in the Middle East*. London: I.B. Tauris, 1993.

—— 'Class and Community in Urban Politics.' In *Etat et ville, et mouvements sociaux au Maghreb et au Moyen-Orient*, ed. Kenneth Brown et al., 57–71. Paris: l'Harmmattan, 1989.

—— 'Is there a Muslim Society?': Ernest Gellner's Sociology of Islam.' *Economy and Society* 24, 2 (1995): 151–188.

—— 'Is Iran an Islamic State?' In *Political Islam*, ed. Joel Beinin and Joe Stork, 103–19. London: I.B. Tauris, 1998.

Newspaper Articles in Arabic

al-'Ashmawi, Muhammad Sa'id. 'al-Irhab al-Fikri wa al-Hisba' [Intellectual Terrorism and Hisba]. *October*, 26 May 1996.

al-'Awwa, Muhammad Salim. 'Bal al-Jizya fi Dhimat al-Tarikh' [But Jizya is in the Realm of History]. *al-Wafd*, 18 April 1998.

'Ba'd Musalsal al-Sidam bayn al-Shurta wa al-Jama'at al-Islamiya ' [After the Episode of Confrontation b'Kalafu Anfusahum bi-Tatbiq Hudud Allah wa Jaladu al-Nas fi al-Shawari" (They Abrogated the Right of Applying the Religious Ordinances and the Flogged the People in the Streets). *al-Ahrar*, 26 December 1988.

'Al-Fikr al-Dini a-Mustanir' [Enlightened Islamic Thought]. *al-Mukhtar al-Islami* 73 (February 1989): 72–7.

Ghali, Shukri. 'Hukuma Khafiya fi Misr Did al-Thaqafa' [A Hidden Government in Egypt Against Culture]. *Ruz al-Yusuf*, 3 January 1994.

'Hamalat Waqiha min Wara' al-Hudud' [Rude Campaigns from Across the Borders]. *al-Nur*, 14 December 1988.

Huwaydi, Fahmi. 'Risalat min Shaykh al-Azhar' [A Message from the Shaykh of al-Azhar]. *al-Ahram*, 16 February 1988.

'Al-Islam la Yatlawwan abdan … Ya Duktur' [Islam Does Not Change Colors … O Doctor]. *al-Nur*, 30 March 1988.

al-Jindi, Anwar. 'Marahil al-Mukhatat al-Marsum li-Iqtiham al-Islam min al-Kharij' [The Stages of the Planned Plot to Invade Islam from the Outside]. *al-Nur*, 3 November 1988.

'Kalafu Anfusahum bi-Tatbiq Hudud Allah wa Jaladu al-Nas fi al-Shawari"[They Abrogated the Right of Applying the Religious Ordinances and They Flogged the People in the Streets]. *al-Ahrar*, 26 December 1988.

Madi, Abu al-Ila, 'Ba'd Hadith al-Uqsur: al-'Unf wa Kayfiyat 'Ilajuh fi al-Hala al-Misriya al-Rahina' [After the Luxor Event: Violence and How to Remedy it in the Egyptian Case]. *al-Hayat*, 25 December 1997.

Mubarak, Hisham, 'Ba'd Indhar al-Suyah wa al-Mustathmirin: al-Ahali Taltaqi fi al-Danmark bi al-Mutahadith al-I'lami li al-Jama'at al-Islamiya [After the Warning to Tourists and Investors: *al-Ahali* Meets with the

Jama'a's Public Relations Spokesperson in Denmark], *al-Ahali,* 9 February 1994.

Muntasir, Salah. 'Mas'uliyat al-Makan' [The Responsibility of Space], *al-Ahram al-Dawli,* 15 December 1992.

'Mustaqbal al-Tabshir fi Misr wa al-Amal fi Makka [The Future of Proselytisation is in Egypt and the Hope is in Mecca], *al-Nur,* 22 June 1988.

'Al-Shaykh al-Sha'rawi Yuwajih Du'at al-'Ilmaniya' [Shaykh al-Sha'rawi Confronts the Preachers of Secularism]. *al-Ahram,* 12 January 1986.

'Ulama al-Islam Yhaddidun Mafhum wa Mazahir wa 'Ilaj al-Tatarruf' [The Ulama of Islam Define the Concept, Symptom and Remedy of Extremism], *al-Nur,* 2 March 1988.

'Wa Islamah!' [O Islam!]. *al-Ahrar,* 24 August 1987.

Documents

Mahkmat Isti'naf al-Qahira, al-Da'ira 14, Isti'naf 278, 1995 (Cairo Court of Appeal, District 14, Case 278, 1995.

Mahkmat Shamal al-Qahira al-Ibtida'iya, Jalsat 15-09-1997 (North Cairo Lower Court, 15 Sepember, 1997).

Index

INDEX

243